The Narrative Study of Lives

The purpose of this Series is to publish studies of actual lives in progress, studies that use qualitative methods of investigation within a theoretical context drawn from psychology or other disciplines. The aim is to promote the study of lives and life history as a means of examining, illuminating, and spurring theoretical understanding. *The Narrative Study of Lives* will encourage longitudinal and retrospective in-depth studies of individual life narratives as well as theoretical consideration of innovative methodological approaches to this work.

Guidelines for authors:

The editors invite submissions of original manuscripts of up to 35 typed pages in the areas described above. As a publication of an interdisciplinary nature, we welcome authors from all disciplines concerned with narratives, psychobiography, and life-history. In matters of style, we encourage any creative format that best presents the work. Long quotations in the protagonists' voices are desirable as well as discussion of the author's place in the study.

References and footnotes should follow the guidelines of the *Publication Manual of the American Psychological Association* (3rd ed.). A separate title page should include the chapter title and the author's name, affiliation, and address. Please type the entire manuscript, including footnotes and references, double-spaced, and submit three copies to:

Ruthellen Josselson, Ph.D., Co-Editor
The Narrative Study of Lives
Department of Psychology
Towson State University
Towson, MD 21204

Exploring Identity and Gender
Volume 2
of
THE NARRATIVE STUDY OF LIVES

Exploring Identity and Gender

■ ■ ■

The Narrative Study of Lives

Amia Lieblich
Ruthellen Josselson
editors

The Narrative Study of Lives ■ Volume 2

SAGE Publications
International Educational and Professional Publisher
Thousand Oaks   London   New Delhi

For information address:

SAGE Publications, Inc.
2455 Teller Road
Thousand Oaks, California 91320

SAGE Publications Ltd.
6 Bonhill Street
London EC2A 4PU
United Kingdom

SAGE Publications India Pvt. Ltd.
M-32 Market
Greater Kailash I
New Delhi 110 048 India

Printed in the United States of America

Library of Congress Cataloging-in-Publication Data

ISBN 0-8039-5568-5 (cloth); ISBN 0-8039-5569-3 (paper)

ISSN 1072-2777

94 95 96 97 98 10 9 8 7 6 5 4 3 2 1

Sage Production Editor: Yvonne Könneker

Contents

Introduction

$\mathcal{A}$s the concept of *narrative* finds its way into more areas in psychology and, generally, the social sciences, those of us who are professors begin to create courses to introduce advanced students to the field. I followed in the footsteps of Professor Yoram Bilu, who has been giving a seminar about life stories in anthropological studies (anthropologists have always been more adventurous than psychologists and sociologists!), and I offered last year, for the first time, a seminar on narratives and life stories in psychology. Fifteen graduate students participated in theoretical and empirical discussions, presenting papers based on life story interviews, biographies, and autobiographies.

At the end of the year, I asked my students to formulate the main lesson they drew from the seminar. Here is what they concluded:

1. Listening to life stories of normal or outstanding people (as distinguished from clinical case studies) is a new, powerful way to study people and therefore to do psychological research. But the way of the narrative is subtle, complex, and more difficult than we expected before trying it ourselves.
2. It is certainly true that there is no truth. Truth is evasive and multifaced and cannot be pinpointed in simple terms. Reality and personality are constructions of a subjective process, taking

place on several levels, within a certain context, in a certain language. We are often insecure in our own conclusions.

3. Yet, within this struggle and relativity, was usually a core of consensus, of a number of facts, traits, or processes about which different subjective accounts seemed to agree. The world, therefore, is not entirely chaotic: We can make some sense of it.

Generally speaking, these points reflect our own sense of the field of the narrative study of lives. In the year since the appearance of the first volume of the annual, Ruthellen Josselson and I E-mailed almost daily from Jerusalem to Cambridge, Massachusetts, and back, discussing manuscripts, reviews, and feedback we received for *The Narrative Study of Lives*. Our involvement with the yearly production of the series has become a major feature of our lives and our relationship. Mutual support flowed across the continents to sustain the constant effort needed for bringing up this infant by its two parents. At the same time, we were also encouraged by the explosion of new books, articles, and conferences, using the concept of the *narrative* in a wide variety of contexts, that people brought to our attention. This is a time of great creativity as people explore ways to tap the meaning of this concept via both theoretical and empirical work by using qualitative and/or quantitative approaches to the story.

But What is a narrative? we kept asking and being asked by our students and colleagues, as when we had prepared the first volume of *The Narrative Study of Lives*. Is it just any story, or history; does it have to conform to a certain structure or carry a message; how is it related to identity, culture, and language; does it differ, in any systematic way, from life-as-lived and constructed by women and men? What is important and what is marginal about a life story? And perhaps more than any other question: What is a good life story worth publishing? Looking at the published literature, as well as the manuscripts we reviewed during the year and the contributions to the present annual, there are a great many ways to use the term *narrative*. We might summarize this variety of voices under the construct of "creative ambiguity." At this stage of the exploration for meaning, which precedes theory building, determining the boundaries of the concept and its exact meaning can only be harmful to progress in the field. We are not yet at the stage of having a theory of the narrative in the social sciences. We are not after definition, but after intelligent applications of the use of narrative and its use for the understanding of human lives.

At the same time, we are attentive to the emergence of a core of consensus. If all chapters of the previous and present volumes of *The Narrative Study of Lives* are taken together, in all their variety, the common denominator that comes to the fore has to do with the contributors' awareness of subjectivity and reflectivity in their means of knowing. Our contributors were sensitive to the interactive linkage of researcher-writer and her or his field of study. They expressed concern about the nature of their data and methods and were aware of their personal relationship with their subject matter. They were open to alternative ways to approach their material and reflected on the choices they made. At present it seems to us that the importance of reflection in qualitative research and analysis, which has become the mark of *TNSL,* cannot be overemphasized.

Of the eight chapters in this volume, five are focused specifically on the lives of girls and women. One of the chapters (Reinharz, Chapter 2) deals with the ways feminist writers experience biographical research about other women. Three of the chapters (Bar-On and Gilad, Chapter 3; McRae, Chapter 7; Stewart, Chapter 8) describe and analyze lives of particular women. One chapter (Rogers, Brown, and Tappan, Chapter 1) presents a study about ego development in adolescent girls. This emphasis on the feminine experience is not incidental. To be sure, the editors of *TNSL* are two women, and although we did not deliberately search for contributions dealing with women's lives, that might be part of the explanation. But, more central, we think, is that feminist research and postmodern approaches to knowledge have developed hand in hand in the last decades. Women have been storytellers in many cultures, yet their different voices were not heard enough in the public sphere. We do not accept the simple notion that the narrative is a feminine domain or research tool or that women speak in the language of stories. Rather we think that the subjective-reflective nature of the narrative coincides with the feminist ideology of compassionate, unauthoritarian understanding of the Other. Although more traditional theory and empirical work in the social sciences concentrated on men and used predominately positivistic, objective models, it is understandable that work by women investigators and/or about women's lives has been in the forefront of alternative research paradigms in the social sciences and the humanities.

Annie G. Rogers, Lyn Mikel Brown, and Mark B. Tappan (Chapter 1) illuminate the puzzle of the statistically significant loss in ego development in girls by counterposing clinical interviews, psychometric measures, and interpretive analyses. Listening to the individual voices of girls talking about their lives and relationships, the authors gain an understanding of the change in the girls' sense of themselves as they move into adolescence. Although a traditional measure of ego development indicates regression or loss at this age, the individual narratives of girls can be constructed and understood in terms of resistance against the debilitating conventions of female behavior.

Shulamit Reinharz (Chapter 2) writes about biographical work in which women constructed the lives of other women. She explores the dilemmas and emotional experience of such writings. The importance of the approach to biography that Reinharz proposes is in going behind the scenes of the writing process and the final product, exploring the experience of the biographer—a topic usually eliminated from the published biography. This focus puts in the foreground the researcher's involvement in her study and her relationship to the topic she writes about, which cannot be ignored anymore if modern epistemological conceptions are used.

Transitions, which are indeed the backbone of so many narratives, are the focus of two chapters of this volume. First, Dan Bar-On and Noga Gilad (Chapter 3) present a narrative analysis of three generations of women in an Israeli Holocaust survivor's family. They demonstrate how a narrative is transferred and reformulated between the generations of a certain family, thus expressing not only an individual identity but also a historical or familial heritage. In the case of Holocaust survivors, each generation has its own way of narrating the past, based on approach and avoidance of the traumatic memory, affected by the passage of time and the process of normalization. Second, Sherry L. Hatcher's (Chapter 6) work deals with the transition of youth, showing that in the absence of clearly prescribed rituals in modern culture, young people create personal rites of passage. Hatcher asked undergraduates what it was like to leave home for college and used their narratives to understand the transition. Coding these narrative data by themes, Hatcher produces a broad, vivid analysis of modern initiation rites.

Richard L. Ochberg (Chapter 4), who writes about the life and personality of a middle-aged man, uses this narrative to demonstrate that stories are not merely told by individuals, after the fact, once they have experienced their lives. On the contrary, people live out the events and affairs of their lives in a storied manner. Ochberg argues that there is no way to disentangle living a life from telling or performing a story: Individuals conduct their life episodes in patterns similar to the plots of stories. So is social science a story told in terms of the forces that shape human behavior. "Storied life" probably will become a core idea in the evolving field of narrative study.

Dalia Etzion and Amittai Niv (Chapter 5) present an innovative narrative study in the field of business administration and organizational behavior. They started from a larger project of studying inventions within organizations and discovered that certain styles of management could be accessed only by concentrating on individual cases over time. For the complex phenomenon of a manager in his organization, the narrative approach is highly illuminating and, in the present study, leads to the description of the "magician" style of management and its pitfalls.

Jill F. Kealey McRae (Chapter 7) starts her chapter with a narrative of her search for the women she writes about, embedded in her own personal-cultural quest as an Australian woman who moved to the United States. Her chapter deals with the ways a story serves to uncover and construct a personal identity, which is a major interest of *The Narrative Study of Lives*. She uses both anecdote and folkhistory to reinforce the case that stories construct identity and life. However, according to McRae, this is not only the case for autobiographical stories, for the short stories that people tell about others and about their moral and social universe also reveal their own selves.

Abigail J. Stewart (Chapter 8) proposes a model of links between an individual's developmental stage and social events, arguing that the focus or impact of a social event will differ according to the life stage during which it is experienced. From dealing with the meanings of the women's movement for one cohort of 91 women, Stewart moves to the narratives of three women who all mentioned the women's movement as a significant event in their lives—in college, in early adulthood, or at midlife.

Thus the second volume of *The Narrative Study of Lives* samples and demonstrates different uses of the *narrative* concept and methodology in the study of women's and men's lives in society. Although the selection of chapters has overrepresented work of psychologists in the area, their work seems to us to include the thinking of other disciplines, merging into issues in history, philosophy, sociology, literature, and anthropology. Narrative work has a universalist core and embraces a wide range of perspectives.

—AMIA LIEBLICH

❦ 1 ❦

Interpreting Loss in Ego Development in Girls

Regression or Resistance?

Annie G. Rogers
Lyn Mikel Brown
Mark B. Tappan

*J*anet is a 12-year-old seventh grader at Laurel School, a private girls' school in the Midwest. As a participant in a 5-year longitudinal study of girls' development, she is engaged in a 2-hour interview in the midst of the school day. Sitting in a small room with a woman interviewer, she begins to describe how she knows when she is being her true self and when she is not being herself, when she is "wearing a mask."

"When I'm with my really good friends, we're all ourselves, and if one of us is doing something that one of us doesn't like, then we'll tell them," Janet begins, describing what it means to be her true self in the vernacular of "being ourselves." She immediately adds, "The people I'm with, they're like part of who I am, we're such good friends," as if to explain to her interviewer

AUTHORS' NOTE: An earlier version of this chapter was presented at the American Psychological Association 99th Annual Convention, San Francisco, August, 1991, as part of a panel entitled "Resisting Silence: Women Listening to Girls."

1

why this question about being her true self evokes her entire group of friends. We notice the sequence of Janet's ideas: Speaking openly about "something that one of us doesn't like" is followed by a chord of connection—"they're like part of who I am," so that Janet's capacity to disagree openly is linked to her sense of being herself in connection with others. Janet also draws clear distinctions between being herself and wearing a mask: "When some people are like in a clique or something like that," she says, "then I wouldn't really be myself. It would be kind of putting on a mask and not being myself because I wanted to be part of this group of people."

Two years later, when she is 14 and in ninth grade, Janet describes herself and her relationships differently: "A good relationship with the people around me means I'm not having conflicts with the other people." Avoiding conflict this year, however, means sometimes not "speaking up." Janet no longer clearly distinguishes when she is being herself and when she is wearing a mask, but instead protects herself from engaging in conflict by silencing herself and leaving relationships:

> When you are in a big group of people and they are like
> saying something like about another person and you
> want to tell them to stop, but you are surrounded by a
> whole group, you really can't say, you just can't,
> because they would get mad at you, you know. And it is
> better if you don't speak up because you can just walk
> away and leave them alone and they can be with their
> ideas and you can still have your own thoughts. But, I
> don't know.

The content of Janet's narrative of relationships has shifted over the years, it seems, from a focus on open disagreement with close friends and a strong sense of connection with others at 12, to avoiding disagreement and leaving others in order to hold on to her own thoughts at 14. Moreover, even the grammar of Janet's speech has changed. Speaking in the general "you" instead of the personal "I," Janet seems to distance herself from the immediacy of her thoughts and feelings. She stops and starts, unable to articulate fully the reason she silences herself, "You really can't say, you just can't."

We have been interested in studying the ways adolescent girls, like Janet, understand themselves and their relationships and how their understanding changes and develops over time. As a number of recent studies document, early adolescence is a time of psychological risk and vulnerability for girls (see Ebata, 1987; Elder, Nguyen, & Caspi, 1985; Petersen, 1988; Petersen & Ebata, 1987). In particular, the move into adolescence affects girls' self-conceptions and, for example, marks a sharp increase in episodes of depression among girls (Rutter, 1986) and a sharp drop in self-esteem and self-confidence, at least in white and Latina girls (American Association of University Women, 1991; Block, 1990). Girls begin to develop disparaging body images at this time (Langlois & Stephan, 1981) and to experience problems around eating (Dreizen, Spirakis, & Stone, 1967; Garner, 1981). In addition, girls tend to lose ground in their assessments of their academic achievement and in their aspirations during adolescence (Arnold, 1993; Bernardez, 1991). There is clearly a need to understand what is happening in the lives of girls and why adolescence is such a time of psychological distress and risk.

We have been exploring girls' changing self-conceptions by using both interpretive analyses of in-depth clinical interviews and a more traditional psychometric measure of "ego development." Listening to Janet talk about herself and her relationships, we notice that her voice seems to change over time, and we believe this shift in voice signals a change in Janet's sense of herself as she moves into adolescence. The changes from her seventh- to ninth-grade interviews reveal developmental strengths, as well as vulnerabilities or losses. In the first interview, for example, 12-year-old Janet reveals particular strengths: She sounds more honest in her relationships, more vital and alive, more consistently in contact with her own thoughts and feelings, and less conflicted about speaking of what she knows from experience. In contrast, 14-year-old Janet can more clearly distinguish and hold different perspectives, also a developmental strength.

She describes herself as someone who can act autonomously of the group, keeping her own thoughts to herself and leaving others when she believes she cannot speak and be heard. It seems to us, however, that along with new strengths the older Janet is also vulnerable in new ways. At 14, Janet leaves the group to hold on to not only her "own thoughts" but also her feelings, her reality, her very self. The older Janet struggles to name her experience clearly, to hold on to the veracity of her perceptions. Again and again she stumbles into confusion during the course of this 2-hour interview. The phrases "I don't know" and "I can't explain it" now mark areas of her experience she cannot fully articulate. "But I don't know," Janet says after she talks about leaving her group of friends, and then her voice trails off into silence. In short, it appears to us that Janet's connection to herself is endangered when she is 14 years old in ways not manifest when she was 12: She seems to struggle at 14 to know what she knew so clearly about herself and her relationships at 12.

Our interpretation that something of importance was lost or endangered between ages 12 and 14 seems to be supported by Loevinger's (1976) Sentence Completion Test (SCT). When we traced changes in Janet's level of ego development, we found that she "regressed" from seventh to ninth grade—moving from Loevinger's conscientious-conformist stage to the conformist stage. In other words, according to Loevinger's theory, she moves from self-awareness edging toward a view of herself as differentiated, independent, and self-critical, to a retrenchment in a simpler and less differentiated conformity to the rules, maxims, and conventions of the group to which she belongs.

Interestingly enough, Janet is not alone in this pattern of "regression"—50% of our sample of 28 seventh-grade girls also regressed in ego development level as measured by the SCT between seventh and ninth grade. In addition, 45% of our sample of 56 10th-grade girls regressed in ego development level between 10th and 12th grade.

What are we to make of this unexpected phenomenon of regression in ego development in this sample of educationally advantaged adolescent girls? Is it possible that Janet and her schoolmates really are moving from a more to a less "sophisticated" and differentiated self-understanding? Or might this phenomenon connect to, perhaps even be explained by, girls' changing relationship to the culture in which they live as they move from childhood to adolescence?

Recent work following girls into adolescence (see Brown, 1989, 1991; Brown & Gilligan, 1992, 1993; Debold & Brown, 1991; Debold & Tolman, 1991; Gilligan, 1990a, 1990b; Gilligan, Brown, & Rogers, 1990; Rogers, 1993; Rogers & Gilligan, 1988) has explained such changes by suggesting that girls move from a rich relational world of childhood in which it is possible to express the full range of human feelings, into a culture of constraining conventions of femininity that pressures girls to narrow their feelings and to modulate their voices. Young girls tell psychologically astute stories of human relationships, rendering in exquisite detail their connections with themselves and with others. A struggle breaks out at the edge of adolescence, however, when these same girls are encouraged to disconnect from their knowledge, to see and hear the world largely as it has been seen and spoken about by men. What girls knew in childhood seems as if it cannot be known, and what girls want to say suddenly seems unspeakable. Facing into this crisis, many girls struggle to remain connected to their childhood knowledge, actively resisting repressive conventions of femininity and fighting openly for authentic relationships.

Yet if girls actively resist the cultural conventions of women's lives—that is, if they engage in a "political resistance"—they are sure to cause trouble in school and in their families and to risk ostracism even in their own peer groups (see Gilligan, 1990a). But if girls cut themselves off from their own knowledge and enter the conventions of feminine goodness, their development from this time on will be marked by signs of what we have come to call "psychological resistance." Capitulating to the culture by learning to muffle or silence their distinctive voices and to speak in another tongue—the voice of the culture—girls withdraw their real thoughts and feelings from relationships, they move "underground" to protect themselves, replacing real or genuine relationships with unauthentic or idealized relationships (Brown, 1989; Brown & Gilligan, 1992;

Gilligan, 1990a, 1990b; Rogers, 1993). In this way girls gradually forget and cover over what they knew as children and then may begin to speak through the bodily symptoms that plague women in this culture: depressive syndromes, anorexia, and bulimia (Steiner-Adair, 1991). Clearly whatever strategy or combination of strategies girls adopt has a psychic cost.

Interestingly enough, when Loevinger and her colleagues (1985) observed a significant loss in ego development among young women attending a private, academically competitive university (participants in her longitudinal college student study), she remarked, "A disturbing possibility is that for some significant fraction of students, particularly women, college is a regressive experience" (p. 960). Although Loevinger's finding of a pattern of regression in college women has not been further explored empirically or explained theoretically, she hints that moving into institutions of higher learning may affect dramatically and negatively young women's experiences of themselves.

Loevinger's theory (like other stage theories—e.g., Kohlberg 1984; Selman, 1980) revolves around the movement into, acceptance of, and movement out of conformity to conventions, ideally a progression toward a critical perspective on those conventions. We wondered whether the regression identified by the SCT might reflect girls' resistance to cultural conventions that negate or devalue girls' knowledge and experience. If this were the case, as girls begin to move into "conventional" stages of ego development, they necessarily would struggle with the distinction between their experiences and those conventions (also see Rogers & Gilligan, 1988). Furthermore girls' struggles with the culture's conventions would not necessarily be discerned through an analysis of ego development levels. The theory itself does not distinguish between the different ways boys and girls may enter conventions of modern Western culture. Rather, ego development theory, like most cognitive developmental theories, assumes a universal path of human development—assumes that development is unconstrained by culture and that all people move into and out of "conventional" ways of thinking and feeling with equal ease. In other words, all people are assumed to be in the same basic relationship to the dominant culture regardless of how they differ from those who have the power to define what is good and right, what is of value, and what is dismissed as of less value.

This constructivist view of the ego, however, does not take into account cultural or gender differences that color the ways individuals make meaning of their particular worlds. According to Loevinger, the ego is a structure of personality, by definition relatively stable, changing very gradually, except during periods of greatest physical and cognitive growth—childhood and adolescence. Ego development theory attempts to explain what Loevinger considers to be a universal human process—changes in the development of the self over time—through a sequence of qualitatively different structures or stages. Nine distinct levels or stages of development have been distinguished from analyses of SCT data: impulsive, self-protective, self-protective-conformist, conformist, conscientious-conformist, conscientious, individualistic, autonomous, and integrated. Structural changes in impulse control and character, interpersonal relations, conscious preoccupations, and cognitive style define the stages of ego development (see Loevinger, 1979, pp. 24-25). Nothing less than a complete pattern of structural changes defines a shift in ego level.

In this structural view of development, the responses or content of the sentence completions are useful only insofar as they are signs of ego level and reliably fit a predefined set of structured stages. We would not expect that the patterns of crisis and struggle with the conventions of the culture that girls experience would necessarily show up as regression in ego development on the SCT. Rather, given the assumptions underlying the structural view that Loevinger's theory epitomizes, we would expect, in fact, that experiences of crisis and struggle with the conventions of any culture, creating disequilibrium, would precipitate growth or movement forward into the postconventional stages of ego development.

Because this was not the case in our sample, we wondered what the SCT was picking up thematically about girls' understandings of themselves and their relationships. To fill out the SCT, girls must grapple actively with conventions of femininity (sentence stems include such items as "A good mother," "A wife should," "A girl has a right to "). In a previous study, we showed that the SCT picks up changes in girls' responses to the sentence stems that mark a struggle with these conventions (see Rogers & Gilligan, 1988). Thus we have an empirical basis for wondering whether the movement through the conventional stages of ego development might take a different turn for some girls. Were these educationally privileged girls facing such strong cultural pressures to conform in adolescence that they were, in effect, moving from a critical perspective on conventions at early adolescence into a capitulation to conventions at middle and late adolescence? Although it is not the way Loevinger herself sees her measure, the SCT can be seen, we argue, as a measure of the way individuals understand their relation to the conventions of the culture in which they live (also see Rogers, 1987, in press; Rogers & Gilligan, 1988). The regression in ego level we found may be interpreted, then, in light of girls' struggle with conventions, a struggle so fraught for some girls that their movement through the conventional stages is diverted and turned back for some period of time during adolescence.

The purpose of the chapter, then, is to explore the phenomenon of "regression" in ego development in adolescent girls by using empirical evidence gathered from our longitudinal interviews. Are Janet and her schoolmates moving from a more to a less differentiated self-understanding; that is, are they regressing—as Loevinger's measure reflects? Or is the regression captured by the SCT a sign of girls' resistance—a political and/or a psychological resistance—to the pressure on girls at adolescence to conform to debilitating gender stereotypes that negate or devalue what they know from their experiences in childhood?

Method

Sample and Setting

The girls in our sample were participants in a 5-year longitudinal study of development involving four cohort groups of girls ranging in age from 7 to 18 in a private all-girls' school in the Midwest. In this school approximately 86% of the girls are white, and 14% are girls of color from various cultures. These percentages are reflected in our two samples. This chapter focuses on two of the longitudinal cohort groups—girls in early and middle adolescence—specifically, 28 girls whom we followed from 7th to 9th grade, and 56 girls whom we followed from 10th to 12th grade. The groups represent intact grade levels in the school.

Measures

The girls filled out the Washington University Sentence Completion Test (SCT) in the first and third years of the study. This test consists of 36 sentence stems, many of them picking up girls' relationships to cultural ideals and values, such as "A good father," "My mother and I," "My conscience bothers me if," and "Rules are." The girls completed the item stems of the test in a group administration, and their responses were typed by item stem. These responses then were scored independently for ego development level by two trained raters.[1]

Each girl in this study also participated in a semistructured, in-depth clinical interview with a female interviewer. The interview consisted of four major sections: The girls were asked (a) to describe themselves in some depth in the first section, (b) to tell a story of their own moral conflict and choice in the second, (c) to think about a set of scenarios about learning and comment on their own experiences of learning inside and outside school in the third, and (d) to consider how society constructs the ideal woman and speak about their own views and plans for the future in the final section. Participants were interviewed once a year for 5 years. Whenever possible, girls were interviewed by the same woman throughout the study.

Drawing on an interpretive method that entails multiple readings or listenings of an interview text (see Brown et al., 1988; Brown, Debold, Tappan, & Gilligan, 1991; Brown & Gilligan,

1990; Brown, Tappan, Gilligan, Miller, & Argyris, 1989; Gilligan et al., 1990), we then read each girl's first- and third-year interview text three different times. Using colored pencils, we literally traced three different voices through each text. The first time through the text, we read or listened for "self": the voice of the "I" speaking in the text, and also the "I" who appears as actor or protagonist in the stories she tells. This reading is underlined in green and allows us to focus on how each girl represents herself and her particular struggles throughout her interview before imposing our own conceptual framework or set of definitions on her experience. As part of this reading, we attended to recurrent words or images, central metaphors, emotional resonances, contradictions, or inconsistencies in style, revisions and absences in the story, as well as shifts in narrative position—the use of first-, second-, or third-person voice.

Our second and third readings were guided by a coding sheet that we developed for this study (see the appendix). The second time through an individual girl's interview, we read for a voice of *psychological distress.* Underlining the text in orange pencil, we garnered evidence of girls' *capitulation* to debilitating cultural conventions of female behavior, as well as evidence of girls' *psychological resistance* to their own voice and knowledge. We read for capitulation by marking the lines and passages in the text where the girl disconnects from herself and her voice sounds as though it has been taken over by conventions that undermine her as a young woman. Reading for psychological resistance (the undoing of her knowledge or the refusal to know what she thinks and feels) entailed following shifts in language that marked her confusion, uncertainty, or dismissal of what she knew, as well as descriptions of physical symptoms or mood changes she did not appear to understand.

The third time through the interviews, we read for a voice of *psychological resilience.* Underlining the text in purple, we garnered evidence of an active *political resistance* to restrictive gender role stereotypes and for evidence of speaking about *genuine relationships.* We read for political resistance by marking a girl's active and conscious resistance to losing her own knowledge, noting when she self-consciously described capitulation strategies as strategies of self-protection and when she spoke out against domination, oppression, false relationships, or debilitating conventions of female behavior. We noted when she shifted from an abstract or highly polished language into a more colloquial, vivid, and at times irreverent language that held together thinking and feeling, mind and body. We also marked passages wherein she spoke about genuine relationships, relationships in which it was possible to be imperfect, to voice disagreement, to feel a full range of emotions, or relationships she described as authentic encounters or as real connections.

After these three readings of each set of longitudinal interviews, we wrote case summaries that included examples from the various voice readings and notes on how prevalent they were in the interviews over time, as well as an interpretation of how each girl changed over 3 years.[2]

Results

We found that although many of the girls regressed or remained at the same ego level over 3 years, only a small percentage actually progressed according to the SCT measure. Girls in both the 7th-grade group and the 10th-grade group who regressed showed stage changes of one or two ego development levels, regressing from various stages of the sequence of nine levels. What is clearest from these data is the wide variability and instability of ego development in both groups of adolescent girls.

In the seventh-grade group, ego levels ranged from Loevinger's self-protective stage through the conscientious stage. Girls at the self-protective stage, according to Loevinger's theory, have a simplified, egocentric, defensive view of relationships, whereas girls at the conscientious stage are both highly self-critical and can understand the differentiated feelings and motives of others. The average stage level was conscientious-conventional, the fifth level in Loevinger's sequence. Girls at this level theoretically see multiple perspectives and possibilities in situations and in relationships and are keenly self-aware. They already have begun to seek out exceptions to conformity and to question the conventions of the culture. In the seventh-grade group, 50% of the girls regressed at least one level in ego development by the ninth grade. Many of these girls regressed from the conscientious-conformist stage to the conformist stage, moving from beginning to question conventions into a simpler and easier acceptance of conventions. Among the girls who did not regress, 38% remained at the same ego level, and 12% progressed at least one level by the ninth grade. The regressors did not differ from the nonregressors in average ego level in the seventh grade.

Among the 10th graders, ego levels ranged from the impulsive stage (girls who theoretically would represent the world and relationships in stark dichotomies) through the autonomous stage (girls who would represent the world and relationships as inherently ambiguous and rich, seeing themselves and others in clearly differentiated terms). In other words, the 10th-grade girls represented all stages in Loevinger's sequence except the highest stage. The average ego level was the conscientious stage, the sixth level in Loevinger's sequence. According to Loevinger, these girls would be self-critical and also show self-respect, and they would see relationships as inherently mutual, complex, and changing. In the 10th-grade group, 45% of the girls regressed at least one level from a range of different levels, 36% remained at the same ego level, and 19% advanced at least one level by the 12th grade. Among the girls who regressed, there were two distinct patterns: girls who regressed two or three levels from the highest stages, and girls who regressed on average one level, from the conscientious stage to the conscientious-conformist stage. Regardless of the level from which the 10th graders regressed, all of these girls moved into a less complex and differentiated understanding of themselves and of their relationships according to Loevinger's theory.

We selected and read first- and third-year interviews of the "regressors" (girls who had regressed at least one ego level) by using the interpretive method we described above. From this analysis, we found surprisingly different patterns in the 7th- and

10th-grade cohorts, patterns we could not have predicted from the Loevinger stage descriptions of their regression.

Seventh-Grade Cohort

We noted certain commonalities among the girls who regressed between seventh and ninth grade. As seventh graders, many of these girls impressed us as unusually lively, intelligent, and vital. Although these interviews were a pleasure to read, they also were difficult to interpret. We found ourselves continually marking rapid shifts in voice and making multiple interpretations of a single passage. Many of these girls shifted back and forth between political resistance (e.g., a clear protest of some form of oppression in a relationship) and psychological resistance—often introduced by the phrase "I don't know," wherein they suddenly sounded confused about what really was happening or sharply dismissed or "forgot" their own perceptions. For example, Janet, the seventh grader introduced at the beginning of this chapter, describes a time when her parents were not listening to her but were listening to her brother. She says, "When my brother is around and he is talking to my parents, you kind of get the feeling that they're listening to him and neither one of them are listening to me." She goes on to describe specifically what she observes: "They'll both be kind of, be like turned in his direction and then they'll ask me to wait until he finishes." Then, quite abruptly, Janet begins to undo her perceptions and to justify her parents' turning toward her brother. "I don't know," she muses, "My brother, either he had a greater problem . . . it was because he had a problem or something, they were probably concentrating on what he was trying to say and then I was telling them something, it wasn't as important."

Many passages could be read in two ways. For example, a struggle for genuine relationship could also be read as capitulation to debilitating norms of female behavior. In these passages the girls evoked in us the sense of living within a double reality— of resisting false appearances and talking behind other girls' backs, while also participating in false relationships in the name of being "nice" or of "not hurting" anyone. Liza, for example, speaks in a long passage about how the "talk" of other girls in her class can cause her suddenly to "regret something" she's said. Learning this year to "be more omniscient" and to "see inside of others in a way," Liza uses her knowledge to silence herself. She explains how this happens: "You can kind of predict what they [friends] are going to do . . . you are like sensitive about what you say so that you don't disturb or hurt them in any way." Thus Liza sees through false appearances, knowing other girls "talk" about her on the one hand, and also participating in false relationships herself by not saying what she really thinks and feels on the other hand.

Clearly these seventh-grade girls were cognitively sophisticated and able to entertain different perspectives on their experiences. This ability was particularly clear when they spoke of their resistance to the ways girls police each other by actively enforcing good girl behavior—what Brown and Gilligan (1992) called "the tyranny of nice and kind." Although very astute in their readings of the social world and keenly self-aware, as is clear in the examples cited from Janet's and Liza's interviews, these 12- and 13-year-olds did not seem to be aware of or concerned about contradictions in what they were saying and did not speak about or allude to the doubleness of voice and vision that our analysis picked up. They often spoke about genuine relationships, open disagreement, and an intense pleasure in being alone or with others. They struck us as curious, as playful, and often as outspoken. Hillary, for instance, asks at the start of her interview, "What do you want to know?" upstaging her interviewer's questions with her own curiosity about the study. Describing what is right or moral as "what I think would be the right thing to do, how I feel, what my feelings are," Hillary asserts that it is not fair to "boss around the first graders just because they are littler," and plans how she will "speak up" and tell the girls who do this to stop it. Toward the end of the 2-hour conversation, she tells her interviewer she can say what she wants because she keeps a diary. "And I'll sit down and write down my thoughts. I don't write in it regularly, just whenever I have this feeling to write."

By their ninth-grade year, much of the vitality and open resistance we identified in the seventh graders seemed watered down; the doubleness of voice and vision was not so striking, and the girls also sounded at times more self-assured, suggesting to us that they may be giving up the struggle to hold on to their own voices as they move into the dominant culture. By ninth grade these girls had entered highly *privatized relationships,* relationships wherein confidentiality became the most frequently mentioned basis for trust. At the same time, they struggled to know when they were being themselves and when they were not. There seemed to be less overt forms of policing among the girls, but they were not off the hook; the group's scrutiny had become more internalized. There was impressive evidence of increased self-scrutiny, including an increased use of visual metaphors. The girls clearly had learned to view themselves through the culture's conventions and to speak in the voice of those conventions. This shift in voice, coupled with a shift in language (that began in seventh grade but is now more pervasive), seemed to indicate they were distancing themselves from their immediate experience—shifting from "I" to "you"—and gave us the impression that they were less fully in contact with themselves and perhaps, in fact, in danger of losing themselves. Liza in the ninth grade, for example, struggles with what it means to be "close" to a friend: "If you can anticipate what she is going to be doing or she can anticipate what I would say, then, I don't know, you can sometimes get mixed up as to who you are, you can sort of lose your individual self."

These girls as 14- and 15-year-olds also sometimes sounded defensively tough in a new way, saying "I don't care" or "I have nothing to lose" by not speaking up in the face of disagreement, rather than showing their real feelings in relationships and risking the loss of important connections. Although these girls described close relationships with others and often wished to be more open about disagreement, they also spoke about elaborate ways to hide their strong feelings, as if open disagreement was taboo. Susan says she is afraid of her friends' sudden "moodi-ness" and "anger": "I don't like to have anyone mad at me," she explains, and "They have real mood swings and you have to catch them at the right moment, or you are doomed." This year, she says, she "stays out of the middle" of a conflict between her two closest friends, though she knows more about their conflict than either one does alone and wants them to "get it out in the open." Susan says she has heard about this conflict in detail from each of the girls and is in a position to bring it up with them, but she decides "not to say anything" because they then may be angry with her for "bringing it up." Susan then goes on to describe her daily life of being "careful" of what she says and wishing her friends were not so "moody." The active struggles to speak that we heard in this group when they were in seventh grade are, by and large, replaced with this kind of carefulness in speaking, or by self-silencing, in the ninth grade.

In short, these girls as ninth graders seemed to have shut down; they seemed less vital and alive to us, and also curiously less complex in their thinking about relationships. Although there was more evidence of abstract language, it sounded a bit odd to us at times, as if they were speaking in foreign accents they could drop quickly. Their voices now picked up conven-tional maxims for a successful and happy life, including con-cerns with doing well in school and getting into a good college, a recipe for "sure" success. And although they also occasionally could protest the pressure they were beginning to feel, they seemed caught in an unsolvable struggle with conventions that would have them be nice and kind, self-sacrificing, passive, and pure on the one hand, and on the other hand also be outspoken, self-confident, independent, and capable of entering any career they chose. Their strategies of dealing with the struggle ap-peared less creative, less critical than they sounded in seventh grade, and also more deeply internalized and perhaps more entrenched. They seemed less likely to resist or fight openly for genuine relationships.

When exceptions to the pattern appeared and there were only two cases, both girls fit the pattern of loss over time, but there was greater evidence of psychological distress in both their seventh- and ninth-grade interviews in comparison with the other girls in the group. Unlike the others, these girls regressed to a preconventional level of ego development by the ninth grade, moving from Loevinger's conformist stage to the self-protective stage, from an unquestioning acceptance of the values and maxims of the culture into a preconventional stance toward the social world that is both simpler and more defensive and wary.

Janet: A Case Study

Returning now to 12-year-old Janet, the seventh grader we introduced at the beginning of this chapter, and following her from the seventh to the ninth grade, we discover that she has regressed from the conscientious-conformist stage of ego development to the conformist stage, as many of her peers have done.

As a seventh grader, Janet not only speaks about open disagreement with her friends ("When I'm with my good friends, we are ourselves, and if one of us is doing something that one of us doesn't like, then we'll tell them") but also stands up for herself with "people I don't consider my real friends." She says that despite "these people (not my friends) . . . saying that I couldn't play softball, just couldn't do it, . . . I thought I was good enough and I decided to stick with it, and now I pitch for the team." Janet also speaks about her fear of the girls in her class and of a need to protect herself. She says, "I'm afraid of what they will say sometimes, if I show them who I really am. Then they won't like me, so I try to put up a front." But this strategy, she hints, is dangerous because she cannot always discern when she is being herself and when she is not: "When I meet new people, I try to be outgoing, see, which I'm usually not. But sometimes I do it and I don't know if it's really a front or not."

Janet is acutely aware of unfairness this year and struggles to speak her feelings. Telling a story about her math teacher in a situation she thought was unfair, Janet says, "It was unfair because she just wouldn't help me, and she said earlier that she would help us if we just came to her. So I went to her for extra help and the teacher refused to help because she said it [the homework] was for points. . . . So I said to her, 'If it's the points that are bothering you, you don't have to give me points, I just want to know how to do it.' " But it is not clear from her story whether Janet wishes she had said this or actually did say this. "I think I should have spoken," she says a few sentences later, "either to her [the teacher] or to somebody else," implying that she has not. Janet may be confused not only about when she is being herself and when she is putting up a front, but also about what she imagines she has said and what she has actually said. Despite this confusion, Janet is able to see clearly through the culture's most idealized images of women and actively *resist* living up to these images. Asked to speak about herself and her future, she says wryly, "Not everybody's going to have the perfect life, the perfect family, and the perfect job and everything. . . . Society, I think, makes women, makes the super-woman look so easy, but there are few people out there who really are that superwoman and who can do everything."

When Janet is 14 and in the ninth grade, she is engaged in an intense struggle to know her own thoughts and feelings from her experience. She has, by this time, taken in many conventions of good feminine behavior. However, the maxims for acceptable behavior that she quotes at times nearly undermine her struggle to know and name her own experience. As a ninth grader, Janet considers what she means by a good relationship: "A good relationship," she says, "means I'm not having conflicts with other people." Avoiding conflict, she admits freely, "means sometimes not saying anything." Janet describes not only silencing herself but also doubting her own desires or wishes. She tells her interviewer that she wishes her mother were not going back to work, "but I have no right to feel that way." Janet also seems to believe that if she says what she really thinks and feels to her mother (about this decision to go back to work), she will talk her mother out of her desire: "If I told her how I felt about her going back, um, that she was not going to be there for me, then she wouldn't want to do it." When Janet does insist on speaking or on having her mother listen to her, she cannot hold on to her own perspective. Speaking, for instance, of her mother not listening to her about a decision regarding a party dress, she says, "I think we should have talked more. I really wanted it. It wasn't really too skimpy really, not really, but we didn't talk about what I had to say." Asked what she would have liked to say, Janet replies, "I'm not sure. . . . I mean it's fine what she decided." The shift away from her own experience, introduced by the phrase "I mean," occurs several times in her interview. Because she clearly can hold multiple perspectives this year, it is striking that her own perspective drops out of her relationships. For example, Janet wants to be "closer to my mom. I feel like we're growing apart so much," but the messages she has taken in as a young woman make it difficult for her to be honest with her mother and with her friends. She says she feels "good" about herself, for example, "only when I help someone else with a problem" and adds, "I need to know that what I am doing is not just for myself."

Carrying this theme into her future, Janet says as a mother she will "always be caring and understanding of other people." Given her uncritical acceptance of an idealized selfless woman, in striking contrast to her wry comments about "superwoman" as a seventh grader, it is not surprising that when she tries to talk about a disagreement with her friends, Janet falls into a densely encoded narrative with no clear referents: "A person in my group wanted to go out with this boy . . . from another school that another person kind of likes, so someone had to tell her not to, and it couldn't be that person, and I didn't want to have to say it, so . . . you don't want to get put in that position where you have to make someone upset at you." This narrative has no specific actions, and it is hard to follow. Janet calls herself "you," distancing herself from herself and her own experience. We wonder whether this encoded speech is the only way she now can speak about real disagreement—in a covered, confusing, diffused narrative that removes her from her experience. This year, she says "I don't know" or "I can't think" in response to many of the questions she had no trouble answering as a seventh grader, and she also qualifies her most astute observations with these phrases. In short, we hear in Janet's seventh- and ninth-grade interviews a struggle for voice and knowledge that continues and intensifies during this time until, by age 14, the struggle itself is in danger of being undermined by the simplified maxims of being a "good" woman she has seemingly taken in and made her own.

Tenth-Grade Cohort

Turning now to the 10th-grade cohort, we noticed that these girls as a group were more politically savvy and more socially sophisticated than the younger group. They knew not only what was expected of them in school and at home but also what they should not know, think, and feel if they were to be accepted in relationships and approved of in school. They often chose to conceal what might be judged unfavorably or what they anticipated may cause a disturbance. These 10th-grade girls knew all about *false relationships* (relationships in which people pretend or play a role rather than risk rejection or disapproval), and they described in detail how they knew when someone else was being false. Yet they engaged in these relationships on a daily basis to protect themselves and others from difficult truths, from the danger of real disagreement. Jillian, for example, finds herself in great distress when, working "behind the scenes" of a play, another girl who appears to be "a nice person" begins to bully her. "She stepped on my hand, and she threw away some of my books, and she spilled my Coca-Cola . . . and she did it in a way that she looked like she didn't do it, or I did it myself." Despite this shabby treatment and Jillian's knowledge of how well this girl could conceal her cruelty and make herself appear "nice," Jillian backs down when her friends "don't believe me" and says, "I had to keep trying to get along with someone who was very rude."

So acutely aware of others' expectations and so intent on meeting these expectations, these girls were willing to engage in what they knew to be false and shallow and even cruel relationships. They capitulated in their relationships with boys, too, often by deliberately hiding their own strengths. Jane, for instance, says she will not tell boys about her successes in sports for fear they "would be scared away."

These 14- and 15-year-old girls ascribed to conventions of maturity and success espoused by their parents and their private, privileged girls' school. They aspired to maturity through "independence" even when this ideal meant cutting themselves off from close relationships, as if the achievement of independence, in addition to "higher grades," would ensure success, or at least a good showing that they indeed were "growing up" and "doing better." Yet they seemed to value themselves so little. These girls frequently spoke about not wanting to "inconvenience others," "hurt others," or "cause a disturbance" in any way, even if this meant dismissing their own needs. The prevalence of their passivity and their willingness to sacrifice themselves in this way was striking, especially in conjunction with the espoused ideal of becoming independent and successful women.

Psychological resistance in this cohort took a new turn—an undoing of their most astute observations, often marked mid-thought by the phrase "I mean" and followed by a confusion or reversal of meanings. Unable to sustain differences in the face of disagreement, for example, a girl might state a clear difference of feeling or opinion and then confuse the different perspectives in her story or undo the difference of opinion by highlighting agreement. Heather begins to tell a story about a disagreement with her father over local politics:

> I got into this big debate with my Dad, uh, he's a debating kind of person, you know, and he almost always wins. . . . So I was saying one thing, and I really did not agree with him. . . . By the end, I could see his point better than mine, so I guess you could say that we agreed.

These girls spontaneously say they do not want to be in conflict, and their narratives reflect this wish. Their psychological resistance also shows up more frequently in the form of reported symptoms—feeling "bad" about themselves even in the face of numerous accomplishments; inexplicable mood changes; and complaints of feeling "tired," "depressed," and "out of it."

Although they largely had given over their own authority to their parents and state they accept their parents' morals and standards, there were glimmers of protest, a quiet protest behind the scenes, but nevertheless, a questioning. Jane talks about getting higher grades this year, looking toward college admissions 2 years in the future. She implies that her increased efforts are her choice: "I know I have accomplished something I want, I want to go to a good college." "But," she says, suddenly wry, briefly protesting, "I mean my mom wants me to go to a good school even more that I do!" Other girls also resisted the high expectations that others, particularly parents and teachers, considered to be unreasonable expectations for exceptional achievement or for flawless moral behavior. At times the girls also quietly protested the image of the "superwoman" (Steiner-Adair, 1986) others hoped they would become—the woman who is perfectly "together": that thin, beautiful woman, with a wonderful husband and children, who is completely independent of them and has a gratifying career.

Despite their tendency to idealize relationships, to gloss over conflict and difficulties, these 10th-grade girls expressed a wish to be real, to be themselves more often, and to reveal themselves more fully and more freely. They not only distinguished between real and false relationships but also saw beneath the surface of others' behavior and accurately read indirect or encoded messages, adeptly translating these indirect messages into others' "real" motives and intentions. Thus they were abler to anticipate others' responses than the younger girls and to make more savvy decisions about when and when not to put themselves in danger emotionally and politically by making a "misstep" or acting on a "misreading" of relationships in the culture of their school. Asked to describe when it is worth the effort to speak up, Kari succinctly says, "It depends on what's involved and what's at risk by not saying anything, or what's at risk by saying anything." In this 10th-grade year, the girls seem to be looking rather desperately for footholds or ideas (e.g., ascribing to independence, wanting to be more self-confident), searching for sanctioned activities (e.g., playing sports, learning to make "well-reasoned" arguments) in order to resist debilitating cultural messages about women.

Following the 10th graders over time, we found two different patterns of change among this group. The first and more prevalent pattern involved moving more deeply into the conventions of the culture by the 12th grade, internalizing these conventions with minimal resistance, and entrenching themselves there, as if for the long haul. Even the glimmers of their resistance in 10th grade became more privatized over the 3 years, so their quiet protests were revealed only behind the scenes of their public lives in the presence of close friends or in a setting such as a confidential interview, while the surface was smooth, polished, perfect. There was nothing to disturb this surface, and, in fact, they told us they felt more "self-assured," more "mature," more "confident" of their successes.

Yet by the 12th grade, many of the girls espoused conformity with conventions, and this entrenchment in conformity went hand in hand with accepting the authority of their parents and taking on a tremendous pressure to do well in school.[3] In fact, these girls (who regressed, on average, one stage in ego development, from conscientious to conscientious-conformist) spoke of the psychological and physical strain of their obsession with doing exceptional academic work for their parents and getting into a college of good standing. Sarah, for instance, who describes herself as "lazy" for not trying hard enough to excel in school and also hold a part-time job at night, says, "I'm just so nervous all the time, my stomach gets upset. I have trouble sleeping sometimes. . . . I'm just exhausted really."

A second distinct pattern of change between the 10th and 12th grades involved fewer of the girls, approximately one-third of the group of girls who "regressed." This group of girls appeared to be more actively and publicly resistant than their peers in the 10th grade. They continued this pattern of public resistance into the 12th grade, becoming more astute in their knowledge of consequences over time, clearly articulating what their actions meant to others and to themselves. These girls also spoke of valuing themselves and their mothers, a theme not common in the narratives of the others who "regressed" in ego development.

These girls seemed to have either sustained or reentered an intense struggle for real relationships, for the veracity of their own perceptions, determined to voice what they knew in the world, and in these ways they sounded more like the seventh graders. But they were far more sophisticated than the younger girls in their knowledge of the political implications of their struggle. These girls also regressed more dramatically in ego development by the 12th grade (moving from the highest ego levels attained by any of the girls in our sample back two to three stages, rather than one stage).

Thus, among the 10th graders who had regressed in ego level by the 12th grade, the meaning of their regression could involve either a more complete capitulation to cultural conventions or an active political resistance accompanied by a move into more authentic connection with themselves and others. The girls who were active resisters in the 12th grade were all working-class girls, girls of color, or girls who hinted at sexual or familial violence in their interviews. What was crucial to their continued resistance, it seems, was a strong relationship with women who spoke openly about their relational experiences—both of pleasure and of struggle—with the girls.

Nawal: A Case Study

Nawal regressed two full stages, from Loevinger's autonomous stage in the 10th grade to the conscientious stage by the 12th grade, yet over time she spoke more clearly of herself, both as a young woman and as Syrian, in relation to her mother.

Listening to Nawal in the 10th grade, we hear a girl who seems to be in an argument with herself about what she should do, about what she should feel and think. Nawal struggles to stay in connection with herself and argues with herself about what she can and cannot know about her experience. When her experience contradicts the messages she has taken in about what it means to be a good student and a good daughter, she has great difficulty staying with her own knowledge. The lines of these overlapping arguments with the culture and with herself are marked by the rigidly moral language of "should" and "have to" and surrounded by the phrase "I don't know." Nawal's struggle to know and name her experience centers around staying in connection with herself while trying to live up to conventions of feminine goodness and cultural ideals of "maturity" this year. She wants to be all-caring and tells stories of "feeling responsible for everyone else's feelings," and at the same time she claims herself entirely "independent" of others, an independence she defines as "mature."

Nawal tells her interviewer that over the previous summer she was able to "relax," although she worked in her father's medical office "full time." She then describes the opening of the school year as a whirlwind of activities and pressures:

> I was on the tennis team. . . . I started running. . . . I play field hockey. . . . I was just in a whirl. . . . Exams were very difficult. . . . I had to make up. . . . I just made the lacrosse team. . . . I'm pulling up my grades. . . . I am really going to try. . . . I am not going to be stupid.

In the midst of this litany of sports activities and efforts to pull her grades up to her parents' and teachers' standards is a quieter voice of complaint: "I just totally tried to unwind. . . . I need to relax. . . . I need to get my mind off school. . . . I feel like I am tired and worn out."

We wonder whether Nawal is "tired and worn out" not only from the sheer number of activities she is engaged in but also because she cannot clearly know or name what is happening to her this year. Her resistance to knowing her own thoughts and feelings is striking in this interview. During the interview, when

Nawal begins to give voice to her thoughts and feelings, this knowledge seems to frighten her, for she abruptly begins to denigrate her experience. For example, after describing her pleasure and skill in playing field hockey, she says, "If I miss the ball or something, I will just go hysterical on the field." As we would expect from a girl at the autonomous level of ego development, Nawal reflects on her own experience this sophomore year as she tells stories about her life and her relationships, marking the changes she feels within herself quite consciously. What is puzzling to us, given this capacity, is her confusion about what the changes signal and also her struggle to speak clearly about when she is behaving in a false way and when she is being real, being herself in relationships. Here she sounds very much like Janet as a ninth grader. Nawal describes "playing up" to a girl on another lacrosse team whom she says she "hates," knowing even as she says this that it is not "right," that although she does not have to be "mean" to this girl, neither does she have to go out of her way to be "nice." But her behavior solves the problem of her discomfort in this social situation: "It saves you from getting into trouble." "But," she says, still uneasy about her actions, "you shouldn't have to be fake." "It's hard," Nawal concludes, "to always do what you really think is right." We hear in her words the doubling of meanings, of both capitulation and resistance, what we would call a strategy of capitulation: A savvy attempt to keep herself from "getting into trouble" turns quickly into a psychological resistance as Nawal herself becomes confused about when she is being a fake and when she is being real. In another excerpt, she describes herself at school: "I will be laughing, coming in, you know, just saying hi to everyone, hi, hi, you know, and just like hugging everyone," but she does not know whether this is real or not. She says, musing, "I mean, I guess I'm being myself today. I don't know." And it seems to us that she really does not know.

At other places in her interview, however, the phrase "I don't know" does not seem to signal real confusion, but rather seems to cover Nawal's astute observations and questions, her perceptions that do not get fully articulated. It is as if Nawal's confusion is itself a smoke screen for a knowledge she cannot bear to claim. In response to her interviewer's question, "Can you tell me about a situation where you or someone you know was not being listened to?" Nawal begins to describe her experience clearly:

> Just like sometimes when I am in arguments with my parents, it's like they don't seem to hear, like they catch certain things that I say and then I'll say things and they will contradict me, but it won't have anything to do with what I am talking about, you know.

Then, as if she has not experienced or known this about herself and her parents, Nawal says, "I don't really think, you know, I haven't really been in that, you know what I mean, I don't really know, I don't think so. I don't know about that one. I can't think of anything." Through the repeated "I don't know" and "I don't think," Nawal chants herself into a waking sleep about her own experience over the course of the interview. And, not surprisingly, her psychological resistance to telling the actual lived stories of her day-to-day life gets expressed physically and emotionally. Nawal speaks about feeling "depressed" this 10th-grade year; she finds herself wanting to "lie in bed" or "eat excessively" and feels "detached" from herself, changes she does not seem to understand. The roots and causes of these changes are not entirely clear to us either, but what is clear is that Nawal stops herself from knowing quite often in this interview; she reveals her psychological resistance in the stories she tells about her life and her relationships.

As we listen to Nawal at age 17, 2 years later in her senior year, she sounds more authentic, more self-confident, and more resilient, and also describes herself at the beginning of her interview as someone who has changed in these ways:

> I am pretty sure of myself. . . . If I'm in a bad mood, I'm in a very bad mood. . . . I'm really resilient. I think . . . I've become more assured, more self-assured. . . . I'm not always confident, but I know what I am capable of doing.

Although she is rated two full stages lower in her ego development, at Loevinger's conscientious stage this year, her voice seems more genuine and clearer to us. What, then, is the meaning of Nawal's regression in ego development? Might her regression actually mark a psychological resiliency and a healthy resistance to conventional norms of femininity and maturity? And in this way might these changes mark a restoration of her knowledge of herself and her relationships that was fast disappearing 2 years ago? What has happened to her in the intervening 2 years?

Nawal tells a story at the beginning of this 12th-grade interview of "a very serious accident" of falling against and through a mirror, of "breaking myself" and, correspondingly, of "breaking a pattern of living" that was making her "miserable." When she fell, she cut "seven tendons, a nerve, and an artery." This accident, which occurred the previous spring, was followed by a period of time she describes as "a nightmare," as a "hell that I had to live through." While she was working to restore her hand and arm in physical therapy in the subsequent months, she also was struggling to understand herself and her mother as Arabic women in a predominantly white suburban culture. This particular struggle culminated in her powerful and public senior speech.

Describing this speech, which she gave before her family, teachers, and classmates, she says:

> It was really a speech about learning to accept myself and was, like, okay, my mom has black, curly wild hair, really dark skin. Dresses like, she wears a huge silver earring, does not fit the stereotypical Laurel mother image, does not. And I love the way she dresses, and I love the fact that she is different . . . but when I was younger, it used to bother me and I hated being Arabic, I hated being different, and I hated having an Arabic name. And I was really almost embarrassed by my mom.

For Nawal it was important to talk about her realization publicly in her senior speech, given before the entire high school, to voice her resistance to conventions of beauty that would have her, an

Arabic girl, wish for "long, long blonde hair" and "blue eyes." "And now," Nawal adds, seeing the political implications of her speech, "my sister goes here and she's in the sixth grade, and her teacher asked me to give that speech for middle school chapel. So I am going to do it because I think it needs to be said."

Nawal also describes a process of sorting out who are "true" friends this senior year, and in this way her voice is reminiscent of the seventh graders. But, in fact, her thinking is much more sophisticated than theirs; Nawal seems to be taking in the history of her adolescence, putting herself back together and coming to know and understand herself and others through the connections she makes at 17: "I might be a little bit different in the way I am with myself now," she begins, and then interjects, "I knew all about me sophomore year, so I thought, but I just didn't connect it with everything around me and now I can connect it with everything around me." Thinking about this, she sums up her journey through adolescence as a time "when you understand yourself, when you can put yourself in relation to everything, you know, everything around you, when it kind of all fits."

Discussion

How do we explain the phenomenon of regression in Loevinger's measure of ego development among these adolescent girls, in light of the different patterns we found in the 7th- and 10th-grade groups from our interpretive analyses of the girls' interviews?

Returning now to Janet, the seventh grader we introduced at the beginning of this chapter, we recall her similarity in specific ways to the other seventh-grade girls who had, in Loevinger's terms, regressed in ego development. In contrast to the girls who either remained at the same ego level or progressed over 3 years—girls who seemed more conventional and bland, less distressed and less troubled to us—Janet and the other girls in her class who regressed struck us as more interesting, intelligent, vital, and alive, more intensely engaged in a struggle for voice and knowledge, and yet also more likely to reveal signs of psychological distress and struggle.

Bringing our interpretations of the girls' interviews in relation to the SCT data, we argue that what Loevinger terms a regression in ego development can be interpreted in light of the intensity of the girls' struggles for clarity in the face of contradictory and confusing cultural messages—messages that would, on the one hand, have girls claim a sense of personal authority and, on the other hand, have girls fit themselves into gender stereotypes of passive, silent women. Given these confusing messages, it is not surprising that some girls in early adolescence "regress" to what Loevinger calls more conventional levels, perhaps seeking the safety of familiarity.

Yet while Loevinger's measure captures the sense of loss we encountered in the girls' interviews between seventh and ninth grade—matching our impression that the seventh-grade girls had entered a feminine "underground" by the ninth grade and, in the process, lost much of their liveliness and resiliency—this measure does not pick up the details of *how* girls actively struggle with debilitating conventions of female behavior.

Furthermore the SCT does not pick up different meanings of regression. Only through the layered readings of the girls' interview texts, carefully tracing shifts in voice over time for each individual girl, could we begin to discern what regression signifies for different girls at different ages. Among the 10th-grade girls, for example, we found that a loss in ego development was accompanied by either increased evidence of capitulation to conventions or increased evidence of authentic relationships and political resistance. We would interpret the former pattern as a sign of developmental vulnerability and interpret the latter one as a sign of developmental strength; yet both of these patterns appeared in interviews with girls who had "regressed" on Loevinger's measure.

Moreover, only by bringing the interview analyses into relation with the SCT data were we able to make sense of findings that seemed, on the surface, not only counterintuitive but also contradictory. For instance, the regression in ego development that was accompanied by increased evidence of political resistance and genuine relationships in the interviews of some 12th-grade girls seemed incongruous to us, and we could not understand at first what appeared to be this contradictory finding. Yet by following shifts in individual girls' voices through their interviews over time and by extending our analyses over two cohort groups, we could trace changes in girls' understanding of themselves from 7th to 12th grade. The pattern among the 12th-grade girls that seemed puzzling at first, we discovered, is, in fact, a logical extension of the crisis girls first face in 7th grade.

Nawal, the Syrian girl who gave her senior speech about learning to accept her mother and herself, publicly resisting the culture of her school, exemplifies this pattern. She regressed from Loevinger's autonomous level of ego development, an unusually high ego level for any 9th-grade girl, to the conscientious level by 12th-grade. During her adolescence we would expect her to progress on Loevinger's stage sequence or to remain at the same level when she had peaked at such a high level so early, but not to regress two levels. As developmental psychologists we wonder, as Loevinger wondered, what this regression means. From our understanding of her interviews and our understanding of the pattern we observed in the 7th-grade girls, we suggest that Nawal's regression marks not a loss, or what would be described according to Loevinger's stage theory as a move to a less full and complex view of herself and of the world, but rather a developmental struggle for knowledge and voice that began in early adolescence and has culminated in psychological resiliency, a healthy resistance to cultural norms of femininity, a new sense of integrity. Perhaps, then, for some girls late in adolescence, the kind of shift in self-understanding that on Loevinger's measure is called "regression" may be interpreted better as girls' resistance: a struggle to restore or bring to the surface an earlier knowledge of themselves, a knowledge that was disappearing rapidly in early adolescence, the period of greatest psychological risk and vulnerability for girls. In other words, perhaps what is called "regression" in Loevinger's terms actually may represent a certain kind of developmental progress in girls' lives toward a more genuine, though less abstract, understanding of themselves and relationships that, because of its irreverence and clarity, may appear on some measures to be a move back into greater simplicity.

It would appear, therefore, that the SCT does not help us distinguish those girls whose loss of voice and knowledge about themselves parallels a loss in ego development from those who actively resist conventional notions of femininity and womanhood. In Loevinger's theory, as in other cognitive-developmental stage theories, such conventional notions must be entered and taken in before they can be challenged or surpassed, a prerequisite to arrival at the highest stages, the endpoint or apex of a developmental order. In Loevinger's theory any movement into or away from conventions will be called either "regression" or "progression"; one is either pre- or postconformist. Although it is possible to trace the ways girls enter and leave the conventional stages in such a system, there is no way to appreciate or understand fully girls' refusal or resistance to enter the very definitions of convention that are built into such stage theories—conventions that are not constructed from their experience, or worse, that may carry assumptions detrimental to their healthy development.

Thus to make sense of the puzzle of our findings, we needed to rely on multiple methods and descriptions of girls' development. Yet, more critically, we needed to consider girls' relationship to the cultural conventions that are part and parcel of constructivist stage-theory models of development; that is, if particular conventions of relationship and of personhood are assumed in the definitions of stage structures of development, then we have to consider what these conventions represent and how they have been defined, before interpreting "developmental" findings.

Notes

1. Ego levels were derived for each girl, based on Loevinger's ogive rules, cumulative frequency distributions of ego level ratings with specific cutting scores (1979). Reliability of ego development rating was assessed in terms of the raters' agreement on ego level ratings (Kappa = .79), as well as a correlation of the raters' assessments of the item responses as a whole (r = .84).

2. Interpretive agreement was determined by the authors' ability to identify evidence of the various categories from extended pieces of interview text, rather than simply to match preselected phrases or definitions to categories. A particu-

lar passage of text could be interpreted in more than one way—that is, marked for evidence of more than one category. For example, there may be signs both of a girl's capitulation to conventions of female behavior—such as her belief that as a good girl she ought to be passive and quiet—and of political resistance—a critique of the Barbie doll image of long legs and blonde hair—within a single piece of text. Comparisons of each reader's interpretations yielded an agreement of 92% (Kappa = .88).

3. This finding corresponds to the Laurel School "Ways of Knowing" data analysis. Although 16% of the 7th-grade girls were "received knowers," 29% of the 10th-graders were coded in this category. "Received knowers" refers to a passive acceptance of authority and a tendency to see things in black and white, a dualistic approach to the world (see Belenky, Clinchy, Goldberger, & Tarule, 1986).

References

American Association of University Women. (1991). *Shortchanging girls, short-changing America.* Washington, DC: Author.

Arnold, K. D. (1993). Academically talented women in the 1980s: The Illinois valedictorian project. In K. D. Hulbert & D. T. Schuster (Eds.), *Women's lives through time: Educated American women of the twentieth century* (pp. 393-414). San Francisco: Jossey-Bass.

Belenky, M., Clinchy, B., Goldberger, N., & Tarule, J. (1986). *Women's ways of knowing: The development of self, voice, and mind.* New York: Basic Books.

Bernardez, T. (1991). Adolescent resistance and the maladies of women: Notes from the underground. In C. Gilligan, A. Rogers, & D. Tolman (Eds.), *Women, girls, and psychotherapy: Reframing resistance* (pp. 213-222). New York: Haworth.

Block, J. (1990, October). Ego resilience through time: Antecedents and ramifications. Paper presented in *Resilience and psychological health,* symposium of the Boston Psychoanalytic Society, Boston, MA.

Brown, L. (1989). *Narratives of relationship: The development of a care voice in girls ages 7 to 16.* Unpublished doctoral dissertation, Harvard University Graduate School of Education, Cambridge, MA.

Brown, L. (1991). A problem of vision: The development of voice and relational knowledge in girls ages 7 to 16. *Women's Studies Quarterly, 19*(1 & 2), 52-71.

Brown, L., Argyris, D., Attanucci, J., Bardige, B., Gilligan, C., Johnston, K., Miller, B., Osborne, D., Tappan, M., Ward, J., Wiggins, G., & Wilcox, D. (1988). *A guide to reading narratives of conflict and choice for self and relational voices* (Monograph No. 1). Cambridge, MA: Harvard Graduate School of Education, Center for the Study of Gender, Education, and Human Development.

Brown, L., Debold, E., Tappan, M., & Gilligan, C. (1991). Reading narratives of conflict and choice for self and moral voices: A relational method. In W. Kurtines & J. Gewirtz (Eds.), *Handbook of moral behavior and development. Volume 2: Research* (pp. 25-61). Hillsdale, NJ: Lawrence Erlbaum.

Brown, L., & Gilligan, C. (1990, August). Listening for self and relational voices: A responsive/resisting reader's guide. In M. Franklin (Chair), *Literary theory as a guide to psychological analysis,* symposium conducted at the Annual Meeting of the American Psychological Association, Boston, MA.

Brown, L., & Gilligan, C. (1992). *Meeting at the crossroads: Women's psychology and girls' development.* Cambridge, MA: Harvard University Press.

Brown, L., & Gilligan, C. (1993). Meeting at the crossroads: Women's psychology and girls' development. *Feminism and Psychology, 3*(1), 11-35.

Brown, L., Tappan, M., Gilligan, C., Miller, B., & Argyris, D. (1989). Reading for self and moral voice: A method for interpreting narratives of real-life moral conflict and choice. In M. Packer & R. Addison (Eds.), *Entering the circle: Hermeneutic investigation in psychology* (pp. 141-164). Albany: SUNY Press.

Debold, E., & Brown, L. (1991). *Losing the body of knowledge: Conflicts between passion and reason in the intellectual development of adolescent girls.* Unpublished manuscript, Harvard Project on the Psychology of Women and the Development of Girls, Cambridge, MA.

Debold, E., & Tolman, D. (1991, January). *Made in whose image?* Unpublished manuscript, Harvard Project on the Psychology of Women and the Development of Girls, Cambridge, MA. Presented at the Ms. Foundation's Fourth Annual Women Managing Wealth Conference, New York.

Dreizen, S., Spirakis, C., & Stone, R. (1967). A comparison of skeletal growth and maturation in undernourished and well-nourished girls before and after menarche. *Journal of Pediatrics, 70,* 256-263.

Ebata, A. (1987). *A longitudinal study of distress in early adolescence.* Unpublished doctoral dissertation, Pennsylvania State University, University Park.

Elder, G., Nguyen, T., & Caspi, A. (1985). Linking family hardship to children's lives. *Child Development, 56,* 361-375.

Garner, D. (1981). Body image in anorexia nervosa. *Canadian Journal of Psychiatry, 26,* 224-227.

Gilligan, C. (1990a). Joining the resistance: Psychology, politics, girls, and women. *Michigan Quarterly Review, 29*(4), 501-536.

Gilligan, C. (1990b). Teaching Shakespeare's sister: Notes from the underground of female adolescence. In C. Gilligan, N. Lyons, & T. Hanmer (Eds.), *Making connections: The relational worlds of adolescent girls at Emma Willard School* (pp. 6-29). Cambridge, MA: Harvard University Press.

Gilligan, C., Brown, L., & Rogers, A. (1990). Psyche embedded: A place for body, relationships, and culture in personality theory. In A. Rabin, R. Zucker, R. Emmons, & S. Frank (Eds.), *Studying persons and lives* (pp. 86-147). New York: Springer.

Kohlberg, L. (1984). *The psychology of moral development.* New York: Harper & Row.

Langlois, J. H., & Stephan, C. W. (1981). Beauty and the beast: The role of physical attractiveness in the development of peer relations and social behavior. In S. S. Brehm, S. M. Kassin, & F. X. Gibbons (Eds.), *Developmental social psychology: Theory and research* (pp. 152-168). New York: Oxford University Press.

Loevinger, J. (1976). *Ego development: Conceptions and theories.* San Francisco: Jossey-Bass.

Loevinger, J. (1979). *Scientific ways in the study of ego development.* Worcester, MA: Clark University Press.

Loevinger, J., Cohn, L., Redmore, C. D., Bonneville, L., Streich, D., & Sargent, M. (1985). Ego development in college. *Journal of Personality and Social Psychology, 48,* 947-962.

Petersen, A. (1988). Adolescent development. *Annual Review of Psychology, 39,* 583-607.

Petersen, A., & Ebata, A. (1987). Developmental transitions and adolescent problem behavior: Implications for prevention and intervention. In K. Hurrelmann, F. Kaufmann, & F. Lösel (Eds.), *Social intervention: Potential and constraints* (pp. 167-184). Berlin: Walter de Gruyter.

Rogers, A. (1987). *Gender differences in moral thinking: A validity study of two moral orientations.* Unpublished doctoral dissertation, Washington University, St. Louis, MO.

Rogers, A. (1993). Voice, play, and a practice of ordinary courage in girls' and women's lives. *Harvard Educational Review, 63*(3), 265-295.

Rogers, A. (in press). The question of gender differences: Ego development and moral voice in adolescence. *Merrill Palmer Quarterly.*

Rogers, A., & Gilligan, C. (1988). *Translating girls' voices: Two languages of development.* Unpublished manuscript, Harvard Project on the Psychology of Women and the Development of Girls, Cambridge, MA.

Rutter, M. (1986). The developmental psychopathology of depression: Issues and perspectives. In M. Rutter, C. Izard, & P. Read (Eds.), *Depression in young people: Developmental and clinical perspectives* (pp. 3-30). New York: Guilford.

Selman, R. (1980). *The growth of interpersonal understanding.* New York: Academic Press.

Steiner-Adair, C. (1986). The body politic: Normal female adolescent development and the development of eating disorders. *Journal of the American Academy of Psychoanalysis, 14,* 95-114.

Steiner-Adair, C. (1991). When the body speaks: Girls, eating disorders, and psychotherapy. In C. Gilligan, A. Rogers, & D. Tolman (Eds.), *Women, girls, and psychotherapy: Reframing resistance* (pp. 253-266). New York: Haworth.

Appendix:
Coding Sheet for Shifts in Voice of Psychological Distress and Psychological Resistance

Voice of Psychological Distress

1. Dissociates from herself; voice is taken over by conventions that undermine her as a young woman.

    a. voice taken over by debilitating conventions for female behavior.

    b. voice taken over by conventions of the independent, autonomous person (the way to go is to go all alone); she uses a language of independence and maturity to justify cutting herself off from other people.

2. When she stops describing her strategies for capitulation and starts adopting them as the only possible way to go, she no longer reflects on or seems to know what she is doing.

3. Psychological resistance

    a. *Language*—pervasive "I don't knows" that mark confusion or uncertainty about what she knows; use of "it" to describe relationships; use of such phrases as, "I probably sound weird."

    b. *Symptoms*—describes mood changes or symptoms that are unexplainable to her, such as depression or eating problems.

Voice of Psychological Resilience

1. Political resistance

    a. When she self-consciously describes capitulation strategies as strategies of protection.

    b. When she speaks out or acts out against domination, oppression, or false relationships, or debilitating conventions of female behavior such as self-silence, self-sacrifice, or self-negation.

    c. When she shifts from an abstract or highly conventional language into a more colloquial, or at times irreverent, language, or a language of thinking and feeling—that holds thought and feeling, mind and body, together.

2. Genuine relationship

    a. When she speaks about relationships in which she thinks it is possible to voice disagreement, wherein there is room for imperfection, for difference and conflict; descriptions of relationships in which she feels a sense of real or authentic connection (as opposed to relationships she describes as false or fake or fraudulent).

❦ 2 ❦

Feminist Biography

The Pains, the Joys, the Dilemmas

Shulamit Reinharz

A study of the experiences of writing biographies of women from a feminist perspective must begin by recognizing that the history of women's lives is largely unknown.[1] In fact, until the development of feminist scholarship, few people considered the history of women to be a history at all. Denying people a history produces socially constructed ignorance and is a form of oppression. Writing biographies about women is thus inherently a form of protest.[2]

This protest has a lengthy past. Each generation has produced a few individuals who have tried to claim a history for women by writing biographies. In the 1890s in the United States, for example, new groups of college-educated women sought information about past women of achievement. To organize their material, they created archives and wrote biographies (Griffith, 1984, p. xix). Another protest against (hi)storylessness is Sadie Iola Daniel's *Women Builders* (1931/1970), a collection of biographies of black women. Her introduction explains that she

AUTHOR'S NOTE: I would like to acknowledge the helpful comments of Lynn Davidman, Ruthellen Josselson, Judy Long, Tema Nason, Alice Wexler, and anonymous reviewers.

wrote "seven sketches of Negro women who have definitely contributed to the development of the Negro youth in the United States" because Negro youth need biographies that depict "achievements of the race." Just as was true in the 1890s, feminists are still likely to be the only people interested seriously in women's ideas and lives. Unlike earlier times, however, the feminist biographer now has two new resources at hand: an accumulation of feminist scholarship, and a "great new audience of women hungry to know about women" (Shulman, 1984). Feminist scholarship offers theories of female development, explanations of family dynamics from girls' points of view, structural explanations of women's roles in society, and ways of conceptualizing relations among women (Bateson, 1989; Raymond, 1986). Scholars who use these theories are feminist biographers; their biographies are feminist biographies. These abundant resources in large part replace male-oriented psychoanalytic theory, a formerly popular framework for writers of biography.[3]

In studying the life of explorer Isabelle Eberhardt, for example, Annette Kobak speculated that there was more to her than male clothing and camelback treks across North African deserts. Feminist theory prompted her to suspect that "some undefined malaise was behind both the cross-dressing and the exceptionally—and often melodramatically—high content of pain that runs through her life, her letters and her diaries" (Kobak, 1988, pp. 40-41).

Others had seen Eberhardt's pain and glamour as contradictions, calling her "enigmatic" and "elusive" and finally "paradoxically empty" (Kobak, 1988, pp. 40-41). Kobak, by contrast, understood Eberhardt's "emptiness" as "a central loss, and not as a failure." She took seriously the possibility that Eberhardt was anorexic, had a realistic fear of incest, and used disguise for multiple psychological and sociological reasons. Because Kobak approached Eberhardt's activities as seriously motivated, Kobak reinterpreted her as mourning a lost true self. Kobak's use of feminist scholarship flowed from her respect for women's concerns and her distrust (Reinharz, 1985) of conventional interpretations.

Today feminists write biographies of women for the same reasons that motivated college women of the 1890s and Sadie Iola Daniel in 1931. Lela Costin's 1983 study of social reformers Edith and Grace Abbott, for example, reflects her concern for contemporary social welfare students who are thrust:

> into a demanding involvement with troubled individuals, families, and communities with little or no awareness that others in the past have confronted equally difficult social problems—often ones remarkably similar to those of today. Without the support of extended experiences that a study of history and of *illustrious figures of the past* can provide, contemporary social welfare professionals and concerned citizens risk a kind of rootlessness and parochial thinking. (Costin, 1983, pp. viii-ix, italics added)

In my view, Daniel's and Costin's careful explanations—even justifications—of their motivation demonstrate the self-consciousness of biographers of women in a society that generally devalues women and considers men alone to be worthy of biography.

The fact that biographies almost always have been written about men is well known. Even female biographers wrote about men. Blanche Wiesen Cook, for example, confessed that she formerly believed women were insignificant. Even though she defined herself as a "professional woman," she did not identify with women's concerns. In 1966, while writing what she calls "hard history" (e.g., history of war, international diplomacy, foreign economic policy), she visited Max Eastman. When he suggested she write instead about his sister and offered to show her Crystal Eastman's voluminous collection of letters and feminist manuscripts, she politely refused. Only when the women's movement altered her thinking did she realize that Crystal Eastman could be important. Only then did she begin to understand that she had been "programmed to deny" the significance of female activists and writers of the past (Cook, 1978).

Carolyn Heilbrun notes that women wrote 6 of the more than 40 essays in *Biography as an Art* (Clifford, 1962). Their subjects, however, were men, royal women, or "women celebrated in the lives of famous men" (Heilbrun, 1988, p. 21). In general, the few women about whom biographies were written were those Heilbrun labels "a man's woman." Biographers of women typically chose those whose "fame was thrust upon them," who "posed no threatening questions," and whose "lives provided no disturbing model for the possible destinies of other women" (Heilbrun, 1988, p. 22).[4] Heilbrun points sadly to Catherine Drinker Bowen, author of six biographies of men and none of women. Wishing to "write of daring, extraordinary accomplishment, legal brilliance, and professional fidelity," Bowen claims to have been unable to think of any woman in these categories (Heilbrun, 1988, p. 22).

Fortunately the situation has changed. Today a woman biographer might actually be uncomfortable writing about a man because, as Alix Kate Shulman wrote, "it would be a diversion from our urgent cause to devote our major energies to men when so many remarkable women were unknown and needed to be heard" (Shulman, 1984, p. 21). Similarly, contemporary feminist biographers want to study not only women but also a particular kind of woman (not a "man's woman"). Simone de Beauvoir's biographer, Deirdre Bair, acknowledges:

> I declined to write the biography of a recently dead woman writer because I found her work so uninteresting that I had no interest in the life that produced it. In declining to write that book, however, I had come to an important realization: namely, that I wanted to write a biography of a woman, but one whose professional life was intellectually stimulating to me and whose personal life was satisfying to her—if such a rare creature existed. I suppose I was searching for a woman to write about who had made a success of both life and work, since I and so many of my friends were having difficulty integrating satisfying work into our relationships. I wanted to know whether there might be a contemporary woman whose life would be of interest to both men and women in this last part of

our century, when the only thing that seems at all
certain is that goals, needs and roles for both are
undefined and in flux. (Bair, 1990, p. 12)

So too, Marina Warner, a biographer of Joan of Arc, sought an
unclassifiable woman, rather than "a man's woman." She:

wanted to learn about Joan not just because her story is
so grand, so odd, so stirring [but] . . . because she has
an almost unique standing: she is a universal figure who
is female, but is neither a queen, nor a courtesan, nor a
beauty, nor a mother, nor an artist of one kind or
another, nor—until the extremely recent date of 1920
when she was canonised—a saint. She eludes the
categories in which women have normally achieved a
higher status that gives them immortality, and yet she
gained it. . . . Joan was presented as Amazon, or as
knight of old, or as personification of virtue, because
the history of individual women and of women's roles
has been so thin. (Warner, 1981, pp. 6-9)

By studying someone who was not a "biological male" but also
not a "cultural woman," Warner hoped to extend "the taxonomy
of female types . . . beyond wife, mother, mistress, muse"
(Warner, 1981, pp. 6-9).

Bair and Warner studied women who challenge us to abandon female stereotypes. An anomalous woman "renowned for
doing something on her own" (Reinharz, 1984b, pp. 19-43) or
"a success in life and work" (Bair, 1990, p. 12) were the types
they sought. Joan of Arc fit one of the bills: "She belongs to the
sphere of action, when so many feminine figures or models are
assigned and confined to the sphere of contemplation" (Warner,
1981, p. 9). Thus Warner's study of Joan of Arc contributed to
the project of defining women's possibilities. Biography contributed to theory, and not just vice versa.

A feminist scholar setting out to write a biography may lack
a specific theory of biography, but she is likely to be familiar
with more general feminist theory. Many biographers, such as

Bair, acknowledge their indebtedness to feminist scholarship in numerous disciplines (Bair, 1990, p. 17). Rebecca Fraser, biographer of novelist Charlotte Brontë, claims that "the feminist revolution . . . has created a major shift" in the writing of biography because scholars suddenly are able to see material that previously seemed invisible (Reinharz & Stone, 1993). Ruth Bordin, a biographer of activist Frances Willard, concurs that the "women's movement of the late 1960s and 1970s and the accompanying growth of women's studies have . . . stimulated new conceptual frameworks through which we can attempt to understand past generations of women and the roles they played in society" (Bordin, 1986, p. xiii). As a start, feminism shows the biographer how to treat a woman's life as significant in itself.

Current feminist biographers, however, recognize that their approach differs from feminists of a previous era. Bordin is explicit about this difference when introducing her biography of Willard. She explains that shortly after Willard died, Anna Gordon wrote a biography informing us of the view of Willard's "colleagues and contemporaries." In a subsequent biography "Rachel Strachey saw the Willard her grandmother had known when they worked together in the Anglo-American woman movement." Later Mary Earhart showed us Willard "at the end of another era when women's values were fast changing." And finally Bordin intends that her own biography will "provide new insights for a later feminist age" (Bordin, 1986, p. xiii).

Feminists produce biographies to feed the "audience of women hungry to know," to satiate their own quest for knowledge, and to repair socially constructed ignorance. They search for women missing from the canon, for neglected works of science and art, and for overlooked accomplishments of all sorts (Abir-Am & Outram, 1987; Reinharz, 1993). If the age of feminist biographies of women is indeed upon us, there are sufficient cases to ask whether any characteristics are shared. My reading suggests that some pains and joys are commonly shared. *Pain* arises in feminist biography from difficulties in locating information, violating the desire for privacy, having to confront oppression, recognizing the special meaning of women's names, and sensing women's anger. *Joy,* in turn, occurs at the "magical moment" of discovery. It flows from the relationship of empathy and succor and from the opportunity for personal growth. In the pages that follow I describe these socially structured experiences.[5]

Painful Properties

1. Lost Information and Surviving Information

Because information about women is hard to come by, it is particularly difficult to write a woman's biography. The editors' introduction to the 1980 volume of *Notable American Women* underscores this problem. They write that although definitive information about the subject's dates, ancestry, parents, birth order, education, marital status, children, and cause of death was intended for each entry, it was often unobtainable, as these were the first essays written on the individual. "Birth dates proved particularly elusive. . . . Information from death certificates could be used only with caution" (Sicherman & Green, 1980, pp. xi-xii).[6] Why is this so?

First, if women's lives were not seen as significant, then careful records were not kept. In addition, women without public recognition leave few records in public places. Modesty, a virtue urged on women, is a further impediment for biographers of women. A "virtuous" woman is not likely to catalogue and carefully store a record of her accomplishments. This "womanly virtue" enables men, for whom modesty is not a particularly valued trait, to appropriate women's accomplishments (Rossiter, 1993). Women who rejected the virtue of modesty, such as pianist Clara Schumann, left ample materials for the study of their lives (Reich, 1985, p. 178).

In addition, women and their associates have a long history of destroying their primary documents. Efforts to reconstruct the life of Elizabeth Cady Stanton, for example, are hampered because of burned or altered records. Joan Mark, anthropologist Alice Fletcher's biographer, carefully questioned the meaning of "the extraordinary unevenness of the resources available." She wrote:

> Alice Fletcher kept voluminous records of her
> professional years, *the last forty years* [italics added] of
> her life. . . . But [she] destroyed everything pertaining
> to *the first forty years* [italics added] of her life. What I
> have been able to learn about Alice Fletcher's early
> years I have had to piece together from extremely
> meager sources. (Mark, 1988, p. xiv)

The mystery behind this selective destruction was solved when Mark discovered correspondence between two contemporaries of Fletcher, showing that the effort to eradicate the memory of childhood sexual abuse may have motivated her to destroy materials pertaining to her early years.

Jacqueline Van Voris, a biographer of women's rights activist Carrie Chapman Catt, also encountered the problem of destroyed materials but had a different perspective. She explains that Mary Gray Peck published *Carrie Chapman Catt: A Biography* 3 years before her friend, Catt, died in 1947. In the process of preparing the biography, Peck altered many of their letters housed in the Library of Congress. Although Van Voris writes, "We are indebted to Peck for saving the bulk of extant Catt materials deposited there," we also suffer from Peck's heavy editing of primary documents. As a result, very little of a personal nature remains. There are no letters to or from Leo Chapman, Carrie Lane's first husband, or George Catt, her second. There are no papers from family members and no personal dairies. Undoubtedly Catt herself destroyed materials of a private nature. Her life was spent so much in public that she guarded what privacy she had.

Van Voris seems ambivalent about the remaining material. She accepts Catt's choice to leave only public materials but criticizes Peck's choice to edit these. Van Voris's resulting book is necessarily subtitled *A Public Life* (Van Voris, 1987, p. vii). One might also feel ambivalent about Virginia Woolf's massive set of papers because Woolf's suicide note requested that her husband destroy all her papers. Louise DeSalvo comments that it is fortunate Leonard Woolf did not comply (DeSalvo, 1989, p. 133). Should we, however, make use of this material despite Woolf's last wishes?

The case of psychoanalyst Melanie Klein, who wrote an unpublished autobiography that differs from "a large collection of early family letters . . . discovered in her son's loft," adds yet another twist to the problem of the availability of a woman's life records. Klein's recent biographer, Phyllis Grosskurth, asks: Why did Melanie Klein not destroy the letters? She must have been aware that they ultimately would be discovered:

> Several explanations are possible. Perhaps certain letters are not destroyed because the subject wants the truth ultimately to be told, even in its unpalatable aspects; yet naturally one is ambivalent about exposing desires, fears, and embarrassment to public scrutiny. In Klein's case, it is possible that she simply could not bear to part with some of the most important areas of her past. (Grosskurth, 1987, p. 5)

Paul Brooks accepted environmentalist Rachel Carson's wish not to be the subject of a biography (Brooks, 1985), and Ann Lane dealt similarly with the wish of historian Mary Ritter Beard (Lane, 1877/1988). In each case the resulting biography focuses on the woman's achievement, rather than on her private life. These women and several others thus become subjects of intellectual, rather than full, biographies. Clearly biographers have been converting the pain aroused by partially destroyed materials into the challenge of theorizing women's selective retention of the records of their lives.

2. The Focus on Women's Personal Lives

Associated with the problem of destroyed materials is many women's (and some biographers') desire to shield their private lives. Bair defines as a feminist dilemma the fact that describing women's personal lives reinforces the idea that their private lives supersede their intellectual activity. Bair mentions participating in a panel discussion:

> At the conclusion of the question-and-answer period . . . I could not help but comment to my distinguished audience that every question asked about Sartre concerned his work while all those asked about Beauvoir concerned her personal life. I must admit I was disappointed. (Bair, 1990, p. 18)

Elinor Langer felt the same way about writer Josephine Herbst: "An elementary tenet of feminism is the validity of discussing a woman in terms of her work alone" (Langer, 1984, p. 9). She also suggested that writing biographies was "politically incorrect" because biographies obscure social forces and present history as the acts of individuals. She called them "bourgeois." Peter Hare offers a biography of anthropologist Elsie Clews Parsons, dealing only with her personality, quoting extensively from her letters and commenting little, thereby minimizing speaking for her but also obscuring her work (Hare, 1985).

Evelyn Fox Keller, on the other hand, suggests that biographies of women in science *should* discuss the woman's personal life and professional work because this connection is falsely denied by scientists (Abir-Am & Outram, 1987). Describing her study of geneticist Barbara McClintock, Keller writes:

> The story of Barbara McClintock allows us to explore the conditions under which dissent in science arises, the function it serves, and the purality of values and goals it reflects. . . . Of necessity, therefore, this book must serve simultaneously as biography and as intellectual history. Its starting point is the recognition that science is at once a highly personal and a communal endeavor. (Keller, 1983, pp. ix, xi, xii)

Clearly these disparate views lay the grounds for a provocative debate concerning a feminist ethic and theory of biography.

3. Confronting Another Woman's Oppression

Anyone who reads biographies of women knows that, to a large extent, they are painful to read. A feminist biographer of a woman is likely to be studying a person who has been oppressed—perhaps in her family as a child, frequently by men she loved as an adult (if she was heterosexual) (Tuck, 1988), undoubtedly by her society in many ways. The biographer knows that the very qualities of being active and creative—if the subject of her biography has these two attributes—made the woman about whom she is writing seem unusual to others, perhaps dangerous, certainly difficult to love. Thus such women as novelist Rebecca West (Glendinning, 1987), labor activist Eleanor Marx (Kapp, 1972, 1976), and Zionist activist Manya Wilbushewitz Shohat (Reinharz, 1984a), rare in having their talents recognized, were nevertheless unfulfilled in love. (Bair knew this and deliberately looked for an exception.) "Recognized talents," furthermore, were unlikely to have had or been able to mother children, despite their wish to the contrary.

It is painful to learn the extent to which women's creativity is hedged in. Fraser credits the feminist revolution for the ability to see how social mores hampered such women as Charlotte Brontë and defined them in inimical ways. Although feminist scholarship has enabled us to overcome the inability to see women (I use the term "gynopia") (Reinharz, 1985), it also has exposed us to hitherto obscured anguish. Reflecting on Brontë's life, Fraser claims that the "different landscape *now visible* [italics added] is particularly electrifying, for Charlotte Brontë offended gravely against the standards of her day" (Fraser, 1988, p. x). Because Brontë's hero-ines threatened the moral order by boldly attacking clergy and religious hypocrisy, her novels were branded pornographic and irreligious. Charlotte Brontë herself earned:

> a notoriety which overshadowed the rest of her life. . . . Nevertheless, she continued defiantly to write as the spirit took her, calling boldly for sexlessness in authorship, regardless of what was considered proper or becoming for her gender, with a missionary

> commitment to the truth, unpalatable as it might be.
> (Fraser, 1988, p. x)

The feminist biographer knows she will have to acknowledge and perhaps even relive the woman's pain.

Thus we have to face the facts that Mary Cassatt, probably the best known American female painter, suffered enormously (Hale, 1975) and that Virginia Woolf, one of the most celebrated writers in the English language, first suffered childhood sexual abuse and then mental illness (DeSalvo, 1989). We must acknowledge that Jacqueline du Pre, celebrated cellist, was isolated by her family because of her talent and died at an early age (Easton, 1990) and that Emily Dickinson, probably the best known American female poet, seemed not to have been able to bear the world (Wolff, 1986). As two of her friends wrote:

> To the villagers of Amherst, she was an eccentric
> recluse, who, in her later years, always wore white and
> never went out of her father's house. It was not until
> after her death in 1886 that her family discovered that
> she had written over seventeen hundred poems. (Todd
> & Higginson, 1978, Preface)

Understanding a woman's pain helps feminist biographers unravel the mysteries around other women. A case in point is the "Judith Shakespeare" metaphor:[7]

> Virginia Woolf wondered, in *A Room of One's Own,* what
> would have happened if Shakespeare had had a
> "wonderfully gifted sister . . . as adventurous, as
> imaginative, as agog to see the world as he was." The girl
> would not, guesses Woolf, have been sent to school, or
> given a chance to learn grammar, logic, Horace and Virgil.
> She would have "picked up a book now and then, one of
> her brother's perhaps, and read a few pages." But then her
> parents would have come in and told her to do something
> practical "and not moon about with books and papers."
> They would have spoken sharply but kindly, for they

were substantial people who knew the conditions of life for a woman and loved their daughter—indeed, more likely than not she was the apple of her father's eye. Perhaps she scribbled some pages up in an apple loft on the sly, but was careful to hide them or set fire to them.

Eventually, however, the time came for her to marry, and to avoid that "hateful" fate she ran away to London, to the stage door, where the actor-manager finally took pity on her. Soon "she found herself with child by that gentleman" and in the end killed herself one dark winter's night. That, surmises Woolf, is how the story might have gone, since "any woman born with a great gift in the sixteenth century would certainly have gone crazed, shot herself, or ended her days in some lonely cottage outside the village, half witch, half wizard, feared and mocked at." (Strouse, 1980, p. xiv)

This haunting, frightening image inspired Jean Strouse to frame her biography of Alice James with "Judith Shakespeare" as model.

William and Henry James did have a sister gifted with fine intelligence, and through her it is possible to look closely at the scenario Woolf imagined. Although Alice James lived a good 300 years after the hypothetical "Judith" Shakespeare, her intellectual life was bound by many of the same strictures. (Strouse, 1980, p. xiv)

During her lifetime, the fictitious Shakespeare was not allowed to be herself and thus could not be remembered. Instead of blaming the victim for the way she lived her life or for what she did not accomplish, theories and metaphors of oppression help us see women as people coping with their environments.

4. Women's Names and Namelessness

Name changing (I was formerly Shula Rothschild) contributes to the difficulty in a woman's being remembered and to a biographer's task in locating material. Cicely Fairfield, for example, was also Rebecca West. Ruth Benedict was occasionally Anne Singleton. Laura Bohanan was once Eleanor Smith Bowen. Harriet Martineau was Discipulus early in her career. Aurore Dupin was always George Sand. Judith Thurman writes about Isak Dinesen:

> She was born Dinesen on April 17, 1885, and christened Karen Christentze. Her family called her "Tanne," which was her own mispronunciation of Karen and a nickname—forever diminutive—that she disliked. She subsequently took or acquired other names: Osceola, her first pseudonym; Baroness von Blixen-Finecke, by her marriage to a Swedish cousin; Tania and Jerie to her white and black African familiars, respectively; Isak, "the one who"—with a certain noble perversity—"laughs." Her admirers often called her after her own characters or imaginary incarnations. To a childhood playmate she was "Lord Byron." To her secretary she was the old battle horse, Khamar. To various literary disciplines she was Pellegrina, Aminae, or Scheherazade. In Denmark, when she was elderly, she was spoken of and to almost universally as Baronessen, the Baroness, in the third person, according to feudal usage. The name on her tombstone is Karen Blixen.
>
> These names had their own etiquette, logic, and geography. They were separate entrances to her presence, varying in grandeur and accessibility. But the name "Dinesen," unmodified either by a sexual or a Christian identity, was that idea of herself and her origins which the child carried into old age. It expressed what she considered essential in her life: the relation to her father, to his family, to a sense that they were a tribe—a stamme, in Danish—a rootstock. When she reclaimed the name Dinesen in middle age to sign her fiction with it, it was a gesture typical of her spiritual economy. (Thurman, 1982, Introduction, p. 2)

Women and men change their names for many reasons. Women change theirs (or have them changed) for the same reasons as men and for two additional reasons: They marry a man and "take" his name; they use a pseudonym to disguise their gender. Historians Bonnie Anderson and Judith Zinsser wrote:

> Many early women writers used anonymity or male pseudonyms to make their writings more acceptable. Jane Austen published all her novels anonymously. Books often appeared "by a Lady" or "by the author of [the writer's previous book]." "George Eliot" was the pseudonym of Marian Evans; "George Sand" of Aurore Dudevant. The Brontë sisters published as "Ellis, Currer, and Actor Bell." Delphine Gay de Girardin, the saloniere, wrote as the "Viscount Charles de Launay." Louise Otto-Peters published initially as "Otto Stern"; her French contemporary, Marie d'Agoult, used "Daniel Stern" throughout her long literary career. . . . [Elizabeth] Gaskell, too, had published her early writings under the male pseudonym of Cotton Mather Mills; her first novel, *Mary Barton,* was published anonymously. (Anderson & Zinsser, 1988, p. 168)

Sophie Germain, mathematician, sociologist, and contemporary of Auguste Comte, called herself Monsieur leBlanc in order to get an education (Bucciarelli & Dworsky, 1980). Josephine Herbst is also Mrs. John Herrmann. Ida Wells was Iola. Contemporary sociologist Matilda White Riley recounts the following incident:

> When a publisher refused to put my name on the book (on gliding and soaring!) that I had written during a college vacation "because no one will read a book written by a girl," I changed my name from Matilda to Mat, and the book sold quite well. (Riley, 1988, p. 28)

Not everyone will take such an accommodating approach. Elisabeth Griffith, for example, wrote about the importance of Elizabeth Cady Stanton's name:

One of the most important aspects of her self-definition was her name. She insisted on being addressed by her full name, Elizabeth Cady Stanton, which she considered her own name, representing her own self. Except for letters to her children, she always signed all three names, even in correspondence with her closest friends. . . . Only her enemies, in an effort to remind her of her traditional domestic status, called her Mrs. Henry B. Stanton. Rather than defer to the prescribed form, Stanton combined her family and married names. . . . By 1847, before she had spoken out on any other women's issue, Mrs. Stanton was defending her right to her own name. As she explained in an argument with an acquaintance:

> I have very serious objections . . . to being called Henry. Ask our colored brethren if there is nothing to a name. Why are the slaves nameless unless they take that of their master? Simply because they have no independent existence. They are mere chattels, with no civil or social rights. Even so with women. The custom of calling women Mrs. John This and Mrs. Tom That and colored men Sambo and Zip Coon is founded on the principle that white men are the lords of all. I cannot acknowledge this principle as just; therefore I cannot bear the name of another. (Griffith, 1984, p. xx)

Sociologist Charlotte Anna Perkins (Stetson), a similar example, chose to be Charlotte Perkins Gilman after she finally found a man to love. Heilbrun, on the other hand, explained her use of a pseudonym:

> I have decided . . . to use myself as an example, to analyze the reasons why I adopted and for many years kept wholly secret the pseudonym of Amanda Cross, under which, beginning in 1964, I published detective stories. . . . There was no question in my mind then, nor is there any now, that had those responsible for my promotion to tenure in the English department of the university where I teach known of the novels, they would have counted them heavily against me; I would

> probably have been rejected. . . . One had one's "real" identity, and if one chose to indulge in frivolities, however skillful, one did it under another name than that reserved for proper scholarship.
>
> I no longer think that this was the whole explanation. I think now that there are layers within layers of significance to a woman's decision to write under a pseudonym, but the most important reason for her doing so is that the woman author is, consciously or not, creating an alter ego as she writes, another possibility of female destiny. So full of anxiety were women, before the current women's movement, when imagining alternate destinies, that they wished to hide their authorial identity from prying eyes. (Heilbrun, 1988, pp. 109-110)

The issue is not dead. Being referred to as we wish to be and having our work respected are difficult goals for many women— black and white, young and old, lesbian and straight. Lesbians in particular have been unable to name their love. The history of lesbian women is thus doubly obscured, doubly erased.

Women choose to change or not change their names on the basis of their assessment of gender-related consequences. Thus "one reason Morisot kept her maiden name was so that people wouldn't think she was capitalizing on the more famous name of her husband" (Temin, 1990, p. 83). As Dorothy Richardson's biographer wrote, "The problems women [writers] have had with their names . . . are one index of the problems they have had with their [literary] identities" (Hanscombe, 1982, p. 17). In an egalitarian world, women would not have to negotiate their identity by trading in names.

5. Confronting One's Own Anger

A responsible biographer of women must consider sexism, misogyny, and patriarchy as she goes about her work. As the biographer tries to understand the woman trying to live her life and society's response to her efforts, anger is likely to be aroused. Langer confronts those who have destroyed the memory of Josephine Herbst and asks angrily, "How could it be that I had never heard of Josephine Herbst?" (Langer, 1984, p. 5).

Katrin Lunde and Luise F. Pusch write about Leonora Christina, who in "Scandinavia is considered a writer of exceptional quality . . . yet about whom there is still neither a historical-critical edition of her collected works nor a definitive biography" (Lunde & Pusch, 1986). Why?

Christine Temin, reviewing Anne Higonnet's biography of Berthe Morisot, ponders with sadness and rage:

> Morisot died in 1895. By then her work had been accepted, celebrated and sold at high prices, and her 1879 "Woman at a Ball" had been bought by the government for the Luxembourg Museum. On her death certificate, her family described her as having "no profession." (Temin, 1990, p. 83)

Why?

Reynolds Price writes:

> Despite the fact that the best of [Katherine Anne Porter's] stories, short novels and essays are as strong as any in American letters—"Noon Wine" alone can stand, calm shoulder to shoulder, with anything in Tolstoy or Chekhov—her work has yet to win the wide and steady attention it earns and rewards. (Price, 1990, p. 1; Copyright © 1990 by The New York Times Company. Reprinted by permission.)

Why?

Cook writes:

> For fifty years our entire culture militated so vigorously against our discovering Crystal Eastman's ideas and finding them usable that she practically disappeared from history. After her death in 1928 there were

memorials and obituaries. But from that year to this not one essay, not one book has been entirely devoted to her work or to her life. (Cook, 1978, p. v)

Why?

Liz Stanley writes:

> One of the great puzzles about Olive Schreiner (1855-1920) is that she was so popularly—and internationally—famous and feted during her lifetime and is now so very forgotten except by a few literature specialists interested primarily in her first novel, *The Story of an African Farm,* and a small but increasing number of feminists interested in finding out more about our political foremothers. (Stanley, 1985, p. 1)

Why?

Langer writes about Josephine Herbst: "Her literary reputation was nonexistent. She was not mentioned by . . . she was not mentioned by . . . she was not mentioned by . . . ." (Langer, 1984, p. 7).[8] So too, Rebecca West has largely been forgotten. Black liberationist Amy Jacques Garvey was not given credit for her accomplishments during her lifetime, let alone remembered after her death (Adler, 1992). The developer of refrigeration—Mary Engle Pennington—forgotten. Rosalind Franklin, a codiscoverer of the structure of DNA—almost completely obscured (see Watson, 1968). Mathematician and physicist Mileva Maric was never credited while working with Albert Einstein and was maligned by his biographers after their divorce (Higgins, 1987; Overby, 1990). Scandalous rumors abounded about writer and political activist Aphra Behn (see Duffy, 1989). Grosskurth (1987, p. x) wrote about her biographical subject: "Few professional women have been subjected to as much distilled malice and rumor accepted as fact as [Melanie] Klein endured both during her lifetime and since her death." Why?

These comments should not come as a surprise. The very fact of leaving a record from which a biography could be written points to a woman's having fought against the definition of what a woman was supposed to be, and this disruption angers others. As an outsider, she is unlikely to have had access to institutions that could perpetuate her name. For this reason it is difficult for future generations to remember her correctly, and easy for her critics to reiterate their criticism. Langer wrote:

> I did not find any serious discussion of [Josephine Herbst] anywhere. . . . It is not as if I could not explain this. On the contrary, I could explain it far too readily. Josephine Herbst was an innate feminist whose strong female characters consistently had a central place in her writing, leading male critics, to whom they were therefore invisible, to conclude that her writing was about nothing. (Langer, 1984, p. 8)

Feminists are as quickly forgotten as are other women because feminist history is not seen as "history" and therefore does not need to be taught to people studying "history." Van Voris wrote with astonishment:

> Carrie Chapman Catt led an army of voteless women in 1919 to pressure Congress to pass the constitutional amendment giving them the right to vote and convinced state legislatures to ratify it in 1920. And then, the first battle won for women, she devoted the rest of her life, more than twenty-five years, to work for peace as the basis of human rights. Catt was one of the best-known women in the United States in the first half of the twentieth century and was on all lists of famous American women. . . . Today, however, her work is little known. (Van Voris, 1987, p. vii)

Griffith wrote:

> In July 1923, on the seventy-fifth anniversary of Stanton's Seneca Falls suffrage resolution, Alice Paul led the National Woman's Party to the site to introduce the

Equal Rights Amendment. The ceremony was planned and the program printed without any reference to [Elizabeth Cady] Stanton. Stanton's daughter, Harriot Blatch, insisted on paying tribute to her mother. She was the only speaker to mention Elizabeth Cady Stanton.

The event concluded with a motorcade to nearby Rochester to lay a wreath at the Anthony memorial. Fifty-four years later, in November 1977, when the national meeting to observe International Women's Year convened in Houston, Texas, it opened with the arrival of a torch that had been carried by female runners from Seneca Falls. Seated on the dais was Susan B. Anthony's grandniece and namesake. The heroine of Seneca Falls, Stanton herself, had been lost to history. (Griffith, 1984, p. xv)

And Alice Walker wrote:

Financial dependency is the thread that sewed a cloud over [Zora Neale] Hurston's life, from the time she left home to work as a maid at fourteen to the day of her death. It is ironic that this woman, who many claimed sold her soul to record the sources of authentic, black American folk art (whereas it is apparently cool to sell your soul for a university job, say, or a new car) and who was made of some of the universe's most naturally free stuff (one would be hard pressed to find a more nonmaterialistic person), was denied even a steady pittance, free from strings, that would have kept her secure enough to do her best work.

It has been pointed out that one of the reasons Zora Neale Hurston's work has suffered neglect is that her critics never considered her "sincere." Only after she died penniless, still laboring at her craft, still immersed in her work, still following her vision and her road, did it begin to seem to some that yes, perhaps this woman was a serious artist after all, since artists are known to live poor and die broke. But you're up against a hard game if you have to die to win it, and we must insist

that dying in poverty is an unacceptable extreme.
(Walker, 1979, pp. 3-4)

Feminist biography has the task of restoring women's complexity and replacing our unidimensional (no)place in history. Beatrice Siegel's purpose in writing about social reformer Lillian Wald was to find the complex woman behind the homogeneous reputation (Siegel, 1983). Bordin had the same goal for her biography of Frances Willard:

> Willard's beliefs and contributions, which spanned a wide variety of reform causes, were reduced after her death to a single dimension, temperance, and that dimension of her life's work was repudiated unequivocally by a later generation. The causes to which she made lasting contributions—for example, the vote for women, the public kindergarten, separate correctional institutions for women, Protestant ecumenicism—became part of the permanent fabric of American life. (Bordin, 1986, p. 6)

It is possible that all biographers think their subject is misunderstood by everyone else but themselves. There is rhetorical utility in establishing a wrongdoing that one can rectify. But feminist biographers are aware of a greater misunderstanding. The unjustified neglect of the few reflects on the total disregard of the majority of women. The feminist biographer knows that she, too, is likely to fall into the same void. To write a biography about a woman is therefore to experience the pain and anger of the subject herself, compounded by knowing the fate of her place in history. But there is also joy.

Joyful Properties

1. The Magical Moment of Discovering the Subject

Because women typically are not remembered, the biographer who does locate records of a woman whose biography she later writes is likely to have a "discovery" experience. The encounter with her subject produces sudden recognition of the subject's significance. Her gaze as a feminist biographer helps lift the subject out of obscurity and into history. The encounter becomes part of the subject's continuing story. Thus a hallmark of feminist biography is the distinctive opening story explaining how the biographer "discovered" her woman. These experiences are a special joy of feminist biography, sometimes referred to as "magical moments." They occur at a particular time and place the biographer remembers and can describe.

Mark writes about the "moment" she "discovered Alice Fletcher fifteen years ago when [she] came across several hundred of her letters to F. W. Putnam, the curator of the Peabody Museum of Archaeology and Ethnology at Harvard" (Mark, 1988, p. xiii).[9] Alice Fletcher surely was known to some people other than Joan Mark, yet Mark discovered her in the sense of meeting someone important to her and feeling she had been waiting for Alice Fletcher, perhaps without even knowing it. Fletcher, too, was waiting to be found.

Sometimes a biographer experiences this encounter as a miracle that infuses her with life and sets her on a new path, a moral mission. Langer mentions "a small, inviting reference to a trilogy by Josephine Herbst . . . enough to send me to the university library the following morning and home with the novels that very day" (Langer, 1984, p. 4). At the moment of discovery and resolve, the feminist biographer experiences a calling, a call to action and self-reflection. Or, to use another metaphor, she uncovers a buried treasure that enriches her—a woman's life.

Bonny Vaught's discovery experience occurred in her local bookstore when a 95-cent paperback edition of *The Journal of Charlotte L. Forten: A Free Negro in the Slave Era* caught her eye:

> Charlotte Forten came into my life ten years ago. . . .
> Her journal touched me, made me catch my breath in
> sympathy as I read it for the first time. Though she had
> begun writing her journal . . . in Salem, Massachusetts,
> [she] suddenly was alive in my home in New Mexico
> more than a century later. (Vaught, 1984, p. 55)

Vaught then explains why this magical moment occurred. What was it about her own background that made her "catch her breath"?

> Before moving to Albuquerque in 1969, I had taught in a California high school with a predominantly Black student body. Social studies curricula were just beginning to acknowledge the Black men and women in American history, so I had been a white teacher sharing my students' frustration about those missing Black people. Where were they to be found? . . . I was totally unprepared for the impact those pages would make on me. Feelings of understanding and sympathy overwhelmed me when I began to read the journal. (Vaught, 1984, p. 55)

The moment of discovery is very powerful. It transforms the life of the biographer, sometimes making her feel that she is recovering (and thus creating) her foremother. If so, she ironically is giving birth to her mother. Perhaps the seductive pull for women who write biographies of women is the very possibility of creating our own mothers.

Also striking in Vaught's story is that during the moment of discovery, the subject breathes life into the biographer. Vaught's excitement in discovering her subject saves her from whatever was troubling her. Similarly, Langer believed she was rescued by finding Josephine Herbst:

> My notes from my first reading of the trilogy are a cross between a sigh of relief and a shout of joy: as if I were a traveler who had somehow gotten detached from my party, and Josephine Herbst were the rescuer sent out to bring me home. (Langer, 1984, p. 4)

The feminist biographer feels like a girl who suddenly meets her lost twin sister. The exhilaration of the moment of discovery is a kind of giving birth and falling in love.

Feminist biography "discovery stories" overturn the fairy tale of the prince who kisses Sleeping Beauty. The prince, it should be remembered, is not transformed by the kiss. In feminist biography the biographer meets her subject and they both "wake up" and are transformed. There even may be religious overtones, as Sara Ruddick implied in her discovery story: "Virginia Woolf changed my life; the melodramatic hint of conversion seems appropriate" (Ruddick, 1984, p. 137). Perhaps the excitement of the discovery moment also reflects a socially sanctioned homoerotic tie between female biographers and subjects. Women biographers are frank about "loving" their subjects. These discovery moments and the associated learning make feminist biographers feel fortunate and enable them to communicate excitement to their readers.

After the discovery the biographer does not remain passive. Instead she typically recognizes that her subject was "buried alive" (was neglected, misunderstood) and that she, the biographer, can set her free. Thus, in addition to being a biographer, the writer sometimes sees herself as a heroine, rescuing her subject from distortion or obscurity. In Shulman's words, "Emma [Goldman] had a hand in rescuing me from what seemed like a dangerously passive life; the least I could do was carry on the rescue operation" (Shulman, 1984, p. 9). Discovery coupled by rescue constitutes the life-sustaining reciprocity between biographer and subject.

The biographer's rescue mission becomes a sense of responsibility to future generations. Elizabeth Scarborough and Laurel Furumoto expressed this sentiment in their study of early American women psychologists. They were "fascinated with [Christine Ladd-Franklin, Mary Whiton Calkins, and Margaret Floy Washburn] as individuals and as our foremothers in psychology" and were "aware of the difficulties of retrieving information about them and others of their period":

> We also came to recognize that the omission of women from historical accounts of psychology placed a serious limitation on our understanding of the past and on women's sense of having a legitimate place in [our] discipline. . . . Our enthusiasm was fueled by two

> dominant elements: our appreciation of the significant
> role played by early women pioneers in opening to
> women the field [we ourselves] had entered and [our]
> conviction that [our] students and *future generations of
> psychologists* should learn of the early women.
> (Scarborough & Furumoto, 1987, pp. xi-xii, italics added)

Thus feminist biographers feel responsible for saving women about whom they are writing, saving themselves and saving the future.

Because the biographer typically presents her discovery story as a chance event, its mystical quality is enhanced: Nancy Reich writes, "My search for materials for this biography began inadvertently: in 1973 I came across the unpublished correspondence (1858-96) between Clara Schumann and Ernst Rudorff" (Reich, 1985, p. 11). Judith Brown's "unexpected encounter" was with a lesbian nun: "I found Benedetta Carlini by chance, while leafing through an inventory of nearly forgotten documents in the State Archive of Florence" (Brown, 1986, p. 3). Kobak writes, "As with any biography, a narrative of my own shadowed that of Isabelle as I wrote this book. Mine included a series of lucky finds and serendipitous introductions to people who have become valued friends" (Kobak, 1988, Acknowledgments).

The narrative device of an uncanny discovery story lends excitement and credibility to the unfolding biography,[10] as in Jean Kennard's story of her unexpected discovery of connections to women writers, her past, and her mother:

> This book was begun in September of 1981 when I
> found myself *trapped* in a small town on the south coast
> of England with *nothing* to read. My mother had
> *suddenly* become *seriously* ill and I had flown home
> without considering what I might do during the weeks I
> spent there. Expecting little of the small local
> bookstore, I *explored* my mother's bookshelves and
> *rediscovered* Brittain's *Testament of Youth* and Holtby's
> *South Riding*. . . . Delight in Brittain's and Holtby's
> work became *fascination* with their lives, particularly

with their relationship to each other and to the women friends who were also writers and whose novels sat *abandoned* beside theirs on my mother's shelves. . . . To this date, apart from Hilary Bailey's short biography of Brittain and a few brief articles, no one has given them the attention they deserve.

This book is an attempt to rectify that omission. It is, in other words, my effort to witness to the lives of Brittain and Holtby as they spoke for their foremothers and for each other. Like so many women writers of the twenties and thirties, they testified to a generation, one they saw as partly lost, destroyed in a war Brittain at least lived to see repeated. They spent much of their lives speaking for those who had no voices of their own, either because they had died prematurely or because they were, in terms of gender or race, underprivileged. It seems, then, particularly *ironic* that their own words should have been forgotten so soon. (Kennard, 1989, pp. ix-x, italics added)

Gloria Hull, too, considered the discovery of material relevant to her research as "uncanny":

Soon after I began teaching one of my first Black American literature courses a few years ago, a student in the class—a young Black woman—came up to me after a session on Paul Laurence Dunbar and told me that she knew a lady in the city who was his niece. . . . From that *unlikely, chance* beginning has developed my single most significant research undertaking—one which has led me into the *farthest reaches* of Black feminist criticism, and resulted in new literary scholarship and *exhilarating personal growth*. (Hull, 1984, p. 105, italics added)

The highly unlikely "discovery" initiates a transformation and a journey. New scholarship and exhilarating personal growth emerge from the biographer's discovery of "her woman."

Sometimes the discovery story is a serendipitous overlap of distant events. Yi-Tsi Feuerwerker reports the magical force at work in her case:

> The death of Mao Zedong and the fall of the Gang of Four in 1976 ushered in a period of relative liberalization, and in the same month that I completed my dissertation, Ding Ling was officially rehabilitated. Indeed, the very day in June 1979 that I received my degree, the news that she had been named a member of the Chinese People's Consultative Conference, the first clear signal that the Party had completely reversed its former verdict against her, was published in *The New York Times*. What happened on that June day in 1979 was by no means the first seemingly *miraculous coincidence* that has marked my relationship with my subject. Nor was it to be the last. Because of such *recurring coincidences* I have come to believe that I have been *fated, "chosen" even* (but by whom is the question) to study Ding Ling the writer. (Feuerwerker, 1984, p. 16, italics added)

When there is no discovery story, there may be a background story of mysterious attraction and shadowing, as Jane Howard writes of her work on Margaret Mead:

> I did not know her or love her, nor did I wince, as some did, at the sound of her voice or the sight of her face. . . . *Somewhere in the back of my mind I had been perplexed by her all along.* . . . She was not only one of the most accomplished and most energetically public women of her time, but one of the most enigmatic. (Howard, 1984, pp. xii, xiii, xv, italics added)

Victoria Glendinning writes about Rebecca West in a way that mirrors the enigmatic quality that Howard saw in Margaret Mead:

> There are several ways of explaining her, and none. . . . She was ninety when she died, and her last twenty

> years were as eventful as any period of her life; I knew
> her for the last ten years, and saw her often with
> pleasure. She left a signed request that two biographies
> of her should be written: a short one by myself, and a
> "full" biography by Stanley Olson. . . . Rebecca West
> lived her life operatically, and tinkered endlessly with
> the story-line, the score, and the libretto. The plot
> remains unresolved. (Glendinning, 1987, pp. xvi-xvii)[11]

There is a plot here with many resolutions and with none. The
mysterious encounters between some biographers and their
subjects resonate in the mystery of the women themselves.

2. Forming a Relationship of Empathy and Succor

A feminist biographer typically reflects on her relationship
with her subject. Sometimes she is a loving friend, treating her
subject with empathy and understanding. At other times she is
a fellow warrior, fighting at her fearless leader's side. The biographer may, in fact, deliberately choose a woman on the basis
of the kind of relationship she seeks just as we do our friends.
Sometimes the relationship itself is mysterious. Langer, for example, can hardly find words intimate enough to describe the
closeness she felt for Josephine Herbst: "A mysterious kinship
linked me with this female stranger as if not only our blood but
the cells of our marrow were somehow matched" (Langer, 1984,
p. 5).

Jacquelyn Dowd Hall speaks of the mysterious alchemy that
springs from sharing geographic roots with her biographical
subject.

> [In] the mysterious alchemy of author and subject, I
> found myself confronting women who were indeed my
> forebears. The Anti-Lynching Association itself was
> launched in the wake of a notorious lynching that
> occurred in northeast Texas midway between Jessie
> Daniel Ames's birthplace and my own. The terrain of

Jessie's childhood evoked memories of my own
upbringing in a small southwestern town. As the first in
the family to seek access to that hazily imagined world
of higher education and professional work, I could not
but recognize her doubt and determination and feel
both sorrow and anger at the damage she sustained.
(Hall, 1979, pp. xii-xiii)

In addition to "mysterious alchemy," there is simple attraction
and commonality, as in the case of Bordin's explanation for
studying Frances Willard:

My life experience quite naturally influenced my
attraction to Frances Willard as a subject for
research. . . . Also, in a personal sense Frances Willard
touched many chords in me. Much of her life was close
to my early life—her religious commitment, her belief in
the equality of women to men, but also her love for the
family. The points of commonality in our views of the
world cannot be denied. (Bordin, 1986, p. xiii)

Over time the biographer better understands the shared geographic roots, the seeming kinship, and the attraction. Even as the
relationship develops, however, the mystery of empathy remains.

Some relationships between the biographer and her subject
are not mysterious. These are instances wherein the biographer
deliberately looks to her subject for help. An example is Ruth
Benedict's effort to write biographies so as to receive help.
Judith Modell, one of Benedict's biographers, describes Benedict's
poignant search to be rescued by the women she studied. Quoting from diaries, Modell writes that Benedict had a " 'desperate
longing' to 'know how other women had saved their souls alive'
and accorded 'dignity' to the rich processes of living" (Modell,
1983, p. 104). To this end, biographer Margaret Caffrey writes:

her "pet scheme" was to steep herself in the lives of
restless . . . women of past generations and write a
series of biographical papers from the standpoint of the

> "new woman." For . . . four years (1914-1918), the
> heyday of suffrage fervor in America, culminating in
> the passage of the Nineteenth Amendment giving
> women the right to vote, Benedict worked on her
> manuscript. . . . She was having trouble writing, but by
> 1916 had refined her "series of biographies" to three:
> Mary Wollstonecraft (1759-1797), the English author of
> *A Vindication of the Rights of Woman,* the classic book
> that sparked the women's rights movement in England
> and America; Margaret Fuller (1810-1850), American
> transcendentalist, author of *Woman in the Nineteenth
> Century,* the classic American argument for feminism;
> and Olive Schreiner (1855-1920), the contemporary
> author of *Woman and Labor.* . . . Her purpose for
> writing this book [was] the affirmation their lives gave
> other women. "I long to speak out the intense
> inspiration that comes to me from the lives of strong
> women," she wrote. "They have made of their lives a
> great adventure." They had proved "that out of much
> bewilderment of soul," steadfast aims could be
> accomplished. (Caffrey, 1989, pp. 78-79)

Through this biographical project, Benedict tried to save her
life, or in today's language, her mental health. Ultimately, however, she realized she could not live through other women. She
had to create her own life. That is when she decided to put her
biographical project aside and study anthropology. Caffrey writes
that Ruth Benedict gradually learned that

> women . . . had to learn to re-see life as a chance for
> "vigorous living." . . . That vision is what the three
> women in her biography had in common, and they
> were its standard bearers. . . . She wanted her book
> [*Adventures in Womanhood*] to have an impact on
> society, but its impact on herself was already
> profound. . . . By writing about them and researching
> their lives, she communed with them and with herself,
> keeping her creative energy alive in what became more
> and more a restrictive, isolated marital relationship. She

got from her biographies "in the heat and depression" of
her own struggle, the belief again "in the existence of
great ends which their lives have already served—which,
if we are worthy of their comradeship, our lives may also
serve." (Caffrey, 1989, p. 89, italics added)

Another example of this type of relationship is biographer
Mary Hill's turn to Charlotte Perkins Gilman for help. Over time,
however, Hill rejected that early relationship:

Many years ago, when I first came across her published
works—witty, insightful, radical feminist critiques—I
was looking for a heroine, for closer contact with a
woman who could articulate my own frustrations and
explain women's problems in ways relating directly to
my life. Her concerns were mine as well: how to
reconcile family responsibilities with professional
ambitions; how to be a responsive mother to small
children and still have time to teach and write; how to
satisfy the human need for love and work. Undoubtedly,
I was looking for historical roots as well, for
intellectual precedents to feminist ideas of the 1960s,
which to many even now seem unsettling and new. In
any case, I had no notion then of what the
research-writing process would involve: poring through
Charlotte's diaries and letters, living through her
roller-coaster vacillations, dissolving my sentimental
admiration, grounding my respect. It led to a rich,
enormously rewarding, decade-long involvement with
her life. For as the heroine image disappeared, a very
human woman came to light, a woman whose brilliance
was matched by her complexity, and whose failures
reflected so many of the ubiquitous destructive social
forces she sought to understand. (Hill, 1980, pp. 3-4)

In some instances the biographer may not consciously turn
to her subject for help, but may find help nevertheless. Joyce
Antler seems to have had this experience in the process of
writing her biography of educator Lucy Sprague Mitchell.

> As my research progressed, Lucy Mitchell's history came to serve as a model, or alternatively, as a warning, for I saw myself grappling with many of the same personal and professional struggles that informed her life. I emerged from the writing of this book with a much clearer understanding of the complicated dimensions of work/family and parent/child relationships. (Antler, 1987, p. ix)

The biographer may find that although her subject differs from herself in appearance or background, she nevertheless is a role model. Judith Modell expresses this idea in her biography of Ruth Benedict, explaining first how they differed, yet concluding that Benedict's way of writing became her model:

> I was . . . alert to temperamental and contextual differences. Ruth Benedict and I were not alike and not contemporaries, but we did share certain situations. I recognized the Vassar that Ruth Benedict went to from 1905 to 1909, surprisingly like the Vassar I attended half a century later. . . . Situational similarities had life-course parallels: I, too, shifted from literature to anthropology after a nonacademic interruption. These similarities supported my decision to compare her statements to instances in my life. I opted for a kind of judgment entailing a large but (I hope) proportioned dose of speculation. [Ruth Benedict believed that] self-reflection became a guide to responsible inquiry. I took a similar attitude in my biography of her. (Modell, 1983, p. 5)

Lane is similarly eloquent about the teacherlike role that Mary Ritter Beard played as her biographical subject.

> She offered me—through her work and through a painstaking reconstruction of her shadowy personal life, which she tried to keep hidden—she offered me herself as my mentor, as my model, in a world in which I found few others. She provided me with an intellectual, political, personal, and philosophical sense

of woman's place in the world's story. My own small,
private existence suddenly had a reality, because it was
part of a past, a woman's past, a past not only of
struggle and oppression and submission and denial, but
also of strength and courage and value and engagement.
I began to work on a biography of Mary Beard, partly to
share with others what she meant to me and what she
had done for me, and partly to repay a debt I felt I owed
her for the life's work she had accomplished and for
which she had been inadequately rewarded by an
indifferent world. (Lane, 1877/1988, p. xii)

Celia Eckhardt, a biographer of social activist Frances (Fanny)
Wright, reflected on her experiences after being criticized by a
"distinguished male critic" for "including so much feminism."
Repudiating this, she reasserted her admiration for her subject:

It was Fanny Wright, in fact, who turned me in middle age
into a feminist—both by way of the positions she argued
so forcefully and because of the way she was treated in
the United States of America. . . . I am honored to have
had the chance to live for a decade with Frances Wright,
and to do what I could to resurrect her claim to be
numbered, as she put it, "among those of the champions
of human liberty and heralds of human improvement."
(Eckhardt, 1986, p. 1)

Clearly, writing these biographies helped the biographers
learn to live and to work.

3. Opportunity for Personal Growth

The feminist biographer's relation with her subject is likely
to be fluid, changing as the work progresses. As Langer writes:
"Biography is not taxonomy with the specimen to be reclassified
according to the latest findings—it is the story of one life as seen
by another, with both always growing and changing" (Langer,

1984, p. 13). Similarly Mary Beth Norton writes that the dialogue between biographer Ann Lane and Charlotte Perkins Gilman changed while Lane worked on the book (Norton, 1990, pp. 10-11). Although it is possible that the magical moment of discovery will be sustained, it is more likely that the feelings of that moment will be joined by many others as the relationship ages and grows.

Because the relationship between the two women always influences the biographer's understanding and writing, a shifting relationship can only enrich the biography by introducing numerous perspectives. Moreover, in the process of writing a biography, the biographer creates herself by entering into a variety of relations with her subject. Her identity at any point results from the fusion of her work on her project and the relation she has with her subject. And sometimes, working on the project makes her realize she no longer needs her subject for help, as in the case of Ruth Benedict's biographical project (Modell, 1983, p. 108).

A tenet of feminist biography is the importance of seeing the biographical subject as a woman who shares the physical and social condition of women in her society. When interviewing Simone de Beauvoir, Bair had that idea in mind. She took to heart "the dictum that we must interpret the facts and events of women's lives in new and different ways." Thus Bair "asked how menstruation and menopause affected her writing life. I am grateful that [de Beauvoir] considered all the questions with equal seriousness and answered them carefully" (Bair, 1990, p. 14). In some cases, however, the biographer resists seeing her subject as a woman until the material compels her to adopt a feminist view. For example, when Mark originally wrote about Alice Fletcher, she was "sex-blind" and:

> treated her no differently than the men. Her sex seemed
> . . . irrelevant, her path to anthropology no more
> tortuous, her difficulties in the field no greater, her
> subjects of study no different, than those of her male
> colleagues. But as I finished that book and turned to a

full-scale biography of Alice Fletcher, my sex-blind
position became increasingly untenable. On the one
hand I felt the gentle prodding of my feminist friends,
who urged me to look at what I had been ignoring.
What about, for example, the extensive female support
system that Alice Fletcher created for herself? Was all
that support necessary if Alice Fletcher's career moved
along as smoothly as did the careers of her male
colleagues? On the other hand, and finally
overwhelmingly, I began to find that the more I worked
on Alice Fletcher in traditional, sex-blind terms, the
less I understood her. (Mark, 1988, pp. xiii-xiv)

Mark originally resisted a feminist interpretation of Fletcher. In
other instances the subject resists being seen as a "woman"
(whatever that means to her) and thus repudiates a feminist
interpretation of her life. Keller provides an example from her
study of geneticist Barbara McClintock:

In her adamant rejection of female stereotypes,
McClintock poses a challenge to any simple notions of a
"feminine" science. Her pursuit of a life in which "the
matter of gender drops away" provides us instead with a
glimpse of what a "gender-free" science might look like.
I am grateful to Barbara McClintock for tolerating—even
while trying her best to dissuade me from—the writing
of this book. (Keller, 1983, p. xvii)

Thus, while having at her disposal the assets of a "a hungry
audience," the feminist biographer of a woman also faces unique
responsibilities and dilemmas. She may find contradictions in
her biographical subject concerning being a woman; if so, she
is likely to consider these to be feminist questions themselves.
Eminent sociologist/anthropologist Elsie Clews Parsons defined
herself as a staunch feminist but "seldom enjoyed the compan-
ionship of women" (Hare, 1985). Florence Nightingale criticized
women for "doing nothing," but then created something for
them to do. What kind of women were they?

But Was She a Feminist?

Barbara Clements similarly struggled to construct a definition of theorist Aleksandra Kollontai. Approaching Kollontai through a feminist lens, she saw her as a feminist, unlike Kollontai herself. Although this contradiction poses a dilemma for the biographer, I believe feminist biographers, just as other biographers, cannot give subjects sole responsibility for defining their lives. The biographer should "listen" to what her subject has to say about herself and then enter into a dialogue with her, asserting her own voice. This dilemma is not unique to biography, but occurs in many areas of social science: Should a participant observer simply report how a community defines itself; should a clinical psychologist rely exclusively on her patient's definition of her problems?

In the following excerpt, Clements struggles with this dilemma:

> Aleksandra Kollontai belonged to the generation of European feminists who won major advances in suffrage and social welfare programs for women. She participated in the campaigns for female emancipation and she made a contribution to the literature on the woman question by exploring the relationship between sexuality and liberation.

> Yet Kollontai vehemently denied that she was a feminist. . . . The distance that Kollontai put between herself and the feminists accounts in part for her being relatively unknown among Western European and American students of the woman's movement. . . . Only in the late sixties did Western feminists begin to rediscover her ideas and the woman herself.

> Western feminists in search of Kollontai found very little to guide them. . . . Yet the story of her life was there, behind the official pictures, in Kollontai's prolific writings and in the documents of Soviet history. The search for her led through these remnants to an extraordinary woman whose life deserved retelling. (Clements, 1979, p. ix)

In a similar vein Marcia Westkott hears a "feminist voice implied in Horney's theory" (Westkott, 1986, p. 5). She views psychoanalyst Horney as a feminist, though Horney might have not concurred (Quinn, 1987).

In a sophisticated twist on this question of self-definition, Paul Roazen attempts to save Helene Deutsch's reputation from what he perceives to be unfair feminist attacks. Instead he wants to rehabilitate her within the feminist tradition. According to Roazen, Deutsch was the "the first psychoanalyst to write a book [1925] on feminine psychology," namely the two-volume *Psychology of Women*. Ironically she since has been attacked for this accomplishment and for her association with Sigmund Freud:

> Her interest in the [psychology of women], along with that of Karen Horney, helped push Freud himself . . . into writing articles about women. . . . The outrage that Freud aroused still surrounds Helene Deutsch's name. To some feminists she is infamous, a traitor to her sex; they have focused their attack against sexism on some of her theories. (Roazen, 1985, p. vii)

Moreover, Roazen argues, as most historians do, that people must be understood within their own context, not measured by a later yardstick:

> In social context [Helene Deutsch] was a leading feminist. . . . Medicine was an exceptional career for women in the early twentieth century; only seven women entered medical school at the University of Vienna when Helene Deutsch did, in 1907; three of them finally received their degrees. . . . Deutsch was writing at a time when middle-class women were confined to the narrow lives of their families; she sometimes thought of herself as a freak for pursuing professional goals. . . . Her life demonstrated that women need not be victims, but that their special abilities, based on social and biological sources, can be translated into active doing in the world. Historically

> Helene Deutsch's career is a leading example of an
> intellectual woman's problems and triumphs. . . . She
> wrote, of course, in a society radically unlike ours, and
> it is unfair to extract her ideas from their proper
> cultural context. For example, despite all that her
> detractors say today, she was trying to use
> psychological theory for the sake of female
> emancipation. (Roazen, 1985, p. vii-ix)

"Is she, or is she not, a feminist?" This question concerns
Caffrey writing about Ruth Benedict, as it does Roazen and
Barbara Clements in their biographies of Helene Deutsch and
Aleksandra Kollontai. Caffrey argues that Benedict's previous
biographers (Margaret Mead and Judith Modell) may not have
seen Benedict as a feminist because their definition of feminism
was limited. Caffrey, by contrast, sees Benedict's:

> life as a case history in cultural feminism, a feminism
> derived from other than political sources, focused on
> changing the values and beliefs that make up the
> framework of a culture rather than working for change
> through laws or the courts, with an emphasis on covert
> rather than overt change. This is a feminism that
> concentrates on internal questions such as definitions
> of masculinity and femininity, and questions of
> selfhood, of individuality, or of independence and
> stresses the necessity of changing inward attitudes of
> men and women and the "shoulds and oughts" of
> American society in order to cause radical change.
> (Caffrey, 1989, p. vii)

Similarly, Costin attempts to bring "professional experts" and
"social engineers" into the tradition of feminism. She understands that such women were not formerly included because:

> the woman as expert . . . did not capture the popular
> imagination in the same way or remain widely known
> beyond her generation as a model of feminine

excellence. A dominant motive in my undertaking this study was to help correct that imbalance. More specifically, I wanted to document the character and achievements of notable women who have been lost in history. Why Edith and Grace Abbott, and not some other early and insufficiently recognized social feminists, became the focus for my study undoubtedly relates to some intriguing impressions about the Abbotts that had lain dormant in my mind. (Costin, 1983, pp. vii-ix)

Katherine Sklar offers a final example of redefining as a feminist, a woman not previously thought of as such. Specifically she interprets educational reformer Catherine Beecher's personality as an expression of protest rather than acquiescence, thus the personality of an "indirect feminist":

Catherine Beecher's female identity constantly intruded into her consciousness and her career. It excluded her from the main vehicle of contemporary social influence, the church, and it persistently relegated her to a marginal social status when she sought a central one. Over the course of her lifetime she accumulated a tremendous amount of animus against male cultural dominance, but she usually expressed this anger indirectly. Her political assumptions led her to oppose the women's rights movement. Nevertheless, her efforts to overcome the marginal status allotted to women constituted a central theme in her career. (Sklar, 1973, pp. xiii-xiv)

Accomplished feminist biographers have brought the lives of many women, known and forgotten, to public attention. Many of these women are now understood as having had a feminist orientation. It is important, however, to not stretch the definition of feminism so wide as to make it a meaningless net that catches everyone. Similarly we need not be compelled to label every woman a feminist for fear of being charged with wasting our time studying the lives of non- or antifeminist women.

The Future of Feminist Biography

Feminist biography will continue to flourish because of the joys of discovery, the existence of a hungry audience, and the desire to right/write the historical record. But the forms it takes will vary. Some, like Griffith, will write "great woman" biographies:

> Elizabeth Cady Stanton was a great woman, and this is unabashedly a "great woman" biography. With the recognition in recent years that populations also contain soldiers, slaves, and shopkeepers, some of whom are women, the "great man" theories of history and the biographies they generated have fallen out of fashion. "Great woman" history, on the other hand, was rarely written. (Griffith, 1984, p. xix)

Other forms of feminist biography may arise from the criticism that biography deepens the shadows on some women when it shines its spotlight on the few. Stanley, for example, believes that feminist biography should focus on networks, not individuals. After reviewing existing biographies of Olive Schreiner, she "arrived at the idea of writing an 'anti-biography' of Schreiner in which 'Olive Schreiner,' a construction of the character or personality of the woman herself, would be a complete absence" (Stanley, 1985, p. 1). Instead, Schreiner's web of relationships would be highlighted.

Feminist biography will continue to be enriched by feminist theory and may help reduce women's oppression as it continues to uncover it. It undoubtedly will continue to succor the women who write it. It also will continue to embody a special type of "double knowing" or cognitive/emotional learning that houses awareness of the facts of a subject's life in a relationship to her. This "connected knowing," described in *Women's Ways of Knowing* (Belenky, Clinchy, Goldberger, & Tarule, 1986), is also Barbara McClintock's scientific approach, as defined by Keller, her biographer:

> She talks about the limits of verbally explicit reasoning; she stresses the importance of her "feeling for the

organism" in terms that sound like those of mysticism. But like all good mystics, she insists on the utmost critical rigor, and, like all good scientists, her understanding emerges from a thorough absorption in, even identification with, her material. (Keller, 1983, p. xiv)

I am not sure that feminist biographers are mystics, but they certainly must be spiritually fortified for the emotional and intellectual challenges—the joys and pains—that are by now standard ingredients of their work.

Notes

1. For example, Palmer and Colton's *A History of the Modern World*, a 1,000-page history textbook widely used in U.S. colleges, contains 28 references to women in its 31-page index: 16 are royalty, 4 are wives of royalty, 1 is the mistress of a king, another is mentioned casually in a sentence about the French Revolution, and 4 are national leaders mentioned in a single sentence about female leaders. Elizabeth Cady Stanton is the only woman who merits a full sentence, and that, ironically, about women's struggle for emancipation.

2. See Reinharz (with Davidman, 1992) for a discussion of ways in which ignorance of the history of women is socially constructed.

3. See Carlson (1988) for a criticism of overreliance on psychoanalytic theory in psychobiography and an endorsement of Tomkin's "script theory."

4. A large group of Wellesley College students rejected Barbara Bush as the 1990 commencement speaker for this reason.

5. I do not claim that only feminists have these experiences. I am simply explaining why they do occur in feminist biography.

6. Because of this problem, the Radcliffe Biography Project was founded to expand "some of the encyclopedia's essays into full-length biographies so that a wider audience could grasp the many contributions women have made to American life—an awareness of which is as yet by no means universal" (Horner, 1988, p. xiii).

7. Virginia Woolf's (1929) speculation is found in *A Room of One's Own*, pp. 80-89.

8. I have omitted the names of the persons who omitted hers.

9. This book is part of the University of Nebraska Press's *Women in the West* series, which includes Maxine Benson, *Martha Maxwell: Rocky Mountain Naturalist;* Emily Fourmy Cutrer, *The Art of the Woman: The Life and Work of Elisabet Ney;* and Emily French, *Emily: The Diary of a Hard-Worked Woman* (J. Lecompte, ed.).

10. I have found one uncanny discovery story written by a male biographer of a woman. See Derek Gill, *Quest: The Life of Elisabeth Kübler-Ross* (New York: Ballantine, 1980).

11. Victoria Glendinning has also written *Vita: The Life of V. Sackville-West* (1983), *Edith Sitwell: A Unicorn Among Lions* (1981), and *Elizabeth Bowen: Portrait of a Writer* (1978).

References

Abir-Am, P., & Outram, D. (Eds.). (1987). *Uneasy careers and intimate lives: Women in science, 1789-1979.* New Brunswick, NJ: Rutgers University Press.

Adler, K. (1992). "Always leading our men in service and sacrifice": Amy Jacques Garvey, feminist black nationalist. *Gender & Society, 6*(3), 346-375.

Anderson, B. S., & Zinsser, J. P. (1988). *A history of their own: Women in Europe from prehistory to the present* (Vol. 2). New York: Harper & Row.

Antler, J. (1987). *Lucy Sprague Mitchell: The making of a modern woman.* New Haven, CT: Yale University Press.

Bair, D. (1990). *Simone de Beauvoir: A biography.* New York: Summit.

Bateson, M. C. (1989). *Composing a life.* Boston: Atlantic Monthly Press.

Belenky, M., Clinchy, B. M., Goldberger, N. R., & Tarule, J. M. (1986). *Women's ways of knowing: The development of self, voice, and mind.* New York: Basic Books.

Bordin, R. (1986). *Frances Willard: A biography.* Chapel Hill: University of North Carolina Press.

Brooks, P. (1985). *Rachel Carson at work: The house of life.* Boston: G. K. Hall.

Brown, J. C. (1986). *Immodest acts: The life of a lesbian nun in Renaissance Italy.* New York: Oxford University Press.

Bucciarelli, L. L., & Dworsky, N. (1980). *Sophie Germain: An essay on the history of the theory of elasticity.* Boston: D. Reidel.

Caffrey, M. M. (1989). *Ruth Benedict: Stranger in this land.* Austin: University of Texas Press.

Carlson, R. (1988). Exemplary lives: The uses of psychobiography for theory development. *Journal of Personality, 56*(1), 105-138.

Clements, B. E. (1979). *Bolshevik feminist: The life of Aleksandra Kollontai.* Bloomington: Indiana University Press.

Clifford, J. L. (1962). *Biography as an art: Selected criticism, 1560-1960.* New York: Oxford University Press.

Cook, B. W. (Ed.). (1978). *Crystal Eastman: On women and revolution.* New York: Oxford University Press.

Costin, L. (1983). *Two sisters for social justice: A biography of Grace and Edith Abbott.* Urbana-Champaign: University of Illinois Press.

Daniel, S. I. (1970). *Women builders.* Washington, DC: Associated Publishers. (Original work published 1931)

DeSalvo, L. (1989). *Virginia Woolf: The impact of childhood sexual abuse on her life and work.* New York: Ballantine.

Duffy, M. (1989). *The passionate shepherdess: Aphra Behn 1640-1689.* Portsmouth, NH: Heinemann.

Easton, C. (1990). *Jacqueline du Pre*. New York: Summit.
Eckhardt, C. (1986, May). *Fanny Wright: The woman who made the myth*. Paper presented at the Conference on Autobiographies, Biographies, and Life Histories of Women: Interdisciplinary Perspectives, University of Minnesota.
Feuerwerker, Y.-T. M. (1984). In quest of Ding Ling (In quest of myself). In C. Ascher, L. DeSalvo, & S. Ruddick (Eds.), *Between women: Biographers, novelists, critics, teachers, and artists write about their work on women* (pp. 15-34). Boston: Beacon.
Fraser, R. (1988). *The Brontës: Charlotte Brontë and her family*. New York: Fawcett.
Glendinning, V. (1987). *Rebecca West: A life*. New York: Fawcett.
Griffith, E. (1984). *In her own right: The life of Elizabeth Cady Stanton*. New York: Oxford University Press.
Grosskurth, P. (1987). *Melanie Klein: Her world and her work*. Cambridge, MA: Harvard University Press.
Hale, N. (1975). *Mary Cassatt*. Garden City, NY: Doubleday.
Hall, J. D. (1979). *Revolt against chivalry: Jessie Daniel Ames and the women's campaign against lynching*. New York: Columbia University Press.
Hanscombe, G. E. (1982). *Dorothy Richardson: The art of life and the development of feminist consciousness*. Athens: Ohio University Press.
Hare, P. H. (1985). *A woman's quest for science: Portrait of anthropologist Elsie Clews Parsons*. Buffalo, NY: Prometheus.
Heilbrun, C. (1988). *Writing a woman's life*. Boston: Beacon.
Higgins, R. (1987, June 29). The passionate young Einstein. *Boston Globe*, p. 45.
Hill, M. A. (1980). *Charlotte Perkins Gilman: The making of a radical feminist, 1860-1896*. Philadelphia: Temple University Press.
Horner, M. (1988). *Sara Lawrence Lightfoot: Balm in Gilead: Journey of a healer*. Reading, MA: Addison-Wesley.
Howard, J. (1984). *Margaret Mead: A life*. New York: Ballantine.
Hull, G. T. (1984). Alice Dunbar-Nelson: A personal and literary perspective. In C. Ascher, L. DeSalvo, & S. Ruddick (Eds.), *Between women: Biographers, novelists, critics, teachers, and artists write about their work on women* (pp. 105-112). Boston: Beacon.
Kapp, Y. (1972). *Eleanor Marx: Family life (1855-1883)*. New York: Pantheon.
Kapp, Y. (1976). *Eleanor Marx: The crowded years 1884-1898*. New York: Pantheon.
Keller, E. F. (1983). *A feeling for the organism: The life and work of Barbara McClintock*. New York: W. H. Freeman.
Kennard, J. E. (1989). *Vera Brittain and Winifred Holtby: A working partnership*. Hanover, NH: University Press of New England.
Kobak, A. (1988). *Isabelle: The life of Isabelle Eberhardt*. New York: Random House.
Lane, A. (1988). *Mary Ritter Beard: A sourcebook*. Boston: Northeastern University Press. (Original work published 1877)
Langer, E. (1984). *Josephine Herbst*. Boston: Little, Brown.
Lunde, K., & Pusch, L. F. (1986, May). *Denmark's first feminist? Leonora Christina (1621-1696), the daughter of King Christian IV of Denmark and Norway*. Paper presented at the Conference on Autobiographies,

Biographies, and Life Histories of Women: Interdisciplinary Perspectives, University of Minnesota.

Mark, J. (1988). *A stranger in her native land: Alice Fletcher and the American Indians.* Lincoln: University of Nebraska Press.

Modell, J. S. (1983). *Ruth Benedict: Patterns of a life.* Philadelphia: University of Pennsylvania Press.

Norton, M. B. (1990, July 15). [Review of Ann J. Lane, *To "Herland" and beyond: The life and work of Charlotte Perkins Gilman*]. *The New York Times,* pp. 10-11.

Overby, D. (1990, April 30). Einstein in love. *Time,* p. 108.

Palmer, R. R., & Colton, J. G. (1984). *A history of the modern world* (6th ed.). New York: Knopf.

Price, R. (1990, May 27). [Review of Isabel Bayley (Ed.), *Letters of Katherine Anne Porter*]. *The New York Times,* p. 1.

Quinn, S. (1987). *A mind of her own: The life of Karen Horney.* New York: Summit.

Raymond, J. G. (1986). *A passion for friends: Toward a philosophy of female affection.* Boston: Beacon.

Reich, N. B. (1985). *Clara Schumann: The artist and the woman.* Ithaca, NY: Cornell University Press.

Reinharz, S. (1984a). Toward a model of female political action: The case of Manya Shohat, founder of the first kibbutz. *Women's Studies International Forum,* 7(4), 275-287.

Reinharz, S. (1984b). Women as competent community builders: The other side of the coin. In A. Rickel, M. Gerrard, & I. Iscoe (Eds.), *Social and psychological problems of women: Prevention and crisis intervention* (pp. 19-43). New York: Hemisphere.

Reinharz, S. (1985). Feminist distrust: Problems of context and content in sociological work. In D. Berg & K. Smith (Eds.), *Exploring clinical methods for social research* (pp. 153-172). Beverly Hills, CA: Sage.

Reinharz, S. (1993, February). *A contextualized chronology of women's sociological work.* Brandeis University Women's Studies Working Papers Series, No. 1.

Reinharz, S. (with L. Davidman). (1992). *Feminist methods in social research.* New York: Oxford University Press.

Reinharz, S., & Stone, E. (Eds.). (1993). *Looking at invisible women.* Unpublished manuscript.

Riley, M. W. (1988). *Sociological lives.* Newbury Park, CA: Sage.

Roazen, P. (1985). *Helene Deutsch: A psychoanalyst's life.* New York: New American Library.

Rossiter, M. W. (1993). The Matthew Matilda effect in science. *Social Studies of Science, 23,* 325-341.

Ruddick, S. (1984). New combinations: Learning from Virginia Woolf. In C. Ascher, L. DeSalvo, & S. Ruddick (Eds.), *Between women: Biographers, novelists, critics, teachers, and artists write about their work on women* (pp. 137-160). Boston: Beacon.

Scarborough, E., & Furumoto, L. (1987). *Untold lives: The first generation of American women psychologists.* New York: Columbia University Press.

Shulman, A. K. (1984). Living our life. In C. Ascher, L. DeSalvo, & S. Ruddick (Eds.), *Between women: Biographers, novelists, critics, teachers, and artists write about their work on women* (pp. 1-14). Boston: Beacon.

Sicherman, B., & Green, C. H. (Eds.). (1980). *Notable American women: The modern period.* Cambridge, MA: Harvard University Press.

Siegel, B. (1983). *Lillian Wald of Henry Street.* New York: Macmillan.

Sklar, K. (1973). *Catherine Beecher: A study in American domesticity.* New Haven, CT: Yale University Press.

Stanley, L. (1985). "Feminist biography"? Some introductory thoughts. In *Feminism and friendship: Two essays on Olive Schreiner.* Manchester, UK: University of Manchester, Department of Sociology.

Strouse, J. (1980). *Alice James: A biography.* Boston: Houghton Mifflin.

Temin, C. (1990, May 24). [Review of Anne Higonnet, *Berthe Morisot*]. *Boston Globe,* p. 83.

Thurman, J. (1982). *Isak Dinesen: The life of a storyteller.* New York: St. Martin's.

Todd, M. L., & Higginson, T. W. (Eds.). (1978). *Favorite poems of Emily Dickinson.* New York: Avenel.

Tuck, R.-M. (1988). *Camille: The life of Camille Claudel, Rodin's muse and mistress: 1864-1943* (L. E. Tuck, Trans.). New York: Seaver.

Van Voris, J. (1987). *Carrie Chapman Catt: A public life.* New York: Feminist Press.

Vaught, B. (1984). Trying to make things real. In C. Ascher, L. DeSalvo, & S. Ruddick (Eds.), *Between women: Biographers, novelists, critics, teachers, and artists write about their work on women* (pp. 55-70). Boston: Beacon.

Walker, A. (1979). Dedication: On refusing to be humbled by second place in a contest you did not design: A tradition by now. In A. Walker (Ed.), *I love myself when I am laughing . . . : A Zora Neale Hurston reader* (pp. 3-4). Old Westbury, NY: Feminist Press.

Warner, M. (1981). *Joan of Arc: The image of female heroism.* New York: Vintage.

Watson, J. D. (1968). *The double helix.* New York: New American Library.

Westkott, M. (1986). *The feminist legacy of Karen Horney.* New Haven, CT: Yale University Press.

Wolff, C. G. (1986). *Emily Dickinson.* New York: Knopf.

Woolf, V. (1929). *A room of one's own.* New York: Harcourt, Brace.

❧ 3 ❧

To Rebuild Life

A Narrative Analysis of Three Generations of an Israeli Holocaust Survivor's Family

Dan Bar-On
Noga Gilad

The Intergenerational Effects of the Holocaust

Most psychological studies dealing with the long-range effects of the Holocaust focus on the second generation. This generation was perceived as being influenced and activated by events experienced by their parents, Holocaust survivors, many years beforehand. We argue that intergenerational studies of the Holocaust have to be carried out within nonclinical samples and

AUTHORS' NOTE: This chapter is part of a research on the aftereffects of the Holocaust on the third generation in Germany and Israel, funded by the GIF (1-43-134.4, 1988-1991). We would like to thank Dr. Gabriele Rosenthal from Giessen, Germany, for introducing us to her systematic narrative and biographical analysis and for helping us apply it to the present research. We would like to thank Miriam Keren and Julie Chaitin for their careful translation of the text into English. We would like to thank Professor Amia Lieblich, Tova Miloh, Gadi Ben-Ezer, Einat Weiss, and Max Lachman for their helpful comments during the analysis phase and Tammy Bar-On for her careful editing and typing.

should include the third generation, thereby presenting the second generation not only as children of their parents but also as parents of their own children.

Results concerning the second generation were not clear-cut. The arguments developed mainly along two dimensions that partially overlapped: the methodological dimension (clinical vs. controlled data) and the dimension of content (negative vs. positive effects). In the first dimension, clinical results of psychopathological long-range effects on the second generation were reported. For example, children of Holocaust survivors had difficulties with individuation (emotional independence) and manifested hostility, developing a stronger achievement need (Kestenberg, 1972; Krystal, 1968). Such findings were not confirmed when random sampling and control groups were used (Reick & Etinger, 1983). It was unclear whether the instruments in the controlled studies were not sensitive enough to identify the effects found in therapy or whether the results found in the clinical, self-selective samples were not valid for the population as a whole.

In the second dimension, many studies asserted that the second generation was impaired due to the burden of the Holocaust that their parents silently carried. A few researchers tried to point out more positive, achievement-oriented responses. Although being an overresponse, people showed a better ability to cope with problems, precisely because they were children of Holocaust survivors. An illustration of the former assertion is found in a study showing that children of Holocaust survivors who suffered from battle shock in the Lebanon War did not adjust as well to daily life as the control group did, 2 and 3 years later (Solomon, 1989). Studies that illustrate the latter approach show that members of the second generation achieve higher economic status and educational accomplishments (Reick & Etinger, 1983).

Later studies were based on other assertions. For example, Danieli (1983) categorized the second-generation reactions according to their parents' objective experiences during the Holocaust (camp survivors, as opposed to partisans) and their own subjective type of coping (fighting vs. resignation). In another study Vardi (1990) stated that families of Holocaust survivors chose one child to fulfill the role of a memorial candle. It is this child who carries the emotional burden the parents have not worked through. According to Vardi the "memorial candle" is the one who generally seeks therapy because he or she is more burdened than the other children.

Probably the above-mentioned categorizations and diagnoses served clinicians in their work with families of Holocaust survivors, in the diagnostic process, in choosing the type of therapy, and in evaluating the prognosis. However, these categories do little to help us understand the phenomena of intergenerational effects in the shadow of the Holocaust. The above-mentioned disputes reflected differences in underlying assumptions: Could the aftereffects of the Holocaust be interpreted as normal reactions to the extreme conditions of the Holocaust, or should they be discussed within the psychopathological context? For example, if the memorial candle seeks therapy, can we assume that his or her siblings are not burdened or that he or she is less verbal about the burden? How do we know? Most Holocaust survivors and their families did not seek therapy. How did they deal with similar traumas by themselves?

What we tend to identify as intergenerational effects of the Holocaust are the combined effects of several parallel processes. The aftereffects of the Holocaust were interwoven with emigration and immigration, absorption difficulties in a new culture (Segev, 1991), as well as individual and family processes. How could we then claim an intergenerational effect of the Holocaust? Even if one assumes that the survivors succeeded in developing a normalization of unresolved emotional burdens (Rosenthal, 1987), one still may pose the question: When was normalization proof of competent functioning, and when was it proof of "malfunctioning" passed on from one generation to the next? Did spontaneous "working through" processes evolve, and how were they similar to or different from those reported by therapists?

We tested these questions by interviewing a nonclinical sample of Holocaust survivors' families, three generations in the family, asking each of them to tell us his or her own life story. We wanted to find out what is being transmitted from one generation to the other. Which new issues evolve? Will the inclusion of the third generation change our perspective of the second generation as portrayed by the current literature?

The Method: Emphasizing the Structuring of the Story by the Storyteller

The issue that concerned us at this stage was the method of interviewing and analyzing the interviews. On the one hand, we wanted to understand the ways people constructed their life stories. On the other hand, we assumed that our interviewees would not talk about certain issues, would even try to hide or distort them. Possibly, after 50 years, processes of distortion were influenced also by what happened meanwhile in the lives of survivors. In contrast one could claim that what has happened during the 50 years was affected by what happened earlier, during and after the war. Who could actually judge when a description was reliable and when it was distorted?

This question became central when relating to life stories of survivors. It is very difficult for researchers to put themselves in their interviewees' shoes (Langer, 1991). Simultaneously it is difficult for the subjects to describe verbally what they experienced there, especially the feelings that accompanied these experiences. The researchers, through their too-strong conceptual framework, may overshadow the fragile language structures that survivors developed to describe those events. In addition the conceptual system of the researchers may, unconsciously, be used to protect them from relating to the survivors' life experiences.

Rosenthal (1987, 1989) described how her interviewees in Germany who had participated in both world wars told their life stories.[1] She compared how each one of them spoke about the two wars: where they spoke at length and where they were brief; what they narrated and what they argued or reported. She tried to raise hypotheses about why they told the story the way they did, searching for the confirmation for these hypotheses in the text itself. She was committed to the original text, the way the interviewees themselves conceptualized their autobiographies, with very little preconceptualization on her part. She saw in their stories an endless process of choice, both forward and backward in time and space: choice patterns that reflected a tension between conservation and change, concentrating on the past, the present, or the future time perspectives.

Rosenthal suggested that the construction of the life story by her interviewees reflected their normalization strategies of facing the threatening past and future. Strategies allow people to smooth out corners in their stories, especially corners they find difficult to confront in the present (Rosenthal & Bar-On, 1992). Whereas other approaches look for a historical truth underlying the subject's distorted report, the present approach asserts a narrative truth (Spence, 1980). Here the question was not which historical truth the story reflected, but rather how the underlying strategy served the narrator's goals from his or her present perspective.

This method of analysis requires an appropriate method of interviewing. The interviewer refrains from presenting directing questions, as these may shape the structure of the interview and thereby produce the interviewer's structure instead of the subject's structure. In effect the interviewer asks the interviewees to tell their life stories the way they experienced them. It is permissible to ask clarifying questions if something is unclear, if contradictions are found in a person's story, or if a noticeable segment of the person's life history is left out of the life story. The interviewer must be careful: Questions may be perceived by the interviewee as value judgments. The purpose of these questions, in fact, is to clarify whether the contradiction or omission is derived from the interviewer's earlier lack of comprehension. However, we find that original omissions or contradictions are usually not accidental.

In our analysis of the interviews, we were particularly attentive to the "working through" process. The initial concept of *working through* was used to explain the laborious psychological process of integrating repressed childhood content (Freud, 1914). Even though the concept was developed to describe the process between patient and therapist (Novey, 1962), it was widened over the years to include a means of coping with posttraumatic stress disorder (PTSD) (Rothstein, 1986). The original goal of the process of working through—letting go the influence of the repressed content—was replaced lately by a more modest goal: the ability to live with the painful traumatic event (Lehman, Wortman, & Williams, 1987).

The concept of *working through* was used in the context of the Holocaust to describe survivors' children's inquiry into the untold stories originating from that trauma (Bergmann & Jucovy, 1991). This use occurred especially when survivors attempted to protect their children from their own horrifying experiences and loss. Paradoxically the pattern of silence that developed around them transmitted this content to the children (Krystal, 1968). A similar attempt was made to describe the process that children of Holocaust perpetrators underwent, struggling with their parents' untold atrocious acts (Bar-On, 1990).

In approaching the grandchildren's relationship to the survivors, the concept of *working through* had to be reexamined. A working through of what? Is there an ongoing need to confront repressed experiences that have been passed on from one generation to the next? For the third generation, on the one hand, it must be extremely difficult to clarify repressed issues originating from the Holocaust, especially if they were silenced by their parents as well. On the other hand, a new generation opens up fresh possibilities that may be used for clarifying issues that previously have been silenced.

Family Interviews,
Three Generations in Each Family

The details of our procedure are described elsewhere (Bar-On, in press). In short, we contacted and interviewed each family member separately, usually two interviewers per family. We usually started by interviewing the survivor and moved down from one generation to the other. Each interviewer transcribed his or her recording, including recalled nonverbal responses, and added a description of the subjects, the interviewing process, and his or her own feelings during the interview. After the transcription, we began analyzing the interviews in a team.

Following Rosenthal (1987, 1989), the analysis of each interview included three stages: First, we listed the biographical details of each interview and started to develop hypotheses based on the life history. We tried to assert for each hypothesis how it might be confirmed later in the text. Second, we defined sequences (according to topic) and identified the linguistic structure of each sequence (was it a narrative, a report, a description, or an argument?). Third, we started with the narrative analysis, one sequence after the other, going into detailed microanalysis in each sequence that seemed to us central. After we identified the central theme or strategy of the interviewee, we then asked questions about what we may find in the coming generation's interview. We repeated the whole procedure in all three interviews, finally summarizing with a discussion of the family intergenerational patterns.

Changing from the role of interviewer to the role of analyst demanded much more than a technical transition. We became so involved in the interviews that it was very difficult to develop the necessary emotional distance needed for the analyses. At this stage our team discussions became very helpful.

A Case Study: The Anisewitch Family

Olga, the Grandmother: ". . . *and that's how we lived*"

We met Olga[2] in her small home, located in a moshav[3] in the southern part of Israel. From the very beginning of the interview, there was a sharp contrast between the trivial language

Olga used, the way she spoke, and the unbelievable events she referred to. Olga, born in Warsaw in 1930, opens: "I had a very happy childhood. I come from a mixed family." In the following sentences, however, it becomes clear that her childhood happiness had nothing to do with having come from a mixed family but, rather, was associated with her mother's home after she had divorced her first husband and married a second, Jewish one. Moreover, at a later stage, it turns out that her coming from a mixed family was a fact that, despite appearing in her opening sentence of our interview, had been kept hidden from her present family for many years. She did not tell her family about it until her brother, Yadek, who had grown up in a Christian home with Olga's father, immigrated to Israel from Poland 8 years ago, shortly after her husband's death. Perhaps Olga wanted to say that her happiness began and ended in her mother's home before the war. She mentions her happiness three times in the first paragraph of her interview, only to end it with: "till the war came and everything—everything changed."

In contrast to the happiness in her mother's home before the war, her father's home was reflected on with contempt. This attitude seemed to be linked to the fact that, being Gentile, her father had saved Olga (and only her) at the time her mother decided life in the ghetto "has come to an end." However, her father became the object of Olga's manifest anger. She started with the trivial: In the beginning it was her habits, unacceptable to her father and his wife; later she was placed in a Carmelite nuns' school to "camouflage the dark color" of her skin. Finally, "I was no longer able to tolerate the oppression of my step-mother." She ran away from her father's house to manage on her own on a nearby farm, where she experienced liberation by the Russian troops.

Olga concludes in irony: "A nice experience . . . my first profession was working as a pig herder." She describes how her father was afraid of her "Jewish appearance and Jewish manner of walking" and her knowledge of Yiddish, all of which might betray him as well as her. "And I was only a little girl, wasn't I?" However, Olga does not tell us anything about the uprising or the destruction of the Warsaw ghetto, which happened while her mother and sister were still there. She had been smuggled out, thanks to her father's being Aryan. Olga suddenly turns to us, directly: "Now, if you want me to elaborate, let me know. I don't know if that is relevant, it depends on what you are interested in." Relevant to whom? The question was put to us, but we understood it as also being posed to herself: Which part of this painful past is relevant from her present, Israeli perspective?

For Olga her experiences with her father were only a link in a chain of devastating experiences. The first warning came from her mother when Olga still could move freely between the ghetto and the outside. She was given the task of collecting sleeping pills from the pharmacies outside the ghetto: "If the situation becomes too bad, then she will end her life with these pills." Afterward, escaping from the ghetto with the help of her stepfather had been considered. However, her mother's decision to stay with her own mother, who did not want to go, put an end to this opportunity. Later Olga witnessed the suicide of her grandmother, who could no longer stand being hidden (she had not obtained a working permit). Being a midwife, "She injected herself with morphine and told us that she wanted to sleep and that no one should wake her up. (pause) I was very close to my grandmother because my mother was always working." Here we could feel the tension between the tone, the words, and the terrible events they tried to represent.

Up to this point, Olga narrated the events as being handled by others. After her narration of leaving the ghetto, she used verbs in their active mode. She bought herself a necklace with a cross in order to hide her Jewishness. She ran away from her father's house to a village where she presented herself as the daughter of a Gentile family who had survived the destruction of Warsaw and, "all in all, I managed quite well and . . . there weren't many problems besides my longing for my mother and my sister who were still living in the ghetto." Did she believe they were still alive? In another place she states: "For a long time I kept thinking that I would still meet them . . . for many years . . . perhaps even when I was already in Israel, I still dreamt." In contrast to the long and angry narration concerning her father, there are only these two sentences telling us how much she longed for the mother and sister whom she left behind, never to see them again.

After the liberation, Olga returned to the ruins of her mother's house, where she found that "only the walls and the cellar remained." Olga tells how desperate she was until she met a woman who gave her tea and some food. To this stranger Olga admitted that she did not "know how to manage," the only time she expresses her helplessness during the whole interview. Then she adds, simply: ". . . and that's how we lived." When asked, Olga said she went to the ruins of her mother's house because, "there wasn't really any connection any more with my father." Was it true? Later she told us about how her brother (who had lived all those years with her father) was disappointed because he had expected her to take him with her to Israel. To begin with, this action shows that her brother felt close to her, while she only experienced being rejected. It also suggests that some kind of contact was maintained with her father's home after the war.

A Jewish acquaintance met Olga in the ruins of Warsaw and directed her to a Jewish children's home in Kraków. From this point, Olga "made a choice" about being Jewish and a Zionist, going to Israel, though the disasters did not stop happening: She joined a kibbutz in Kalytcz. While she was in Kraków for an ear treatment, a pogrom took place in Kalytcz and her best friend, with whom she shared a room, was murdered. Shocked, she stayed in Kraków and joined another kibbutz there. It took them 3 years finally to immigrate to Israel during the war of independence. When she arrived, her ear problems kept her in a hospital in Haifa, while most of her friends from the kibbutz were killed in the battle of Latrun.[4] Fate was following her, but Olga persistently moved forward "to rebuild life."

Olga tells her story in eloquent Hebrew, much better than the other survivors we interviewed. She now tries to make a clear distinction between what had happened there and what she has created here. The use of verbs is still in the active mode, but the narration becomes much more condensed, as if telling us that there is not much more to tell: She married a Holocaust survivor; they joined the moshav to become farmers in the south of Israel, where she is still living. She gave birth to three children. Her husband, who was very ill all those years ("He had lung problems from the concentration camps"), died 8 years ago of lung cancer. She recently started a new relationship.

Unexpectantly her youngest son, Benny, joins in, changing the course of the interview. Olga laughingly just told us what she had told her children: "They know everything. Whenever they asked, I told them. What they didn't ask—I didn't tell." Her son, referring to this comment, says, "We understood that over there it was bad, really bad . . . so you don't ask any more questions." Did her children know what she had told us about her stepfather ("who had actually been a real father to me"), that he still was living, in London, not interested in renewing contact with her after the war? We do not know. We could only imagine how difficult it would be for her to tell them.

Besides the Jewish-Gentile estrangement that these two fathers embodied, we found an ambivalence in Olga's attitude toward her being Polish. On the one hand, it was her mother tongue. On the other hand, these were the people who helped in the extermination of her family and who perpetrated the pogrom in Kalytcz. This ambivalence is revealed when she relates negatively to the Poles they met in the moshav she and her husband had joined. Olga explains that her son does not know Polish because she and her husband had decided "to speak Hebrew when the children were born." But a few minutes later, she recalls a record she had bought in Tel Aviv: It had "a beautiful Polish lullaby which made me swear to protect my little son." It is this record that calmed her fears, fears Olga was able to talk about only after her son mentioned his own.

Olga, originating from an educated family, was unable to obtain a proper education due to the war. Olga puts the responsibility, though indirectly, on her father. Because of him, she had to move from one place to another, and this uprooting interfered with her studies; thus she became a "maid for these different families." This lack of education later made Olga doubt her authority as a parent. She urged her children to get an education, thereby guaranteeing their future. "Study whatever you wish. The main thing is that you study." Also here, Olga speaks out of a conflict. On the one hand, education was the only legitimate component of the family before the Holocaust, still valuable after a sign of continuity. On the other hand, education did not save any of the Jews (e.g., her mother and her grandmother), just as she argued earlier that the Jewish religion did not help its believers.

It is precisely Olga's attempt to present a feeling of normality in her life story, in light of the extraordinary events of her life history, that made her untold story powerful. For Olga this probably refers to the divorce of her parents, the war ("till the war came and everything—everything changed"), and the refuge her mixed family background provided her with in the terrible constellation of the Holocaust. This was a relative advantage, in comparison to her mother and sister, who could not escape from the ghetto. She later deliberately puts herself on their Jewish side. Still we could feel that there was more in it than she could tell. We do not know what her untold stories contain: Being attracted to the Christian religion during her stay with the Carmelite nuns? Feeling at some point more Polish than Jewish? Olga only provided hints in these directions.

The untold story showed in the way Olga tried to hide her mixed background from her children. For example, we were told about her brother's arrival in Israel first by her son, only then by Olga. Yadek's arrival forced Olga to tell her children about their then still-living grandfather and his family: "How could I tell them earlier about a grandfather who was not a father to me?" she asks bitterly. Her inability to clarify the untold story also showed itself in the apologetic way she describes her brother's failed attempt at absorption into Israel and his emigrating to Germany. On the one hand, she was saddened by his not having succeeded in adjusting and, on the other hand, she stated: "His attempt was doomed to failure," as if serving as a proof that her way of deciding, of "rebuilding life," in Israel was the only possible way to live in the present, to overcome the past.

Benny hinted at the untold story when relating to his difficulties during the Intifada. He had a hard time defining "on whose side I am," that of the Israelis or of those "carrying the cross," referring to the Palestinians. In the context of the interview with Olga, however, carrying the cross had an additional meaning, especially when considering "what side I am on." Not by coincidence, Olga reacted immediately, with an obvious contradiction: On the one hand, she tells how she taught her children that an Arab is a human being; on the other hand, "in the army, in order that this child protect himself adequately, perhaps, he must be told that the other side is not exactly like him." It is as if she wanted to tell her son, "Know who you are, just as I had to decide who I was."

Olga has difficulty expressing emotions. When Benny talked about his fears concerning his father's health and death or about the compulsiveness he believes that he has absorbed from his parents, Olga was unable to deal with his outbursts. Using trivial jokes and comments, she tried to lessen the level of emotions expressed to the degree she had established earlier in the interview. Only once, when she spoke of the Polish record, did she give in to her fears, meshed with those expressed by her son. It is interesting to note that it was Benny who made his home near his mother, whereas his two sisters chose to live farther away. Was he chosen to be his mother's memorial candle (Vardi, 1990), representing Olga's two fathers who failed, her husband who died?

Looking ahead to the interview with Dina, Olga's daughter, we were curious to find out how she would relate to her mother's past. Would she continue her mother's farming activities? Would she accept her mother's urge for education? Did Dina have fears as her brother did, or would she minimize them as her mother did? How did Dina react when her mother told her she still had a grandfather in Poland? Did she also try to trivialize the past, to go on, creating a new reality rather than experiencing it?

Dina, the Older Daughter:
Between Restoration and Survival

Dina, like many other members of her generation, told her story, reducing its importance in comparison to that of her parents: "My parents settled in the moshav. . . . They were pioneers, but pioneers of the fifties are not like pioneers of the eighties." Olga used trivialization for reducing the impact of the events she had experienced during the war. Dina trivializes her own doing, in relation to her parents's deeds, emphasizing the continuity of what her parents have achieved during their life in Israel. She reminds us of Olga when she turns to Noga, her daughter, and says, "I don't know if you're interested in that at all." It seems as if Dina is also asking herself, Can my story be of interest to anybody? Her last sentence was, "It is probably characteristic of a hundred million other families, right?"

In her life history Dina had her own pioneering experience. As a teacher, she helped establish a school in Lehavim, a new urban settlement in the desert. This motif reminds her of her childhood. She recalls from the stories of her parents how they had joined the moshav "at the edge of the desert," where Dina was born. In the tiny first-grade class in the moshav, Dina already was given an important task: She was the only one who understood the Hebrew of the teacher, as well as Polish and Rumanian, spoken by the other pupils. When Dina became involved in building a school from scratch at Lehavim, she remembers, emotionally, the pioneering spirit of her childhood.

Words like *create* and *strong* appear over and over in different contexts—as expressions of action and novelty. Mixed with narrating novelty are expressions of temporariness, danger, and fear. In the moshav "members were sitting on their suitcases," there were "poverty and backwardness." Near her parents' house, saboteurs stalk, stealing cows and killing people. When she is asked about her own memories, Dina's opening sentences are, "I was rather frightened as a child. I guess I caught some of those fears. I don't like darkness and things like that." Did these fears relate to issues beyond the moshav's reality? Dina did not explain such a possibility, at least not in the course of our interview.

While narrating her early memories, Dina's expressions of pleasure are always interwoven with fears. The loaded wagon of hay overturned, and all of the children fell off, along with the bales of hay. It must have been rather frightening, but Dina describes it as a celebration. She tells about the neighbor's son, who fell sleeping from the wagon on the way back from the beach, as if it were a funny incident. However, the boy's mother "almost had a heart attack because her son had suddenly disappeared." The British army camp with the huge hole in the ground is a source of mystery and fear, but the ground was also "full of flowers of all colors" like in a Nature Preservation Society's poster.

Out of the lively description of events something else emerges: the Israeli identity of the child-woman, which helped Dina not relate to her parents' pre-Israeli past. It was not that she did not know. For example, "I simply had no grandparents. That's how I grew up. It seemed natural; that is, I didn't feel I was missing anything, and that's that!" Only with the appearance of her mother's brother (when Dina is already a mother herself), something new occurred: "Beforehand [before Yadek came] it was us, and our present-day lives, all of that was strong enough, there were enough experiences and stimuli that . . . I, at any rate, did not bother myself with their past." Had Yadek not appeared, perhaps Dina still would be absorbed in that strong present.

According to Dina, settling in the moshav was an ambivalent issue for her parents: On the one hand, there was a legend of pioneering, accompanied with hospitality, adventures of farming, and nature. Dina very much identified with this part of her parents' story, "something that has tremendous strength." On the other hand, her father suffered from severe physical problems ("He's not cut out to be a farmer") and her mother felt inferior to their city friends—for not "having concerts or enough books." There was a mixture of sarcasm about the "bejewelled women with their high heels" who had no idea what physical work and life in nature was like, with a feeling of envy toward their cultural superiority. The story was Dina's; were the feelings Dina's or Olga's?

Were these expressions of ambivalence, of fear and temporality, meaningful to Dina? During most of the interview, she tried to mitigate their significance. She insisted that neither she nor her siblings felt any less fortunate than those city children who used to come to visit them: "All of us have overcome the gap, and we are all well off." The push to learn, to obtain an education and a profession, had its source in Olga's educational deficit. Only recently has Dina come to enjoy studying at the university "for its own sake," as compared with her early training for the teaching profession. Now it was even difficult for Dina to return to the narrow framework of teaching elementary school after "the new world opened up for me."

Insight requires tranquility, free time. Dina had no time because she was in constant action—for example, her failed attempt to keep the Shabbat. Identifying with her father, whose attempts were unsuccessful, Dina tried to practice the Shabbat in her own home. She had this ideal image of "lighting candles, the children sitting quietly around the table in a festive atmosphere." However, she did not accomplish this ideal. Was it due to the children, who did not go along with it? Or was it Dina, who seemed too busy with her housework? "When do I have time to do the laundry and cleaning?" Partially admitting failure, partially on the defensive, Dina stated, "So that's religion—without religion." Dina avoided the opportunity to reflect on it. Following Olga's path, Dina cast doubt on the religious ceremonies, as well as on the existence of God after the Holocaust.

Secular family celebrations such as birthdays, which are of central importance to the family, are celebrated with religious zest—a response to the void left by the loss of family in the Holocaust. The phonograph, bought with Olga's reparation money, became the catalyst of "joy and dancing." Again and again, it is Dina, like her mother, who creates reality, rather than experiences it. It is as if she still is participating in a latent controversy regarding the success of the restoration.[5] Whereas her younger brother expresses his anxieties, struggling with his parents' reflection in himself, Dina gives no sign of similar feelings or reflections.

This detachment became obvious when Dina spoke of the Holocaust. To begin with, there was a difference in her mind between "restoration and survival." She grew up on the idea "from Holocaust to restoration" and brought it into her teaching, in accord with the Israeli norm of heroism that characterized the 1950s and 1960s (Segev, 1991). At home the hard times in the moshav were discussed widely, but no horror stories from the Holocaust. When, a month after her father's death, his friends came and spoke of their experiences in the concentration camp, Dina added that they did not talk "about the exceptional, only the regular things that had happened." Although she knew she had no grandfathers and grandmothers because they were massacred in the Holocaust, these were "external words—I didn't feel any trauma. . . . I had no problem with this."

It was surprising, therefore, to hear Dina's response to a question about whether she recalled any objects in her parents' home. She recalled a red kerchief her mother had kept—the only reminder of the time her father had been in the concentration camps during the Holocaust. Perhaps this was an indication that, for her, the Holocaust was associated emotionally (without words) with her father, rather than with her mother. Dina said her father was not talkative, just as it is difficult for her to "talk about her father in the past tense."

When Olga, as a result of her brother's arrival, started speaking of her father's home, Dina was shocked. She found that she still had a grandfather (Olga's father) in Poland. However, she tells us about it with mixed feelings: "A grandfather was born, that was the funniest thing!" We feel her anger and embarrassment in this response. At this point in the interview, Dina calls her mother "Olga" and stops referring to her as "my mother." Dina immediately tries to give reasons for calling her mother Olga ("Don't see it as a sign of estrangement"). However, we believe it was not coincidental that she started to relate to her mother in this way at this exact point in the interview.

Here we find a first sign of a boundary between mother and daughter not expressed before. On the one hand, the change of name could be seen as a sign of intimacy between Dina and her mother (she had called her mother "Olga" in her childhood). On the other hand, it may be a sign of anger—anger at the mother who tried to conceal her past, perhaps also anger at the lack of boundaries that, until then, she could not establish. Dina was the eldest child and felt very close to her mother (quoting her sister: "When you are with Olga, no one else exists"). Olga concealed her Gentile background (and that part of her past) from Dina. As that aspect of her mother's past was uncovered, the myth that she was very close to her mother, as well as the myth that the past "was finished with," were both torn down for Dina.

Now Olga told her daughter how she survived in the ghetto and after the war. Dina adds, "Her stories about how she survived, I think they built me up, too." She does not explain how they helped build her, but we may surmise that, for Dina, Holocaust no longer meant restoration or heroism, but pride in her mother's act of survival. In the Israeli context, this change constituted crossing a very fine, yet clear-cut line: those who associate themselves with here, versus those who associate themselves with there. Dina stated, "Nothing came as a surprise for me, nothing . . . but now, it is finally connected." And we assume the link that had been missing for Dina had been the effect the past still has on the present, combined with the legitimacy of human weakness and survival.

At the very time this happened, several other important events were happening in Dina's life. Dina went to study at the university, for the first time "for its own sake." At that time Dina and her sister settled the problems that had caused tension between them. Dina, the older, responsible sister, could not afford to do what the younger one could. Her sister could "make trouble for her teachers," while being recognized as the gifted one. Dina, living up to her parents' expectations, saw herself as an "average child."

Dina tells us with great emotion about an incident at the police station, which Olga had only hinted at when she said she had been braver than her father ("If they catch us together, don't you dare say that I am your father"). Whereas Olga reports on her father's fear, Dina emphasizes the element of rejection ("Get away from me so that I won't have to see you again"). Dina added, "And to this day I feel inside—a twisting—how can a father say such a thing?" Here Dina is still identifying totally with her mother.

Was Dina aware that Olga's stepfather was not interested in renewing contact with her? Olga wanted to spare her daughter these complex and embarrassing details, and Dina willingly cooperated with this wish. Indeed Dina asserted that her mother still "uncovers one detail while concealing a lot." She assumed there may be other facets to her mother's story that she still does not know about. Dina did not ask, however, and her mother prefers to give letters and pictures from the past to her grandson, who is doing a school project about his family, rather than show them to Dina.

There was only one clue to the way Dina imagined the past during her childhood, beyond her expressed fears, dangers, and feelings of temporality. Dina was describing "the fascination of that hill"—the mystery of the British army camp to which Dina felt herself drawn in her childhood. They played "Will You Fall In Or . . . Not" near the frightening hole in the ground. There were remnants left by the army—objects such as a fork, a pocket knife—and "we were rather poor, actually quite poor." In contrast were flowers of beautiful colors on the hill. We asked ourselves whether this place entailed an unconscious representation of the past for Dina. Was it something like "Father's concentration camp" or "Mother's ghetto" and "a cemetery for lovers who were not buried"? A place where children could play dangerous games, like the "games" the parents had "played" under the Nazis?

Dina tries to present a conflict-free life story. We asked ourselves whether this presentation reflected her way to handle the tension between Israeli restoration and diaspora survival. Dina has come a long way as she has described the process in her own mind: no longer only restoration, but also respecting the act of survival. Being Polish has recently become a part of her identity through her relationship with Yadek. Still the change in her consciousness may be due to her growing up and becoming a woman, or to the self-confidence she had acquired as the vice principal of the school. It also could be accounted for by changes that have occurred in Israeli society as a whole. Nevertheless we thought Dina's unspoken question still was: In what ways do I belong both here and there?

We now ask, What did Orit (Dina's eldest daughter and Olga's granddaughter) absorb from the stories of her mother and grandmother? Orit is not obligated to concern herself with the complicated issues of the past. As a second generation in Israel, she lives at a distance of 50 years from the events that shaped Olga's life and, to a certain degree, influenced her mother's life. She was born into a wider family framework with grandmothers and grandfathers. She was born into the complicated Israeli reality (tensions between Arabs and Jews, the religious and the secular, the various ethnic groups, a difficult economic situation), where the past is no longer represented but through the myths and slogans of the elderly. She is a 16-year-old, busy building her own identity. Will Orit try to ask further, new questions?

Orit, the First Granddaughter: Old Stories—New Choices

After a brief attempt to follow directions and tell her life story, Orit turned to Dan, almost as her mother and grandmother did: "But I didn't think you have come here to listen to my childhood memories." Orit had her own a priori ideas of the interview. She did not think Dan was interested in her in her own right, but rather as the granddaughter of Olga. After two short stories of her childhood in Yerucham[6] (shoplifting from the stores, and the death of her beloved dog), Orit comments, "I don't have a marvelous life story like some people." This comment was not surprising for an interview with a 16-year-old, especially because she was referred to by her mother as "not being the type who talks much." However, Orit's next phrase, "I am just an ordinary girl," reminded us of Dina's and Olga's self-representations.

For us the interview held a surprise: Neither Olga nor Dina had mentioned anything about Olga and Orit's trip to Warsaw last year. For Orit this was a key experience: "My visit to Poland changed my way of thinking." Alas, Orit did not clarify in what way. She traveled with her grandmother to her home ground. She tried, indirectly, to ask her about the Holocaust, but Olga told her, very much in the spirit of what she said to her children, that it is difficult for her to talk about it freely but that she is ready to answer any questions that Orit might have. Orit asked, and Olga told her, why her mother sent her to live with her father as "things got bad in the ghetto" and about the problems she had with her father, as well as her grandmother's suicide.

Orit acknowledged the feelings between Olga and her father: "Since he was her father, it was clear that she loved him, but she didn't feel good there." Was this the naïveté of a 16-year-old who could not imagine not loving one's father? Or perhaps it was her insight into the complexity of the relationship between Olga and her father. At any rate, it was very different from Dina's (and Olga's) formulations. Dina did not consider the possibility that Olga loved her father, a futile love that did not work out. Olga only spoke of being rejected.

Further in the interview, Orit showed an unusual talent in identifying people's feelings. Her definitions were clear and concise, without going into motives. When she referred to Olga at the time of their Warsaw visit, "Grandmother doesn't really show her feelings; it is difficult to be emotional with her." She described Dina as, "She's nosy like me," her uncle Yadek, "He's like my grandmother—both of them are quiet and so cultured . . . no cursing." Again reflecting on Olga, "My grandmother has such a quiet way of speaking, but it always sinks in at the right spot." She described the lack of effect the past has on her parents: "That didn't influence them, because the two grandmothers made it clear that what was, was; the main thing is the present and the future." In all of these references, not judgment or anger or fear were expressed. It was more than the "black and white" thinking we had expected of a girl her age.

It was Orit who asked to accompany her grandmother in the first place: "I said jokingly: 'Me too' . . . sort of a 'small revenge.' " Even if her first motive was the jealously she felt toward her brother's planned trip to the United States, Orit exhibited a more serious approach later on. Her curiosity about her family's past was striking. Orit knew how to listen to Olga "between the lines": "Then I could feel her excitement, 'Here I am, back home,' " accepting her grandmother's difficulty in showing emotions as part of telling her story. This curiosity was not satisfied after hearing her grandmother's personal story in Warsaw. When Orit states later that she wants to serve in the intelligence section of the army in order "to do something for this country," she adds with a smile and a bit of irony, "From this family, I already have experience in spying." There was no need for her to prove that she had missed or lacked anything.

All of this information reflects Orit's own choices, rather than her conformity. She became an investigator of the past in her own right. Even when she verbally accepted the family's norm—"The main thing is the future, it's not so important to scrape around in the past"—she tries to find out, to understand those things that were not discussed in the family. She bypasses the lack of influence of the past on her parents, trying to make sense of the complexity of the past. In a few simple statements about Olga, Orit showed that she has captured something that Dina and her mother could not clarify in their life stories.

Our question remains: Why did neither Olga nor Dina tell us about last year's trip to Warsaw? After all, it was a central event in Orit's life that "changed her way of thinking." Did her mother or grandmother not notice it? Moreover, in the interviews with both Dina and Olga, no mention is made of Orit's unique interest and sensitivity. Both related to the child and grandchild in a very general way: "Orit is an ordinary child," said Dina when describing her daughter's schooling.

One may suggest that not mentioning the trip was a by-product of a biased interview. Orit stated the subject of our research: "You didn't come to hear my childhood stories, but to hear about my grandmother's memories from the Holocaust." Dina knew about our research subject and possibly her mother did, too. Perhaps they assumed that we were not particularly interested in their relationships with their children and grandchildren. In Dina's interview, however, are detailed descriptions about the move to Lehavim, about her first teaching experiences, including the phase in which she taught her own son, Gideon. It must be asked: Why was it Orit who was left out of her mother's narration? Why did this omission include her daughter's and her mother's trip to Warsaw?

It is more difficult to believe that this trip was unimportant for Olga. One can sense, through Orit's descriptions, how Olga's feelings and memories were aroused by this visit. Nevertheless Olga made no mention of the trip whatsoever! However, Olga "uncovers one thing and conceals a lot," according to Dina. Olga tells only what she is being asked for, according to both her and Orit. If it had not been for her son's arrival during our interview, we may not have learned about her brother's trip to Israel and what it opened up in her family.

Therefore we may assume that it was not an omission at random, but rather an intentional one. What was it that led Dina to pass by the trip of her mother and daughter? According to Orit, Olga suggested that Dina come, but it was not possible "due to financial reasons." Was that the only reason Dina did not come? Orit related to the issues of Olga's father, of Olga's feeling at home in Warsaw, in a different manner from Dina. She related to Olga's feelings, not by seeing them through Olga's eyes. Perhaps Dina did not tell us about the trip to Warsaw because she could not share her daughter's insights.

It is more difficult to explain why Olga "forgot" to tell us about her trip with Orit. After all, Olga contributed to Orit's interest in the past by sharing her stories and feelings with her. She could be proud of herself: Why did she not show us this pride? It seems that Olga was not inclined to feel proud about what Orit got from this trip. It must have been a difficult experience for her, as Orit stated: "Then I could feel her excitement . . . 'Here I am, back home.' " If Orit sensed correctly, it must have been difficult for Olga to feel at home *there* after she worked so hard at rebuilding her life *here,* repressing feeling at home there. Perhaps the trip to Warsaw meant so much to Olga that she could not handle it within the same interview in which she narrated about the past.

Olga could not say what Orit so simply stated about Olga's father: "Since he was her father, it was clear that she loved him, but she didn't feel good there." During Yadek's visit in Israel, new opportunities opened up to clarify this relationship. Olga shared with her family her mixed background and feelings, the hardships she faced in order to survive both physically and emotionally. If her brother's visits opened up an opportunity for her to work through her anger toward her father, this chance probably was gone when her father died during Yadek's visit in Israel. Thus another dimension was added to the irreversibility of pent-up emotions. Perhaps her father's death sealed the fate of Olga's relationship to the past, a seal that the trip to Warsaw reopened, but not her narration of that past.

Summary: Intergenerational Patterns of Strategies in the Anisewitch Family

Olga survived a range of devastating experiences, accompanied by identity dilemmas (Jewish, Christian, Polish, religious-nonreligious, educated-noneducated). In her life history, she became an Israeli farmer-pioneer. In her life story, she developed a strategy oriented toward the future ("to rebuild life"), cutting herself off from the other parts, not really using new life events to work them through. Dina, having her own childhood experiences of dangers and uncertainties, adopted her mother's strategy, thereby defending herself also from her mother's unresolved conflicts. Orit, we thought, had a different childhood and more freedom of choice to formulate her own relationship with the past and the present. Unlike her mother, she did not have to make the transition from restoration to survival. Orit, not obliged to identify with Olga, also had no need to distance herself from Olga. She may be in a position to test what "rebuilding life" is about in this family.

Olga and Dina have contributed in no small measure to Orit's relative freedom. Olga put all of her energy into rebuilding life under harsh physical and emotional conditions. Together with her husband, she established the foundation for the physical security of her newly established family after their former families were destroyed in the Holocaust. Dina, still exposed to some insecurity, went on establishing her family, developing a professional career, and building a new school in the community. Dina also had to develop a strategy that would enable her to maneuver between her mother's manifest expectations and unresolved feelings toward her past while bringing up her own children in a more complex social environment in which new values of pleasure and self-realization emerged. All of this she did under one roof of a three-generational family, a kind of family she herself did not have in her own childhood.[7]

Dina's strategy may have afforded Orit new options to look into the unresolved psychological aspects of her grandmother's past. It seems that by asking questions and trying to find answers, Orit could formulate, without fear, the relationship between Olga and her father, Olga's feeling at home in Warsaw, and the late appearance of Yadek as "natural" life events. This conception may have helped Orit develop a deeper psychological understanding beyond the more simplified ones her mother and grandmother tried to present in their life stories (Bar-On, 1992). Although she is still very young, too young to say anything conclusive about her own life history, we could identify early signs in her life story pointing in this direction.

Discussion: Some Methodological and Theoretical Issues

We can imagine a wide range of methodological arguments this analysis raised: We interviewed only three persons (and Benny, who joined in Olga's interview) in a family that has several other influential figures: Olga's late husband, Dina's husband, Dina's sister, Orit's siblings. Probably every additional interviewee could shed some new light on the complex family case study, as we witnessed in Benny's unexpected contribution to Olga's interview. We did interview one family in such an extensive way (Weiss & Levi, 1990) to find out that every additional family member added a new variant, thereby developing a kind of "Rashumon." This interview had the effect of making the picture more complex, adding information about the relationship between individual stories, between the issues discussed in the family and those that were not discussed.

By interviewing only one member of each generation, we undertook the risk that some of our interpretations would not have strong enough interpersonal validity, especially while trying to evaluate intergenerational effects. We therefore always started analyzing each story separately, looking for interpersonal coherence: The proofs in the text helped us identify an interviewee's strategy. When we talked about Olga's normalization strategy, trivializing the nontrivial, we could find it both in the way she talked and in what she said, repeatedly. For example, after each story, we would hear a phrase such as, ". . . and that's how we lived," or, "and then we went on." Only after identifying such coherence would we look at interpersonal coherence—in Olga's case by experiencing her reactions to Benny's emotional accounts, finding it in Orit's words "Grandmother doesn't really show her feelings; it is difficult to be emotional with her."

This was the technical part of the analysis. The more difficult part was to try to imagine, to understand, how our interviewee had lived through the situations she was describing. What was it like for Olga to watch her beloved grandmother slowly becoming "more and more yellow" after taking her morphine injection, until she was "defined as being dead"? What was it like for a 12-year-old girl to wander around in the "Aryan" part of Warsaw with a cross as a necklace, seeing and hearing the ghetto being destroyed after the uprising, wishing her mother and sister were still alive, knowing that she came out only due to her "Aryan" father? How was it for Dina to grow up in a village where saboteurs were stealing, killing people at night? How was it to meet her uncle Yadek, a person never mentioned before, and to find out suddenly that there is a grandfather still living in Poland?

Answering these questions was a much more difficult task to accomplish. On the one hand, we tried to do it within the context of the life story as the experiences were told. On the other hand, we wanted to understand the life experiences these stories stood for. In the above-quoted stories, the tension between the two was very difficult to handle as interviewers and as analysts, especially when presented to us as a matter of fact by our interviewees (Langer, 1991). However, this tension helped us interpret the functionality of normalization strategies for a person who wants to go on with life (always being confronted with new hardships to overcome), without investing his or her limited energy in the (lost) past. This being a functional strategy, one probably does not consider its limits, except when there is no other choice (e.g., for Olga when Yadek suddenly appeared). As psychologists we now could see that *working through* is a concept, not always an ultimate necessity in people's lives.

In addition to the difficult issue of validity is an issue of representativeness. One could argue: Assuming you found these strategies, even the intergenerational patterns, what relevance has the Anisewitch family for other families? Quite obviously we were telling a story of an unusual (mixed) family background. Why should their story be relevant for other, very different experiences and life stories coming from the Holocaust?

We would like to clarify what representativeness stands for. If one thinks about representativeness in terms of extracting value (e.g., a mean, median, or mode) for complex issues such as intergenerational effects, the number of uncontrolled variables does not allow such an extraction. Giving up looking for an average, we had to compromise for descriptions of the unique. We had to search for a way to formulate the variance of the "active variables," rather than representing them by a single value.

Within this variance, Olga showed an outstanding optimism ("to rebuild life") under extreme circumstances, transmitting this vitality to her daughter. Clearly not all survivors (even within our limited "sample") showed such a drive to go on under all hardships and to be able to transmit it to the following generation (Bar-On, in press). Furthermore not all grandchildren had an opportunity or the wish to look back into the unresolved issues of their grandparents and parents, especially not at the age of 16. So we could understand the issue of representativeness as a way of "mapping out" the variety of experiences and narrations, relating them to some crucial aspects of intergenerational effects. Within such a map the Anisewitch family represented a certain variant that now could be compared with other similar or different variants in terms of life histories, life stories, and the relationship between them.

Our study taught us how important it was to look at life stories of three generations, rather than at two, as earlier studies did, trying to identify intergenerational aftereffects of the Holocaust. Within our limited case study, Orit added a very important aspect to the earlier texts. More so, she added a new outlook of narrating the past. In this conclusion we join in with others who have stressed the importance of looking at three generations while studying intergenerational effects, especially when stressful and traumatic experiences are involved[8] (Carter & McGoldrick, 1988; Chang, 1991).

Notes

1. Rosenthal's method was discussed extensively in her article in the first volume of *The Narrative Study of Lives* (see Rosenthal, 1993).

2. The Anisewitch family, presented here, was interviewed in the spring of 1990 and analyzed by the two authors. The full account of the interviews appears in Bar-On (in press). All names and locations have been disguised.

3. A cooperative settlement in which each family runs its own farm.

4. A famous battle during the war of independence (1948), to uplift the siege on Jerusalem, in which many freshly trained new immigrants were killed.

5. *Restoration—Te'kuma* in Hebrew, meaning rebuilding the Jewish life in Israel, being close to the religious idea of redemption (*Ge'ula*).

6. A poor development town in the south of Israel, where they lived before moving to Lehavim.

7. I (Dan Bar-On) grew up in a generation that had almost no grandparents. My parents left Germany in 1933. My mother went back in 1936 to take her parents out before it was too late. Thanks to her, I could listen to their stories in my childhood. The children I grew up with had no grandparents. Almost all of the grandparents of European-originating Haifa-citizens of the late 1940s met in one cafe on Saturdays.

Although in other immigrants' cultures mostly no grandparents were present, they lived somewhere left behind. My friends, mostly of European origin, being survivors of those who fled "in time," had none left, anywhere, whatso-ever. Therefore one can understand this urge to reestablish grandparenthood for your children, a task Dina's (and my) generation became totally committed to. This task was quite different among the Oriental Jewry whose families immi-grated to Israel in the early 1950s. It also gives a new perspective to the relationship between Western and Oriental Jews in Israel at that time: The latter were not so much looked down upon, as envied: They had grandparents.

8. We would like to mention here Kurosawa's movie *Rhapsody in August,* which shows the three-generational differences in dealing with the trauma of the atomic bomb experienced by the first generation in Nagasaki.

References

Bar-On, D. (1990). Children of perpetrators of the Holocaust: Working through one's own "moral self." *Psychiatry, 53,* 229-245.

Bar-On, D. (1992). Israeli and German students encounter the Holocaust through a group process: "Working through" and "partial relevance." *International Journal of Group Tensions,* pp. 81-118.

Bar-On, D. (in press). *Fear and hope: Narrative analysis of five Israeli families of Holocaust survivors.* Tel Aviv: Hakibbutz Hameuchad & Lochamei Hageta'ot.

Bergmann, M. S., & Jucovy, M. E. (1991). *Generations of the Holocaust.* New York: Columbia University Press.

Carter, B., & McGoldrick, M. (1988). *Changing family life-cycle: Framework for family therapy.* New York: Gardner.

Chang, J. (1991). *Wild swans: Three daughters of China.* New York: Simon & Schuster.

Danieli, Y. (1983). Families of survivors of the Nazi Holocaust: Some long- and short-term effects. In N. Milgram (Ed.), *Psychological stress and adjust-ment in time of war and peace* (Vol. 8). Washington, DC: Hemisphere.

Freud, S. (1953-74). Further recommendations on the technique of psycho-analy-sis: II. Remembering, repeating, and working through. *Standard edition of the complete psychological works* (Vol. 12). New York: Hogarth. (Original work published 1914)

Kestenberg, J. S. (1972). Psychoanalytic contributions to the problem of children of survivors from Nazi persecution. *Israeli Annals of Psychiatry and Related Sciences, 10,* 311-325.

Krystal, H. (Ed.). (1968). *Massive psychic trauma.* New York: International Universities Press.

Langer, L. L. (1991). *Holocaust testimonies: The ruins of memory.* New Haven, CT: Yale University Press.

Lehman, D. R., Wortman, C. B., & Williams, A. F. (1987). Long-term effects of losing a spouse or child in a motor vehicle crash. *Journal of Personality and Social Psychology, 52,* 218-231.

Novey, S. (1962). The principle of "working through" in psychoanalysis. *Journal of the American Psychoanalytic Association, 10,* 658-676.

Reick, M., & Etinger, L. (1983). Controlled psychodiagnostic studies of survivors of the Holocaust and their children. *Israeli Journal of Psychiatry, 20,* 312-324.

Rosenthal, G. (1987). *"Wenn alles in Scherben fällt . . .": Von Leben und Sinnwelt der Kriegsgeneration.* Opladen: Leske & Budrich.

Rosenthal, G. (1989). Leben mit der NS-Vergangenheit heute: Zur Reparatur einer fragwürdigen Vergangenheit im bundersrebuplikanischen Alltag [Proceedings]. *Zeitschrift für Bürgerrechte und Gesellschaftspolitik, 3,* 87-101.

Rosenthal, G. (1993). Reconstruction of life stories: Principles of selection in generating stories for narrative biographical interviews. In R. Josselson & A. Lieblich (Eds.), *The narrative study of lives* (Vol. 1, pp. 59-91). Newbury Park, CA: Sage.

Rosenthal, G., & Bar-On, D. (1992). A biographical case study of a victimizer's daughter repair strategy: The identification with the victim of the Holocaust. *Journal of Narrative and Life History, 2*(2), 105-127.

Rothstein, A. (1986). *The reconstruction of trauma: Its significance in clinical work.* New York: International Universities Press.

Segev, T. (1991). *The seventh million.* Jerusalem: Keter. (in Hebrew)

Solomon, Z. (1989). A three-year prospective study of post-traumatic stress disorder in Israeli combat veterans. *Journal of Traumatic Stress, 2*(1), 59-74.

Spence, D. P. (1980). *Historical truth and narrative truth.* New York: Basic Books.

Vardi, D. (1990). *The memorial candles.* Tel Aviv: Keter. (in Hebrew)

Weiss, E., & Levi, Y. (1990). *A narrative analysis of my grandfather's life story, his four children's, and their elder children.* Unpublished manuscript, Ben Gurion University.

❧ 4 ❧

Life Stories and Storied Lives

Richard L. Ochberg

*W*hat do we mean when we refer to the "storied nature" of human lives (Rosenwald & Ochberg, 1992; Sarbin, 1986)? Put practically, what do we hope to learn about the way people live when we interpret interview transcripts from the perspective of storytelling? The question arises out of the growing success that narratively inclined investigators have had in transforming the way we pay attention to personal reports.

Traditionally psychologists, sociologists, and anthropologists have turned to interviews on the reasonable faith that well-placed informants—the village chief or the town thief—can describe their ways of life with unrivaled accuracy and detail. Much interview research continues to be done for just this reason. More recently, however, narrative interpretation has turned its attention to the styles in which informants recount their experience. What images or turns of phrase do they employ? What larger structures organize their accounts? What purposes do these choices serve? In short, interpretation has shifted its focus from the told to the telling.

What do we learn when we interpret a personal account in this fashion? Broadly, we see how individuals make sense of their lives (Cohler, 1988). Each life story selects, from an unlimited array, those moments that the narrator deems significant and arranges them in a coherent order. This fashioning of order is much more than a chronology. For example, a life story establishes what counts as the main line of the plot and, thereby, which incidents should be construed as making progress or as retreats or digressions (Gergen & Gergen, 1983; Mishler, 1992). Similarly, life stories create narrative tension: How did a series of events build up into a significant problem, and how was it overcome (Ochberg, 1988)? In these ways a story establishes what sort of life this has been: a comedy of fortuitous salvations, a tragedy of unrealized chances, an epic of storms encountered and weathered.

This sense making may be directed toward several audiences. First, of course, is the storyteller, who is simultaneously the narrator, the protagonist, and the first audience of the tale. Most stories, however, are addressed also to an interlocutor: minimally the interviewer, and more largely all of the potential audiences this interviewer represents (notably including those projections of self-criticism with which narrators invest their witnesses). The public credibility of any story depends not only on the facts it reports but also on the narrator's skillful deployment of those local rules of discourse that make storytellers and audiences intelligible to each other. In turn the response of the audience determines both the success of the story and the identity of the narrator (Behar, 1992; Greenspan, 1992). In sum, then, life stories are a way of fashioning identity, in both the private and public senses of that word.

This approach, however, has a potential problem. If life stories and the identities they justify depend, in part, on their reception, then a life story must be a part of an individual's public life. The story must, in some fashion, be told. How often does this really happen? Most of the personal accounts that we analyze come our way in the course of research. (A notable exception is the narration of psychotherapy.) Because we cannot very well predicate a theory of narratively formed identity on the participation of a social scientist, we must explain how something like personal narration occurs in everyday life. Two recent examples illustrate what this might mean—but also, why public personal narration may be rare.

Concerned United Birthparents (CUB) is a national organization of support groups for parents, chiefly women, who surrendered their children for adoption. At CUB meetings women recount their experiences of the adoption, framed in the narrative line favored by the group: a story of institutional neglect and compulsory surrender. Modell (1992) shows how this form of narrative reconstruction honors these women's grief and legitimates their desire to reestablish contact with their children.

Susan Harding (1982) reaches a similar conclusion about a very different account: a story told by Reverend Cantrell, a Baptist minister, about accidentally killing his infant son. Harding argues that Cantrell's retelling of this tragedy is a form of witnessing. The story takes place within the tacit context of a Biblical tradition of sacrifice stories. Further, by telling his story to potential converts—in this case, Harding herself—Cantrell reaffirms his identity as a man of God: ready to turn his personal loss to doing the Lord's work.

The interpretations that Harding and Modell offer show us what is accomplished by the stories' style of telling. The events themselves—a child surrendered for adoption, or an infant accidentally killed—are only the raw ingredients of these narrators' identities. More fully, their identities depend on the stories' narrative coherence and the audience's response that Cantrell or the CUB mothers are able to elicit.

But which audience interests us? Harding suggests that Cantrell told his story in an attempt to convert her; this time, Harding herself was the audience. However, we cannot imagine that Cantrell's identity as a religious witness depends on the likelihood of another anthropologist stumbling into his church. The broader point is that he and the CUB mothers live in communities in which public testimony is frequent and formative. Members of these communities are often called on to bear witness or to listen to the testimony of others. These repeated tellings and hearings establish membership in a circle of fellow-believers, give meaning to old tragedies, and, at least for the CUB members, legitimate what might otherwise seem unreasonable action. This is ideally what we mean when we say that identities are formed by the public telling of life stories.

This much said, however, we must notice that narratively constituted worlds of this sort seem unusual. Public testifying

may characterize various communities of faith—religious or secular—but for most of us there is no counterpart to the institution-
alized narration that Harding and Modell describe. Most of us tell
our stories on rare occasions: in court, or in an employment
interview, or perhaps on a first date—and these hardly add up to
a means of identity formation.

Of course, we can examine the connection between stories
and lives without insisting that telling a story has any formative
effect on identity. The life stories that individuals tell reveal their
sensibility, just as thematic apperception stories do. Further, an
individual account may clarify the codes and practices within
which it is rendered (Fish, 1979). Ultimately we learn not merely
how an individual is making sense, but what sort of tacit local
rules make this instance of sense making sensible. Harding and
Modell, for example, each interpret their informants' accounts
within the context of their communities' narrative practice. In
a more critical vein, feminist interpretation has shown how the
stories women tell about their lives may be constrained by the
narrative forms—and the forms of living—that our culture currently legitimates (Gergen, 1992; Riessman, 1992; Rosenwald &
Wiersma, 1983). In this way our understanding of individuals'
stories clarifies the structure of their worlds; this is what makes
interpretation distinctly more than idiography.

Plainly, the stories we tell about ourselves are shaped by our
personalities and by the intersubjective codes of our communities. The direction of influence, however, is one-sided. Is there
a sense in which those personalities or communal practices are,
in turn, shaped by our stories?

In this chapter I argue that individuals do not merely tell
stories, after the fact, about their experiences; instead they live
out their affairs in storied forms. This relationship between
stories and lives can be seen in three ways.

First, there appears to be a structure to sequences of lived
action that is similar to the structure of a traditional plot. A plot,
conventionally, is a way of organizing events into a rising crescendo of tension that reaches its peak in a climax and then
resolves into a denouement.

Second, individuals appear to address these plotlike sequences of action to various audiences. In turn, the identity of the protagonist/performer depends on the audience's response. It is in this sense that a life lived in the form of a story is part of an individual's public record.

Third, by virtue of how the plot turns out and how the audience responds, life performances justify the idealized images that narrators hold of themselves. Here, too, is a connection between living a life and telling—or performing—a story. For a life, again like a story, is a kind of *argument*. It is a way of claiming that one construction of experience should be privileged and that some other, negative alternative should be dismissed.

What unites each of these dimensions of lived action and connects them to more literary perspectives on narrative is a specific conception of the *work* accomplished by both a story and a life. Briefly, a story brings to a head the possibility of being undone—and then attempts to rescue itself. This confrontation with the possibility of negation occurs at the three levels just described. As a *plot* a story exposes its protagonist to the possibility of defeat. As a *performance* a story risks the disbelief or disinterest of its audience. As an *argument* a story risks being supplanted by an invidious alternative. This much is true of stories in the ordinary, literary sense. Storied lives run the same risks. The lives we perform expose us to the same dangers of negation. In turn, our self-idealizing identities depend on our success in meeting and overcoming the possibility of our being undone.

Putting the matter this way alters the connection we might see between stories and lives. First, rather than ask, How do people talk about their lives? it asks, How do people perform their lives in storied form? This emphasis on action rather than talk frees us from the embarrassing possibility that telling one's story may be a rare occurrence. Few of us go around telling our stories to each other, but all of us are continually living out sequences of purposeful action. Second, rather than ask, How are the devices of life storytelling like those of literary narration? it asks, How does performing a life accomplish the same work

as performing a story? This question emphasizes the consequences rather than the technique of living one's life in a storied
form.

How is a life like a story? Here is an account that one man,
Lew, told me as part of an interview study on the meaning of
work in the lives of middle-aged men (Ochberg, 1987).

A Risky Life

Lew Myjer, a large man with the booming voice of an ex-
actor, sprawls back in his chair and tells me about his weekend:
"I just got back from spelunking." I am impressed. Later he will
tell me he likes to entertain people with the adventurousness of
his life.

We are talking about his plans. Lew is currently an administrator at a mental health agency, a job for which his previous
experience on the stage and as a disc jockey leaves him notably
and proudly unqualified. But life in the conference room has
grown stale; he is thinking of becoming a union organizer. He
explains, "It is not the same as getting up in front of a micro-
phone or camera, but it has the same appeal. Getting up in front
of people, getting them stirred up and motivated, almost like a
campaign. What unions do is campaign all the time."

It almost seems a reasonable choice, except for the state of
the economy. This is 1983, the nadir of Michigan's auto slump,
and everyone I know with a job supported by the shrinking state
budget is fearful of being laid off. Lew, meanwhile, has managed
to become the president of the local union and therefore has the
highest seniority of all. Of course, he would lose his seniority
the moment he quit his job, and with his lack of credentials, in
a dismal economy . . . Leaving his job now does not seem wise.
Lew, though, insists:

> It really does not take a whole lot of ingenuity to do
> what you want, because everyone else is fearful. You
> are one step ahead of everyone else who is afraid. They

take one, or two, or three major risks in their life, and
that is it. And a lot of times they regret it the rest of
their lives, and don't know how to move away from it. I
like risky people, who assert what they want. They
seek out the things that make them happy.

What does the risky life represent to Lew? Gradually it becomes clear that it is his escape from a dismal alternative: a life
of anxious, depressed paralysis. His first job after graduate school
was as an actor in a one-man traveling show.

I would drive to some school, set myself up, perform,
pack everything up, drive to another school, perform,
sometimes two, three, four times a day, then find
myself a motel or drive to the next city and find a
motel, and do the thing all over again. I did that for 5
months, and I succeeded. I blew an engine in the car
and got another one. Sometimes I ran out of money and
had to sleep in my car. I really just pitted myself against
the worst conditions. It gave me the sense that I was a
good survivor.

Being a good survivor is important to Lew. He explained that
for years he doubted himself. The risky life is his way of proving
his mettle. Lew was the first among his friends in the theater
department at college to try for a professional job in summer stock.

Let me describe what it is like being an actor. It is a
very difficult experience for someone who is not sure
of himself. You have to sell yourself. A constant,
repetitious selling yourself. And I had been the first in
my peer group to take that step, to go out and look for a
job. I broke the ice here too. And I was proud of myself.

The constant selling recalls what he said of union organizing:
Each is a constant campaign against the odds.
    He had planned to try out for bit parts, but the company
director encouraged him to audition for the lead. Lew won the

part and did creditably well for his first professional performance. At the same time, he became involved with the woman
who played the female lead.

> I was working with this woman who just saw through my
> ability. She said, "This guy can't do it." Every chance she
> put me down. I took so much grief from this woman that
> for the rest of the summer I was in a depression, this
> feeling that I will never be able to support myself. She had
> her own problems; she was heavily on tranquilizers. The
> irony of it was that she was also coming on to me. We
> started seeing each other, and she was just as caustic and
> malicious personally as she was on stage. But I was
> challenged. It became like a life or death situation.

After the season ended, he went home. He describes a period
of intense depression that lasted a month, and then a characteristic escape by way of decisive movement.

> When I say depressed, I mean I woke up and it hit me.
> I'd spend the day alienated from everything going on. I
> would just walk in a daze. And then I survived again. I
> got in this new Volkswagen that my brother gave me
> which I didn't know how to drive. He gave me a
> 15-minute lesson and said, "Okay, you are on your
> own." I drove to Atlantic City, where I knew some
> people who were working on a Shakespeare festival,
> and got a job in about a day.

Once again he recovered by way of movement: jumping in a
car that he could barely drive, with no money in his pocket, and
landing on his feet. But let us back up. A woman has entered the
piece, a woman who "had her own problems" but who nevertheless intimidated him. She and her various sisters reappear in
Lew's life. Sometimes he emphasizes their neurotic helplessness; at other times he fears they will unmask him.
     That winter he moved to Cleveland, got a job at a radio
station, and started dating the woman who did the morning

news. When the station was sold, they moved together to Ann Arbor.

> Carol wanted to get her strength back together. We were unemployed 3 months. I managed to get odd jobs, but she was incapacitated, so she wanted to build up some confidence. Both of us had lost our jobs, but I am a resourceful person; although I was depressed, I don't sit around moping about it. I do something, even if it is not what I want to do. It keeps me interested and involved.

As it happens, Carol eventually moved to Hawaii. Lew, who had planned to move with her, stayed behind. As he tells the story, however, he emphasizes Carol's depressive lethargy, his own energy. When disc-jockeying seemed a dead end, Lew again moved on, decisively.

> I didn't see myself growing in radio, so I went down to CETA and told them, "I want to do a career change; I don't know in what. I think social service might be something I'd like to try." I applied to one job; told them I had no credentials. But what I learned in my previous background was how to act. I can sell a line of bullshit real well. I didn't get in initially, but the woman they hired quit the first day and they called me.

A year and a half later he applied to be director. "I came in a squeaky second to an MSW. I said to myself, 'I think I have reached my ceiling here; better start looking around.' I made a few phone calls, got hired by the Mental Health Center in a new program. Six months down the line the coordinator left and I got promoted as coordinator."

Again notice the contrast between himself and women. Women mope, they lose confidence, they quit after a day. Lew acts, lands on his feet, and carries off the job despite his lack of training. However, it soon emerged that women are more dangerous figures in Lew's life than these portraits of helplessness suggest.

Even when they are neurotic, women threaten to call his bluff. The first summer stock acting job ended in despair. There have been similar occasions.

Lew's first performances in graduate school were tremendously successful. At the same time, he was flunking out of school. Once again he was involved with a woman who threatened to see through him.

> There was this older woman I wanted to impress. If I had thought about it, she was impressed anyway; she had her own hang-ups. But two or three times I just wasn't able to do it with her, and it scared me: "Is this an indication that I am gay?" I felt I could never do as well again as I did on the first performance of that play. I feared every night it would get worse. I still have this fear that if someone took a good look at me they would see a sham. I am still scared that it is not real. Every year I think less of that.

Eventually I asked whether his fear of being uncovered entered into his sexual relations. He said, "Well, let me tell you how I impressed her. It was all the preliminaries. I don't think I ever really screwed her. It was the initial sample that was outstanding."

The big first impression and the less adequate follow-through are the themes of still another early job. During his first summer home from college, Lew talked someone at a tool and die company into hiring him as a draftsman. At first all went well. Lew took on more sophisticated assignments than the owner expected him to handle and carried them off successfully. Still, his drawing on more basic projects remained a shade imprecise. "So he kept me doing the basic stuff, over and over again. And the anxiety of having to do this, and coming to work, was too much. I began to feel claustrophobic; a real heavy sense of being trapped."

The drafting boss, Lew's girlfriends, and the audiences at the theater all provoke Lew's anxiety that his initial impressiveness will not stand the light of close scrutiny. Interestingly enough Lew is quick to reverse the charge of fraudulence and ineffectuality. His descriptions of women emphasize their inability to meet a challenge. More generally he has a caustic eye for the pretensions of people around him. One summer he worked at a bank; he recalls an incident with his boss.

> This supervisor covered a book with brown paper, but so accurately that it took 2 or 3 hours. I said, "I hope you are going to read that book, because you sure are taking a lot of care with it." It was obviously one of the first hardcover books he'd bought; I couldn't see him reading it.

Then there was a young woman at work, who went to Barnard, with whom Lew tried to strike up a conversation. "I thought I could talk with her because I read a lot. But she gave me the impression she had no time or wasn't interested. She wasn't really an educated person. She was doing a mechanical job. She wasn't really a thinker." If Lew fears being the object of damning scrutiny, he is also an expert at seeing through others. His is a sardonic, piercing gaze.

To sum up what we have heard so far: Although Lew is often afraid that he is not competent, he takes on exceptional challenges and seems deliberately to court risk. He is often afraid that someone—especially some woman—will see through him. In apparent defense, he is quick to see through the pretensions of others. When he does feel beaten down or depressed, he feels immobilized, but soon restores himself by decisive movement. Overall, his is a style of attacking danger head-on. The meaning of these themes lies in his childhood history.

Lew's parents married late, after a long courtship. Before his marriage the father had been a musician. Lew believes that his father married ambivalently and never made his peace with the decision. In fact, he disappeared for 2 years shortly after the marriage to live with another woman. Even after he returned, he spent much of his time out of the house, involved in a dozen local political organizations and causes. Lew recalls his mother complaining about his endless "outside interests."

If Lew pictures his father with at least the virtue of a romantic past, his portrait of his mother is unrelieved. Lew describes her as a nagging, fear-ridden woman who depressed everyone around her. The father escaped to his outside organizations when he could. (Lew, who never actually witnessed this part of his father's life, imagines him as a passionate orator.) When he was trapped at home, the father absented himself emotionally. He was forever preoccupied with his music or a crossword puzzle. When these escapes failed, he walked around distractedly in what Lew describes as an "anxiety cloud." Meanwhile the mother nagged and worried; Lew recalls that she fed on misfortune.

> I remember one woman who was having a divorce and gravitated toward my mother because my mother dealt with tragedy. Then when this woman started stabilizing, my mother was still dealing with the tragedy, and this woman didn't want to deal with it anymore. My mother couldn't understand that.

Over the years Lew's mother became increasingly hobbled by anxiety. For a time she taught school, but the school children made her nervous and she had to quit. Later she took a job two blocks from the house. Lew recalls her saying, "Thank God it isn't any further, because you know I can't make the bus."

The mother brought her sense of impending disaster to everyone else in the family. Lew says, "It was always look out, because around any corner there might be another catastrophe." When Lew's brother, Paulie, wanted to play high school football, the mother refused to sign the letter of permission: too dangerous. Football can be a dangerous game, but Paulie was a big, aggressive kid.

Lew recalls his mother's reaction when he got into Brooklyn Tech, one of a handful of elite high schools in New York.

> I remember the first words out of her mouth were something like, "Are you sure you can do it?" It wasn't

like a pat on the back, or, "My son did so well." What I was left with after the phone call was, "God, I made a mistake; I shouldn't have accepted going to this school." She scared me all the time. Because I was stubborn, I would take on risky things, but I never enjoyed what I did because I was always so fucking scared. I carried that almost into my middle 20s, this fear of life.

Elsewhere he described his perpetual self-doubt.

There was a lot of internal talking. Could I do this or not? A Ping-Pong game. A simple thing like a date. Could I go out with this person? I would build a case, "Yes, I can." Then I'd build a case, "No." It was a constant rumination. Never a simple thought; always pulling it apart. "No, you can't do that; who are you kidding? Yes, you can; no, you can't."

By this point we can see a good deal of what decisive, "risky" movement means to Lew. It connects Lew to the romantic image of who his father once was—and holds out hope of escaping the dreary paralysis to which both parents have succumbed. Lew's chronically anxious mother was house-bound, unable to drive, take the bus, or manage a job more than two blocks from home. His father had traded away the best part of his life for a safe but stale marriage. His only pleasures were his mysterious "outside activities." Lew determined not to make his father's mistake; he pictures vitality in terms of breaking out. Don't get stuck: inside the house, in a bad marriage, in a dead-end job. Speaking of the choices now before him, he says:

I am really beginning to miss the creative part of my life, the acting. I see my father becoming the amateur musician, you know, [instead of] a professional. It sort of means a defeat for me. That the next step is that I am going to find me a woman who will drive me into the clouds. And I think there is a lot of fear, even though I don't express it a lot, that that may happen to me. I don't think my father ever truly made the commitment.

If Lew's mother represented stagnant paralysis, while the father of Greenwich Village days stood for zestful chance-taking, the father Lew saw every day around the house was a more ambiguous figure. It would have helped had his father been a more decisive and joyous man: He could have supplied a counterweight to the mother's gloominess and a more attractive figure for identification. There is evidence that Lew tried to imagine his father in this light. Lew built a world of fantasy around the father's oblique references to another, happier time. He pictures his father hanging out in the Village coffee houses in the 1930s and 1940s; discussing Schopenhauer and the Communist Manifesto with intellectual friends; writing a bit of poetry. In Lew's mind the details of this time are indistinct; they have the soft focus of myth.

> Sitting around in the coffee shops with the same pair of pants on, and shoes; living in a one- or two-room flat in the Village with two or three other people. The books they read were great works of Kant, that kind of stuff. Playing music, being articulate, knowledgeable about art and poetry. That is my image. They had a lot of fun together; they partied a lot. A lot of images come from old photos and little pieces my father would tell me.

Not only bygone days were romantic; Lew tried to believe that his father was still living the old life in his mysterious "outside activities." Apparently the father encouraged the illusion; Lew recalls, "He used to hint around. I got the impression he was always doing other things. I don't know where I got it. Maybe I thought he was still sitting in the coffee shops." Interestingly enough, Paulie also made up stories about the father. For years Paulie told his friends that his father was a banker, though he actually sold pharmaceuticals. Only the mother refused to go along. "My mother used to put my father down all the time, degrade him. 'Oh, your father is never home; he is finally making a living. He spends more time showing his affections to other people; he never brings anything home.' "

Did Lew himself believe the myth? Certainly he tried. At the same time, there was always a doubt in his mind. At one point he remarked, "Maybe I needed to make my father mysterious." As Lew now sees it, he clung to the romantic image of his father in order to stave off his doubts and his lack of respect. "What didn't you respect?" I asked.

> His relationship with my mother. The fact that I was getting a lot of shit from her, and he seemed to take a lot of shit from her, and sort of resigned himself to it. He would storm out of the house at times. But he seemed to deal with it by being away, out of the house or into himself. I would get, "I'll give you money but don't tell your mother. Don't tell your mother we did this." Not that we did anything unusual. A lot of times he would start off the conversation with, "Don't tell your mother I told you this."

A few minutes later Lew began telling me a story about his brother. Paulie was in a gang and was arrested several times. He stole a car and ran away to Florida. He shot a BB gun at Lew and once came at him with a knife. Yet, although he made life unnaturally interesting for Lew, Paulie redeemed himself by a magnificently direct sense of fraternal loyalty. When Lew got himself in trouble with the bullies at school, Paulie passed the word. "The word got out that Paulie was going to kill anyone who beat me up; so nobody touched me. It was like the tide went out." Another time, at summer camp, Lew was burned through the carelessness of a counselor.

> My brother then—this was never proven—burned down the bunk, the entire cabin, with his football uniform in it. I remember the camp directors made me lie to my mother and say it was my fault. They told me to say I had burned myself playing with matches.

The contrast between Paulie and the father is stark. His father offered no protection. Paulie was terrifying, but when Lew needed him, he was effective. Significantly Lew remembers the camp directors' admonition, "Don't tell your mother." Lew's ineffectual father had the same refrain.

Lew recalled how his father would try to build up his confidence.

> He'd say, "You're tall; you have lots of attributes; why are you insecure?" I was just indecisive about whether to believe him. It was hard for me to say, "Oh, you're right, Dad." I doubted his knowledge; I didn't doubt his sincerity. There must have been a part of me that just didn't respect him.

These last passages explain more clearly the problem Lew faced and the solution he has chosen. A truly adventurous father—or even an ordinary, hearty one—would have been a welcome antidote to Lew's fear-ridden, immobilized mother. However, the anxious, absent, ineffectual father of Lew's real experience needed the continual refurbishing of fantasy. Lew exaggerates his father's adventurousness and ignores his ineffectuality in order to provide himself a worthy model for identification.

To make this defensive image plausible, Lew acts out the "risky" life that the father of his idealizing fantasy—but not the father of his disappointing reality—might have led. Doing so allows Lew to ward off the anxiety that he is really like his mother or the ineffectual man he half-acknowledges his father to have been.

Earlier I said that Lew fears being unmasked. In counterattack he is quick to point out the frailties of others. However, there is another side to Lew's piercing gaze. If Lew saw deeply and acidly, he also kept his opinions to himself. He was more than quiet; he was sealed off from the world.

> I lived with a guy for a year and a half. Once he said, "How come you never talk to me?" I saw myself as talking all the time, in my head. I had a running dialogue with myself, but I didn't let any of it out. Most of my life as a younger person was seen from inside, like encased in a shell, walking around with this piece

of translucent concrete around me. I always felt I was
seeing what was going on around me. I was collecting
images of people. On the subway I would see how
people read, how they farted, how they fidgeted around.

When Lew saw through the pretensions of others, he kept
his opinions to himself. This silence makes sense as an attempt
to preserve his father's dignity. Lew could not afford to believe
that both parents were inadequate, and so he refused to admit
to himself what he actually suspected. His piercing, unmasking
gaze is turned away from his father, but inevitably it finds other
targets, against whom he directs the scorn he cannot direct at
his father.

We might even speculate that Lew's sense of being a fraud
serves an unconscious, defensive purpose. Instead of accusing
his father of being a sham, Lew redirects the accusation against
himself. However, this business of disavowing what one sus-
pects is problematic. Lew pays a price for charging himself
instead of his father with fraudulence. If Lew's father suffered
his wife's contempt, now Lew feels that a string of women are
ready to expose his incompetence.

Why should he go to these lengths, redirecting against himself a charge that should be laid against his father? One reason is
that Lew's father seems too vulnerable, and Lew cannot afford
to lose him. The adventurous father is really Lew's only model
for adult competence. The second reason is that Lew may have
been afraid, if only indistinctly, that his disappointment might
lead him to become violently angry.

How much did he have to fear? We must consider not only
what Lew suspected about himself but also the models provided
by his family. Paulie—whose teenage violence Lew partly admired—ended his life in a blaze of rage gone amok. He was
thrown out of the Navy for stabbing a man; he then murdered
his wife and committed suicide. Lew tries to explain Paulie's life:

Paulie's wife kept saying, "You know, this is related to
all the anger you feel. You never resolved any of it, the
anger toward your mother or your father." My brother

and I, we had never talked about it! I wasn't aware of
my own yet, and his was channeled into this real hatred
toward society. And of course he died before he ever
recognized it—or maybe he did recognize it and couldn't
handle it. I really have no idea. Maybe she got to places
he didn't want to be gotten to. Because I was angry
with my father, he was really pretty ineffectual in terms
of getting between my mother and her vibes.

Lew's explanation of Paulie's life is useful to us chiefly for the
way it indicates Lew's own anxieties. What Lew tells us is that
Paulie was pushed to feel, too clearly to be borne, the anger both
brothers felt toward their parents. Expressed in the raw colors
that were Paulie's style, that rage led to murder and suicide. Lew
took the other road, choosing not to see, toward the emotional
deadening of the concrete bubble.

Did Lew fear the same rage in himself? During his first year
in graduate school, the pressure of acting became intolerable.
Eventually he checked himself into a psychiatric hospital. His
parents finally drove him home while Lew, semidelusional,
imagined the police were chasing him to pay for a water bill.
Back at home Lew entered a period of depression and irritability.

It was just a strange part of my life. I was not getting
along with my parents, I almost choked someone; I
tackled him. That was the beginning of heavy acting
out toward my parents. I fought the draft and got out.
The psychiatrist said I would kill—the wrong people.

Usually the low periods in Lew's life begin with the fear of
incompetence, often provoked by feeling unmasked, and lead to
depression. He describes that depression in terms of lethargy and
also what he calls "alienation": feeling sealed off from others. Now
we suspect that his numb isolation is itself a defense against seeing
too sharply, too accusingly, and acting out his anger.

Lew's father died of a heart attack the night after playing a
concert in Fort Lauderdale. Lew flew down from Cleveland.

I have pictures taken of him the night before he died, playing the violin. And I look at them, at his face–trying to see any signs that he is going to die. There is an intensity to the way he played the violin, and I am looking at his face, knowing that in the middle of the night he died.

I got ready to go down there on my own. I told a friend across the street, and another friend. Just a strange kind of drifting sense until I got down there. My mother was distraught. And I was a mixture of being an observer and being emotionally involved in the sadness and loss. I was sort of drifting.

I didn't want to deal with my mother's grief, and I didn't believe my mother. I believed she was hurt and lonely and upset, but I think I was angry at her. My experiences of my parents were always of them yelling at each other. And now here is my mother wailing that she has lost her husband, and I wanted to tell her to stop acting. It seemed genuine, but I knew that my mother was crying for herself more than my father. I just remember my anger toward her, feeling, "Why is my mother grieving so much? She didn't like him when he was alive." She always belittled him and put him down.

I felt numb. All my life I had felt like this alien in this nucleus of strange people. And when my father died I still felt that. I didn't feel very real about myself, and in tap with other people. I still felt in a box. When I came down there–you know the book *The Stranger*? They are burying his mother and he is following and he doesn't know what to feel; I felt that way. I remember the anger toward my mother, and a real sense of loss.

And we seem to be looking over Lew's shoulder, wondering what he hopes to see in that photo. Lew says he is trying to see what killed his father, but I think he is trying to see his father's life. Looking at the photo, Lew attempts to discern not only the passion that killed him but also the glow of his mysterious "outside" life. Who was he, this father? What did he really love?

Lew tells us, and lives his life to show us, that he and his father shared a bond. They were both adventurers. Why then, at the end, did Lew feel once again numb, detached, alienated? Perhaps the answer is that Lew's identification has not been with the father of real life, but with a romantic myth. This symbolic father has been purged of ambiguity. The shadings of admiration and contempt, love, and anger that Lew felt toward his real father do not register on this half-tone symbolic image. However, suppression of this sort is always threatening to come undone: Memory and emotion threaten to corrupt the purified image. Lew cannot afford this, and so, while his mother wails, he wanders through the funeral, wondering what he might truly be feeling.

By accepting this version of his father, Lew hopes to evade the troubling questions of his childhood. Why could the father not rescue the family from Paulie's violence, the mother's pessimism, Lew's self-doubt, his own anxiety? Why, in short, was he not more of a father? Lew's answer is that his father really was heroic—somewhere else. The alternative would be to accept his mother's view: that the father was an old fool of a dreamer who abandoned his family once and might do so again. To save his father from his own agreement with this assessment, Lew collaborates with the romantic myth. Later, in his own life, he plays out a career that preserves this interpretation of what it means to be a man. The risky life saves Lew from recognizing how he really feels about his father.

This segregation of heroic and degraded images, however, exacts a cost. Lew cannot escape the suspicion that his father was really inadequate. Unconsciously Lew identifies not only with the heroic myth but also with the father he holds in contempt. Fearful of replicating his father's marriage, Lew has remained single. He is not comfortable with his independence, but he seems unable to sustain a relationship. He said:

> I don't feel as intimate as I can be or would like to be.
> There is a lid on my emotions. But I feel I'd better let it
> rest. It is hard to describe the feeling of constantly
> going over in your head why you can or can't do things.

> When you don't have that conflict, you want to just
> leave it rest. It's like a den of snakes; you open the
> wrong lid, and it's going to come out at you.

Similarly Lew's fear of being trapped in a safe but dull career continually leads him to toss aside hard-won security for a new risk. He has prospered in this fashion, though we notice that no job sustains very long the vividness Lew expects of life. Although he works hard and well, Lew lives for his weekends. He is the adventurer of his circle. While his friends drone on interminably about their ordinary jobs, Lew talks about spelunking. Sometimes, though, he wonders why there is nothing in his work that he finds interesting enough to talk about for hours at a time.

Lew and I spoke 8 years after his father died, absorbed in his private passion, 7 years after Paulie's life ended in a blood-splattered room, almost 6 years after Carol left for Hawaii. He said that in the last year or two he had started to change.

In his previous occupations, Lew's training as an actor allowed him to move quickly into any role without troubling to understand the details of the job. He still boasts about his ability to carry off the performance: "I like the show, the cream. I have spent my whole life siphoning off the cream. I will do clinical work up to a point. As soon as it gets to the nitty-gritty, where I really have to apply clinical skills, I'll back off."

Recently, however, Lew became troubled by his estrangement from the people with whom he works. In an organization of clinicians, his role as administrator makes him both more and less than everyone else.

> Because I can get to the essence of the job, the details
> will come as I go along. And what I have realized is that
> I still need the details; you can't just know the essence.
> You know, in any field there is a whole language that is
> used. People communicate to each other in that
> language. I may be able to perceive, but if I want to
> function in that field, I have to convey what I perceive.
> And much of that detail is the common language.

As Lew's view of himself changes, so too does the story he tells about his father. Toward the end of our last interview, Lew offered a revised version of his father's career:

> I think what my father eventually did in life was get to the nitty-gritty and actually apply himself to a trade. And although he still liked the showmanship aspects, essentially he was a salesman. He was not ashamed of it at all. He would say, "People like me to come into their stores. They look forward to it." And yet I liked the drama, the fantasy stuff.

Lives, and stories told about them, are not immutable. Lew seems to be moving toward a life of more ordinary but deeply felt engagement. As he does, he may revise both the story he tells about his father and the way he lives.

Plots, Audiences, and Arguments

Earlier I noted that if identity depends on the way others see us, then to affect identity a life story must be part of an individual's public record. Telling one's story to an interviewer or to oneself is not enough; the story must in some fashion be told to a community of significant witnesses. However, it is far from clear that such public self-narration is commonplace. Therefore it seems useful to see whether the psychological work supposedly accomplished by life stories may be accomplished also by the lives that individuals perform. Can we extend our notion of "story" to sequences of lived action (cf. Ricoeur, 1979)?

We can anticipate that action does not have at its disposal the wealth of rhetorical device available to oral or literary narration. However, action and narration may share at least these qualities: Like a story, action may have the structure of a plot; like a story, action may be addressed to an audience. Further, the protagonist/performer may experience the success of the plot and the audience's response as vindication for one preferred version of the life, rather than a less palatable alternative. In this sense a life, once again like a story, presents an argument.

These similarities between lives and stories are of psychological significance because of the *work* that each accomplishes. To anticipate: Stories and lives focus the latent danger of their own negotiation in order to see how the protagonist will emerge. This focus is what makes literary stories compelling to readers and makes lives compelling to we who live them. With this, we may return to Lew.

Stories as Plots

We might begin by observing that Lew lives his life in the form of a *plot,* a pattern of transformation.

Repeatedly Lew finds himself in jobs for which he is unqualified. However appealing these jobs are at first, he gradually starts to feel trapped, stagnant, up against the ceiling of possible promotion, and thus depressed. Further, he starts to worry that his lack of qualifications has been noticed by some potentially dangerous critic. Faced with mounting depression and anxiety, Lew transforms the situation and himself: He breaks out. He jumps in his car and drives off to the Shakespeare festival, or to a new college campus, or he moves from Ohio to Michigan. The movement is "risky": He does not know how to drive a car with a stick shift; the engine periodically breaks down; he changes careers with no preparation. By luck (though really, he suggests, well-deserved fortune) he lands on his feet: The Shakespeare company hires him; the woman who beat him out for a job loses heart, and Lew gets the call. Often enough the dangerous critic is revealed, by subsequent events, to be less competent than Lew himself. Finally he lands in a new job for which he is once again formally unqualified. Although this ending proves that Lew is a survivor—he can maneuver in the world even without the proper credentials—it sets the stage for a reenactment.

Why does Lew conduct his life in terms of this particular plot? Apparently it is to persuade himself that he will not end up as depressed, anxious, trapped, and unmasked as his parents. I deliberately put the matter in this negative fashion to emphasize that Lew is not so much trying to arrive at any particular goal as to escape from a particular danger (cf. Gergen & Gergen, 1983; Mishler, 1992). Describing a plot in terms of the danger that it overcomes points to one similarity between the work accomplished by a story and life.

Traditional plot forms—comedies, tragedies, adventures, even some histories—carry the protagonist through a phase of rising tension to a climactic crisis and a denouement. This structure brings to a head the latent danger in a situation in order to discover how the protagonist will prevail or be undone.

This form, I suggest, is not only typical of literary stories but of the plots people live. Lew lives his life in such a way that he continually brings to a crisis the terrors of his imagination. This mode allows him to demonstrate that he can transform these situations in ways that his parents could not; therefore he will not suffer their fate. It bears emphasizing that the plot Lew enacts would be savorless without its danger. Just as a story is no good if the lovers find each other too soon, or if the murderer is discovered in the first chapter, so Lew's story would be spoiled were there not a risk to be overcome. It would be insufficient for Lew to be like the romantic father of his idealizing fantasy; he must reclaim this romantic ideal from the edge of defeat. It is the overcoming that matters. This is the sense in which Lew acts out a plot—and it is the heart of the matter.

Although the structure of rising tension, crisis, and denouement may apply to many lives, each individual's style of living a plot is as distinctive as anything else in personality. Compare, for example, Lew's style of risky movement to Nixon's imagery of hunkering down and holding on—"stonewalling," "hanging tough."

Further, although the plot of a story is a composite of many elements—characters, situations, moods, forms of action—not all of these need be represented at a given moment. In fact, psychodynamic repression may be facilitated if the plot is represented metonymically, by a single element. Elsewhere (Ochberg, 1988) I have described a man who seemed to reenact his (largely suppressed) memory of childhood abuse through the imagery of a crescendo. His relationships and his conduct of business displayed a theme of unstoppable rising action followed by a crash. This imagery of plot movement—largely split off from representations of characters—was almost all that remained (at least consciously) to represent the original and still unconsciously vivid experience of his father's unstoppably rising temper. Similarly Lew seems to condense the interpersonal and affective significance of his experience into the image of "risky movement." To return to the puzzle with which we began: When Lew explains his decision to change careers by saying, "I like risky people," he is unconsciously pointing us to everything else.

Stories as Appeals to an Audience

The second way that a life may be similar to a story lies in the appeal each makes to an audience. Individuals do not merely regale themselves with their personal narratives, they put their lives on public display. A portion of their self-regard depends on how their audience responds.

Lew, for example, believes he is continually being scrutinized by some skeptical witness who threatens to expose his fraudulence. Much of the zest in his life comes from the danger of being unmasked and the corresponding satisfaction of being impressive.

Who are the audiences in Lew's life, and how do they matter? We probably should begin by ruling out the literal audiences he has faced: as an actor, as a disc jockey, and as a research informant. (A theory that applies only to professional performers is of little interest; an account of audience response that deals only with the special circumstance of being a research informant is absurd.) Fortunately we can point to other audiences in Lew's life: his first boss, who scrutinized his drafting; or his girlfriend, who threatened to unmask his inadequacy as an actor. A more positive audience seems to be composed of Lew's friends, whom he likes to entertain with his adventurousness. These examples suggest the more general point that although very few people perform before literal audiences, all of us may recruit our friends, families, or even casual acquaintances to be our witnesses.

It is significant that these various audiences in Lew's life are not under his control. Lew's old boss might have fired him; his old girlfriend might have left him for someone else. Because Lew can never be certain of his audience's reaction, his performance is always at risk. Paradoxically this jeopardy is essential to Lew's satisfaction. Each time Lew exposes himself to the possibility of being publicly unmasked and instead escapes with an accolade, he solidifies his idealized identity. Here we see the significance of the fact that Lew's "story" is a public performance, and not merely a private narrative. Lew might tell himself he is adventurous rather than ineffectual, but unless he is wholly lost in a world of private delusion, he must doubt his own self-regard. It is a far greater success for him to win over a live audience, who might disagree, than to tell himself stories of his valor in the safety of his own imagination.

In putting things this way, I am returning to the agonistic theme of this interpretation. The plot of Lew's story leads him to encounter and overcome dangerous situations. Similarly, as a performance, Lew's story risks being unappreciated by various audiences and instead wins them over. What Lew seems to savor—in the plot of his life and his appeal to an audience—is the way he overcomes the risk of failure.

We may wonder whether Lew's combative relationship with his audience is idiosyncratic. After all, we commonly think that personal narrators desire a more welcoming reception—from their therapists, for example. Is Lew exceptional, or does he illustrate a more general principle? Consider two examples.

Earlier I described Harding's (1992) interpretation of her interview with Reverend Cantrell, a fundamentalist minister who recounted, in an attempt to win Harding over to born-again Christianity, the horrifying accident of his son's death. In so doing, Cantrell reaffirmed his own faith (and, we might suspect, resurrected the possibility of meaning in a world where personal tragedy had rendered it vulnerable).

Now we might speculate about what sort of reaction Cantrell ideally desired. Harding suggests that Cantrell hoped to convert her, and no doubt he did. Suppose, however, the conversion was easy. Suppose Harding said, at the end, "You know, I've been on the verge of joining the church for quite a while." Might Cantrell not have felt cheated, as if the magnitude of his tragedy were out of all proportion with what it accomplished?

A second example: Evans (1992) described the satisfaction that two choreographers take in creating dances that touch their audiences. For each woman the connection to the audience reenacts and improves childhood experiences of being heard and understood. However, modern dance is by no means a transparent medium. Audiences are often perplexed, and Evans argues that this potential for being misunderstood, disconnected, is fundamental to the satisfaction his choreographers feel in ultimately evoking a response.

These two examples seem similar to Lew's. In each case we see that the performance is satisfying, not simply because the audience responds, but also because the audience's potential resistance is overcome. Audiences that comprehend too easily or convert too readily or, in Lew's case, suspend too lightly their disbelief are not what we want. The success of the performance depends on overcoming the possibility of failure.

Stories as Arguments

As a plot, Lew's life overcomes dangerous situations; as an appeal to an audience, it overcomes skepticism. Together these two suggest a third way of appreciating the storied nature of what Lew is up to: Again like a story, his life is an argument.

Every story presents a particular version of events. Versions differ, and it has been the thrust of most contemporary theorizing to acknowledge the subjective truth of each. However, this catholic tolerance is not the attitude adopted by any one story itself. Each version of a story attempts to persuade us that it alone is credible. Stories, however, may be more complicated affairs, indicating a preferred reading and at the same time hinting to us that this preferred reading is suspect. It is in this sense that a story may be an argument: One version tries to overcome the voice of a suppressed alternative.

Psychodynamic self-representations share this fundamental, constitutive doubleness; so do lives. This is the third and most fundamental sense in which Lew's life is like a story. It is not enough to say that the story Lew acts out in his life serves the purpose of overcoming the dangers he fears. More exactly the story serves to suppress those dangers. Lew must persuade himself—by way of persuading others—not merely that he can rise above those moments when he feels stagnant and ineffectual but that he does not really fear becoming trapped or ineffectual after all.

This is a somewhat different way of thinking about how a story "overcomes" a danger in the world or in one's own character: not by facing and defeating a threat, but by excising it from recognition. This sort of psychodynamic "overcoming" is what I mean when I say that a story functions as an argument.

Lew's story satisfies him not merely because it preserves his idealized image of himself but also because it overcomes the chronic possibility that this idealized image will be undermined by a negative alternative. It is the tension between these two accounts that makes the idealized version important.

The contemporary trend in interpretation has made us all leery of suggesting that any account is less true than another (Rosenwald & Ochberg, 1992). Therefore, when Lew seems to alternate between telling us that he and his father were adventurers and that they were both incompetent frauds, we are tempted to say that each is a valid version of his story. We fall back on the doctrine that subjective truth is open to multiple constructions. However, this excessively tolerant view of the matter misses the point. We can only grasp the significance of what the idealized version means to say if we also notice what it means to avoid saying; that is, the meaning of this story is connected inextricably to the way it is an argument.

At this point, however, we encounter a methodological problem. Lew makes explicit the idealized version of his story in everything he says, but how are we to recognize its suppressed alternative? We cannot compare this story to the "facts of the matter," partly because Lew is our only informant, and more significantly because it is Lew's construction—not that of some objective witness—that matters. (Nor, of course, can we very well ask Lew, because he is the interlocutor that he is most interested in deceiving.) We are forced to rely on indirect hints. This dependence will be a problem for anyone who hopes to convert interpretation to positivism—to base interpretation on what is incontestable in the text (Taylor, 1979). It seems unavoidable, however, if we are to take seriously the notion that a story is fundamentally an internal argument between what is said aloud and what is on the verge of being said.

How do we know that Lew's preferred version is not the whole story? Partly because Lew himself is suspicious. He tells us he had his own doubts about his father. He also admits there are some things he prefers not to think about: "It would be like opening a can of snakes." He invites us to unmask him, telling us he is a master at "selling a line of bullshit." To these direct but minimal statements we can add a host of indirect clues. Lew's account is brimming with suspicion and the possibility of unwelcome discovery. Sometimes Lew is the object: His boss or his girlfriend might discover his inadequacy. Sometimes Lew is the spy: He notices "the way people fidget and fart on the subway." Both Lew and Paulie made up stories about their father: Once again the theme of false images is raised. Even Lew's description of staring at his father's last photograph, trying to discern a hint of what might have killed him, is of this theme. Again and again Lew seems to be asking, half longingly, half fearfully, "Can anyone see the truth behind the public image?"

Still, the ways Lew alerts us to look deeper are only a beginning. We suspect that something is being concealed, but we do not yet know what or why. Drawing on indirect clues and our presuppositions about how self-deceiving stories operate leads us to juxtapose vignettes that Lew himself does not explicitly connect. For example: Lew reports that Paulie burned down the cabin after Lew's camp counselor, who accidentally burned him, said, "Don't tell your mother." We are led to draw the contrast. Paulie avenged Lew by his decisive action (at cost to himself: Recall, his hard-won football jersey also burned in that fire). Lew's father, like the cowardly camp counselor, says, "Don't tell," and as Lew tells us in still another fragment of the interview, "seemed unable to get between [me and] my mother's vibes." Thus the vignette of Paulie and the fire points us to what the official account denies. Instead of seeing the father as a hero, we see that Lew half-accuses his father of being inadequate.

Still, this is *our* construction; Lew never pulls the fragments together. There is no final debriefing, no place where Lew lines up the pieces and says, "Here is the unexpurgated text of what I have been trying to show you." The meaning of this story does not lie directly in these fragments—neither individually nor in their sum—rather, the story is in their relationship. However, this relationship—between what is said and what is disavowed—is a construction; it is not fully inscribed anywhere.

We might note that we can only reach this understanding because we anticipated it. Before ever sitting down with Lew, a psychodynamically inclined interlocutor would assume that any account is likely to display this tension between an officially avowed and unofficially repudiated version. Our ability to recover this structure depends on our preunderstanding. To say this is not to point to anything unusual or suspect; it is the usual situation of all interpretation (Fish, 1979).

What, then, is the true story? If Lew is not exactly the daredevil he would like us to believe, neither is he the anxiety-paralyzed cripple he sometimes seems to fear becoming. The "truth" of this story lies neither in its idealized heroics nor in its suppressed fearfulness, but in the relation between the two; that is, what is "true" about this story—what Lew finds emotionally compelling about it—is the way it is an argument between possible versions. Only when we see that Lew lives out one version of his life in order to first evoke and then overcome the damning alternative do we appreciate what he is up to.

Conclusion

What does this interpretive perspective allow us to notice about lives? In a usually ambiguous phrase, it reveals how people go about "making something of themselves." To "make something" of oneself means, colloquially, to be successful. At the same time, a more literal meaning suggests the effort that goes into maintaining a positive self-image. This work is continual. At least psychodynamically one does not make something of oneself once and for all, say, by becoming a doctor or a company president. Instead individuals continually rediscover themselves in new situations in which they might be unmade: revealed as flawed. The work they do, via narratively structured and publicly performed action, rescues their self-ideal from the risk of its negation.

Most of social science is a story told in a more passive voice. Our theories lead us to frame questions and answers in terms of the forces that shape human behavior. To ask, Why does Lew act this way? seems inevitably equivalent to, What makes him act as he does? but not, What is he trying to accomplish? Yet not only are people the objects of social and psychological forces, they also are purposeful agents.

Lives, like stories, are the way we fashion ourselves: encountering and temporarily surmounting the projected demons that would diminish us. This is what a narrative perspective allows us to notice: not only about the way we talk, but also about the way we live.

References

Behar, R. (1992). A life story to take across the border: Notes on an exchange. In G. Rosenwald & R. Ochberg (Eds.), *Storied lives* (pp. 108-123). New Haven, CT: Yale University Press.

Cohler, B. J. (1988). The human studies and the life history: The *Social Service Review* lecture. *Social Service Review.*

Evans, J. E. (1992). Language and the body: Communication and identity formation in choreography. In G. Rosenwald & R. Ochberg (Eds.), *Storied lives* (pp. 95-107). New Haven, CT: Yale University Press.

Fish, S. (1979). Normal circumstances, literal language, direct speech acts, the ordinary, the obvious, what goes without saying, and other special cases. In P. Rabinow & W. M. Sullivan (Eds.), *Interpretive social science* (pp. 243-265). Berkeley: University of California Press.

Gergen, K. J., & Gergen, M. M. (1983). Narratives of the self. In T. Sarbin & K. Scheibe (Eds.), *Studies in social identity.* New York: Praeger.

Gergen, M. M. (1992). Life stories: Pieces of a dream. In G. Rosenwald & R. Ochberg (Eds.), *Storied lives* (pp. 127-144). New Haven, CT: Yale University Press.

Greenspan, H. (1992). Lives as texts: Symptoms as modes of recounting in the life histories of Holocaust survivors. In G. Rosenwald & R. Ochberg (Eds.), *Storied lives* (pp. 145-164). New Haven, CT: Yale University Press.

Harding, S. (1992). The afterlife of stories: Genesis of a man of God. In G. Rosenwald & R. Ochberg (Eds.), *Storied lives* (pp. 60-75). New Haven, CT: Yale University Press.

Mishler, E. G. (1992). Work, identity, and narrative: An artist-craftsman's story. In G. Rosenwald & R. Ochberg (Eds.), *Storied lives* (pp. 21-40). New Haven, CT: Yale University Press.

Modell, J. (1992). "How do you introduce yourself as a childless mother?": Birthparent interpretations of parenthood. In G. Rosenwald & R. Ochberg (Eds.), *Storied lives* (pp. 76-94). New Haven, CT: Yale University Press.

Ochberg, R. L. (1987). *Middle-aged sons and the meaning of work.* Ann Arbor: University of Michigan Press.

Ochberg, R. L. (1988). Life stories and the psychosocial construction of careers. *Journal of Personality, 56*(1), 173-204.

Ochberg, R. L. (1992). Patterns of unhappiness in men's careers. In A. Collins & R. Young (Eds.), *Interpreting career.* New York: Praeger.

Ricoeur, P. (1979). The model of the text: Meaningful action considered as text. In P. Rabinow & W. M. Sullivan (Eds.), *Interpretive social science* (pp. 73-101). Berkeley: University of California Press.

Riessman, C. K. (1992). Making sense of marital violence: One woman's narrative. In G. Rosenwald & R. Ochberg (Eds.), *Storied lives* (pp. 231-249). New Haven, CT: Yale University Press.

Rosenwald, G. C., & Ochberg, R. L. (1992). Life stories, cultural politics, and self-understanding. In G. Rosenwald & R. Ochberg (Eds.), *Storied lives* (pp. 1-18). New Haven, CT: Yale University Press.

Rosenwald, G. C., & Wiersma, J. (1983). Women, career changes, and the new self. *Psychiatry, 46,* 213-229.

Sarbin, T. R. (1986). *Narrative psychology: The storied nature of human conduct.* New York: Praeger.

Taylor, C. (1979). Interpretation and the sciences of man. In P. Rabinow & W. M. Sullivan (Eds.), *Interpretive social science* (pp. 25-71). Berkeley: University of California Press.

❦ 5 ❦

The "Magician's Predicament" as a Managerial Hazard

Dalia Etzion
Amittai Niv

*C*ertain managers in organizations acquire the status of "magicians," apparently by virtue of their being able to do things that are vital to the success of the organization and that others—subordinates, colleagues, superiors—are unable to do. We use the word *apparently* advisedly because it is impossible to know whether the magic of the magicians is real or not. The magician and those in his[1] environment cooperate in creating an enchanted world in which it is impossible to determine what should be attributed to the extraordinary powers of the magician and what is inherent in the opportunities afforded by his position or to the evolving patterns of perception, thinking, and actions of those populating this enchanted world.

AUTHORS' NOTE: This chapter is based on the experience of the authors in ongoing consulting during the late 1980s to a number of fast-growing firms in Israel and on retrospective interviews with their general managers. Professor Don Schon of the Massachusetts Institute of Technology was a partner to the consulting, the research, and the development of some of the ideas on which the chapter is based. Thanks are due to the Institute of Management for its financial support and for enabling the ideas to be developed and permitting the interviews to be carried out under its auspices. The project was also partially financed by the Israeli Institute of Business Research. Gerda Kessler was extremely helpful in translating the original material from Hebrew into English.

Under certain conditions—and in time, these do indeed develop—the function of the magician becomes a trap. He must go on performing his magic even when he has become tired of doing so and despite increasing doubts concerning its effectiveness. Solutions that saved the day in the past are not suitable to the present reality, and subordinates are not able to deal with new problems independently. The trap is exposed in all its severity when the big successes of the past (which came about because of the initiative and daring of the magician) lead the organization into a new competitive environment in which the powers of the magician no longer work. By virtue of his status, and with no one to question his infallibility, the magician is likely to start making faulty decisions that even may bring about ruin to the organization and, in the end, to him too.

How can a talented and successful manager escape from the magician's trap or, better still, stop himself from falling into it in the first place? How can he help others in his environment to follow in his successful footsteps and to free themselves of their exaggerated dependence on his magic? These questions are discussed here in the context in which the enchanted world usually develops—conditions of fast growth, or the contrary, conditions of extreme crisis. The intricacies of the possibilities and dangers inherent in these conditions are illustrated by means of narratives of magicians we have come to know well during the course of our work as organizational consultants.

Managing Organizations in a Turbulent Environment

The growth of organizations and their managers is effected through an ongoing exchange among the three partners to the process: the manager, the organization he heads, and the external environment in which they function. Throughout this exchange, dilemmas develop that reflect the complex total environment in which the process of growth takes place. These dilemmas usually represent difficult choices, such as to purchase or manufacture in-house, to bring in managers from outside or develop them from inside, and to concentrate on the domestic market or focus efforts on developing foreign markets. The complexity of the dilemmas is due not only to the large number of factors involved in their creation but primarily because they impinge on the system of values of the decision maker. Dilemmas, by definition, are problems that have no unequivocal solution; thus the managers confronted by them learn sooner or later to live with them at a more or less satisfactory level. The concrete choices that they make around the various dilemmas crystalize into very personal management patterns. Whatever the pattern, the managers grow by learning about themselves and their organization while dealing with the dilemmas they face.

The main source of the dilemmas that managers face in organizations is the external environment in which they function. The management literature calls the reality in which most economic organizations function today "turbulent," describing it as being characterized by frequent and rapid changes and ever-increasing difficulty in identifying the factors that bring about these changes. The changes in the environmental conditions are described in detail by Tushman, Newman, and Nadler (1988). They use the term *discontinuities* in describing the phenomenon of processes and trends that are broken off or change direction suddenly and unexpectedly. Morgan (1988) sees the risks and opportunities accompanying this reality and calls their management "riding the high waves." Vaill (1989) emphasizes the permanence of change and surprise as daily features in the lives of many firms and refers to them as "permanent white water." The combination of frequent changes and the difficulty in diagnosing their sources makes the unexpected in all areas of the organization's activity an inextricable part of its experience.

The turbulent environment not only demands an ever-increasing degree of managerial attention but also renders most of the classical management tools obsolete and ineffective. The classical tools are based on a large measure of stability in the world of the organizations. Such is the importance attached to planning and control by means of methodical tools and a quantitative approach. But reality creates one of the most difficult paradoxes in modern management: Today's manager is called on to take on more and more responsibility in precisely those areas over which he has less and less control. The significant lessening of conventional control ability highlights the present weakness of most premises on which classical management was, until recently, based. The changes taking place before our eyes in the environment of most complex organizations turn these assumptions into myths that do not accurately reflect reality, and other qualities become essential in affecting and controlling the turbulent reality in which the manager functions. Thus the repertoire of behavioral skills required of today's general manager, claims Vaill (1989), turns his or her job from ordered theory and methodical process into a performing art.

Quinn (1988) calls the manager who succeeds in making the transition from the classical pattern of management to that required by present circumstances a *master*. The double meaning of the word, which signifies both expert and overlord, reflects well the complexity of the job of the general manager in our times. Thus much of the stability, method, and absolute control that characterized the senior manager's job in the past have disappeared. These features supposedly are replaced by characteristics that border on the mystical and magical, such as charisma and transformative leadership, which, in the present circumstances, constitute an appealing alternative for management in turbulent times, but one that is not devoid of pitfalls (Burns, 1978; Conger & Kanungo, 1987; House, 1977; Yukl, 1989).

Bass (1985) claims that the charismatic leader has a sort of inner mystic belief that evokes in his followers an admiration bordering on worship. The conditions that give rise to this phenomenon are change and crisis that evoke fear, stress, or anxiety. According to Bass, charisma is adopted as a method of leadership when formal authority fails to handle a severe crisis and traditional values stand in question. Such difficult situations are more common in new organizations struggling to survive or in those that are aging and failing. The difficulties become particularly great in times that allow or call for rapid growth. These conditions, as we shall see, constitute the background against which "magicians" rise and fall.

Economic Growth and Individual Initiative

Economic development is, to a large extent, a product of the initiative and drive of capable individual managers who pull their organizations far ahead of the mediocre establishment of their economic sector or specific industry. Some of them become living legends, entering management textbooks as vivid illustrations of the role of individuals in contributing to the well-being of society.

One important characteristic of these pioneers is their ability to combine technological and business vision within the framework of a manufacturing organization. Indeed this triangle of leader and visionary, technological and business expertise, and a dynamic organization constitutes the main recipe for economic growth. But nothing lasts forever. Many heroes of the past on the economic growth front turned out to be stars whose meteoric rise was all too soon followed by a very painful fall. Steve Jobbs, co-founder of Apple computers, started as a small entrepreneur. He became, within only a few years, IBM's main challenge in the area of personal computers, but he was able to enjoy the glory of this victory for only a short while. The recession in the computer industry of the mid-1980s took its toll, and Jobbs had to leave his own creation and let a bureaucratic executive put it back on the rails. John Reed, an industrial engineer, was brought to Citicorp (First National City Bank of New York) in the late 1970s to help its large Operations Division (8,000 employees) absorb new technologies and reorganize as the backbone of the bank's future growth. Reed performed what appeared to the old-fashioned bankers to be pure miracles and turned the Operations Division into the spearhead of the whole operation. It was just a matter of time before Reed was promoted to chief executive of the bank. Six years later Citicorp plunged into deep troubles. It lost significant parts of its market, its profit shrank, and the value of its stock fell to a third of its value 6 years earlier. The miracles that worked for Reed so well 10 years earlier are not helping at present.

Such stories about the rise and fall of economic legends make good reading and have spawned many and varied explanations for these fateful upheavals. The most widespread of these explanations are the following:

1. *The fog of uncertainty:* Success, like failure, is attributed, according to this explanation, to constraints encountered by most of the managers heading fast-growing organizations in dealing successfully with the uncertainty surrounding them. The sources of this uncertainty are several: (a) technological innovations that at the same time make for great possibilities and serious risk, (b) frequent and fundamental changes in the world's economy that all too often restructure the conditions of competition, and (c) the changes that take place with similar frequency in the economic policy of governments and international institutions. The combination of these factors envelops the "growth arena" in a thick fog and makes it impossible to deploy a "security network" capable of preventing a downslide into ruin.

2. *Improvisation:* Improvisation is at the root of the dynamics of fast-growing organizations. In their early years, it makes for flexibility and prompt adjustment to bureaucratic obstacles and unexpected difficulties. But at later stages, it becomes a prescription for disaster because of the tendency to dismiss the value of orderly deliberation and meticulous planning.

3. *The character of the heads of the organization:* This very common explanation relates to the mercurial character of the managers and to the misfit between their personal characteristics and the objective situation of the organizations they control. Many sudden failures of fast-growing organizations have been attributed to critical mistakes, made by those heading them, around such issues as an initiative in developing a revolutionary product, breaking into a new market, and joining forces with a strategic partner. "Gambler," "success went to his head," "he fell prey to his intuition"—these are the kinds of accusations made to explain

the behavior of the head of an organization that has stopped growing. In its early stages, according to this view, an organization seeking fast growth needs an entrepreneurial manager with a fertile and even wild imagination and an aversion for anything resembling order and method. However, an organization that has gone successfully through its birth pangs needs a more establishment oriented manager who knows how to make use of tools and method, adheres to procedures, and creates rigid frameworks for those working around him. The greater the gap between the maturity of the organization and the characteristics of its head, the greater the likelihood that the two will suffer a painful fall (see Adizes, 1979; Greiner, 1972; Torbert, 1987; Weinshall, 1975).

4. *Luck:* Why did one firm in the area of military electronics manage to survive and grow despite a long list of crises it went through, while another in the same industry soared high in its first years but was brought down by a minor shakeup in the defense establishment? For lack of an alternative explanation for the difference in the fate of the two firms, we turn to plain luck. This is an acknowledgement of the inability to interpret the facts in a more rational manner. The shrugging of shoulders that usually accompanies these explanations says something about the nature of people and the way of the world.

As organizational consultants we had the opportunity to follow, over long periods, the careers of managers at the helm of fast-growing firms in Israel. We also learned of the difficult conditions under which they forged their paths. We came to appreciate the challenges accompanying rapid growth and the pain involved in the disappointments. During these years our attention was focused mainly on the ongoing dialogue between the growing firm and its general manager, which makes a complex and rich mosaic of many and varied details that make up the main dilemmas accompanying the organization's process of growth. We have named the most salient of the dilemmas facing general managers of successful and fast-growing firms "the magician's predicament." In the following pages we describe this dilemma in detail and discuss its significance, adopting what we hope is a human approach to understanding the phenomenon.

Who Is a Magician,
and How Are Enchanted Worlds Created?

The *magician* is a manager, usually the head of his organization, who is surrounded by subordinates and worried directors in a difficult and fateful period. The magic attributed to him arises from his ability to carry out a broad range of leadership functions, such as (a) getting the members of the organization to work together as a team in achieving a difficult objective, (b) creating a meaningful and exciting vision, (c) making difficult decisions and sticking to them, (d) formulating complex strategies, and (e) maintaining employee loyalty and responsibility to the organization, even under difficult circumstances. The enchanted world is not restricted to the top of the organizational hierarchy. It can extend to all parts of a large organization—to the marketing or the finance department, to the R&D laboratories, or even to a project framework. It is the unusual manager who is able to scan a complex profit-and-loss statement for a few minutes and delineate a broad picture of the state of the organization, identify mysterious malfunctions in the production system, or to determine, on the basis of a short interview, the suitability of a candidate for the position of deputy general manager for human resources.

Four conditions contribute jointly to the development of an enchanted world:

1. An organizational reality characterized by uncertainty and much anxiety. This is usually the outcome of a turbulent environment that accompanies the growth of new organizations or crises in existing organizations.

2. The presence in a position of leadership of a talented individual having a repertoire of skills suited to the needs of the actual situation.

3. The inability to transmit the complex skills that this unusual manager possesses to others by any simple explanation or brief training. His inimitable actions, which he himself is often unable to explain, are thus given labels such as "intuition," "intelligence," "charisma," or simply "brilliance."

4. The presence of others (subordinates, colleagues, superiors) who hold the manager in high esteem and are willing to cooperate with him and to follow him blindly.

The manager becomes a magician during the course of difficult circumstances or critical undertakings in which he is perceived by others (and perhaps by himself) as the organization's builder or savior. His heroic deeds, though visible, cannot be imitated easily, and it is thus only natural that henceforth an aura of magic will encompass this miracle maker's every action.

Magic, in whatever form, is a matter of context and timing. A manager can act as a magician or be perceived as such in a specific organizational context. In other situations he behaves as any other mortal. The magic we are talking about does not necessarily cross organizational boundaries and does not last forever. A talented and successful manager is likely to find himself with the status of magician for a limited period of time and, just as he managed to establish this status for himself, so he can lose it, suddenly or within a short period of time.

The Study

This chapter is based on the narratives of 10 senior managers who were magicians during a certain period in the history of their organizations. The magic they wrought is their only common denominator. Otherwise they differ in the content of the work they undertook and in the way they carried it out. We met them all during the course of our work as organizational consultants. Two years or more after our consulting activities in their organizations had concluded, six of them agreed to cooperate in a study evaluating the contribution of the organizational consulting. They were asked to reconstruct the organizational measures they had taken during the period under discussion and to evaluate the effect the consulting had had on them. We cross-referenced their narratives with our own reconstructions as consultants and with documentation from the period. Thus we obtained the stories of the cases, which served as our raw material (see Runyan, 1982, and Mann & Pedler, 1992, for methodological considerations).

From the thematic content analysis that we carried out on the material, magic stands out as the central motif of the personal tales of our interviewees. Alongside it were other salient motifs, such as contending with crises, loneliness at the top, learning from experience, and dependence and responsibility. It was difficult to detect the magician's predicament in a one-time observation. Only in long-term follow-up was it possible to discern how, in the headiness of success, the seeds of future failure are sown. We also learned from the retrospective analysis that awareness of the danger accompanying success can enable one to take appropriate preventive measures in good time (on the advantages of the "clinical" approach to organizational analysis, see Schein, 1987).

We chose to illustrate our thesis by sketching portraits of two general managers, very different in their managerial styles, heading large organizations. For us they very clearly portray two archetypes of magicians. On the one hand, David has a strong sense of his magic; he believes he has extraordinary talents that he cannot transmit to others. Josh, on the other hand, may be defined as a reluctant magician who tries to shake off the magic aura in which others have enveloped him. David became ensnared in the magician's trap and paid for it with his managerial career. Josh managed to escape.

Magicians' Tales

We met *David* when he was at the peak of his career, during which he had managed to turn a small family business into a flourishing corporation in the electrical equipment industry. David is firm in his belief about his ability to perform miracles. He frankly reflects on his unusual intuition, which he defines as "the stigma of experience," in the following manner:

> Our firm turned into a success story thanks to my unusual
> talents. However, unfortunately, I am surrounded by
> people who are incapable of doing the things I do so
> well. Apparently there are two kinds of people in the
> world. I belong to one, and they belong to the other. My
> actions are for the most part spontaneous and intuitive. I
> cannot describe them in detail, and others certainly
> cannot. These are things you are born with or that you
> acquire somehow through your cumulative experience.
> The whole thing is rather mysterious, and you cannot
> transmit it to others. The truth is, I derive great
> satisfaction from the fact that I succeed because of my
> unusual intuitive powers. At the same time, it annoys me
> that I have to do everything myself.

From the point of view of the firm's senior managers, David's
immediate subordinates, the picture appears something like
this:

> We have a very unusual boss. He can do things,
> essential to the organization, that we cannot. We don't
> understand where he gets his unusual ideas, and he,
> apparently, can't explain it. But he's here, thank
> goodness! At the same time, he drives us crazy. Every
> day he calls to check how the monthly production plan
> is going and interferes in anything we try to do by
> ourselves.

When *Josh* came to his current job as chief executive of a
medium-sized consumer goods manufacturer, the firm was badly
in need of rehabilitation. He had come to the job from the public
sector, where he had held a senior position in one of the
country's biggest utilities. In his new role, he decided to keep
the existing senior management intact even though most of
them were getting on in years and lacking in education. They
were also suspicious, wary, anxious, and very low in morale.
Josh attributed this demeanor to the authoritarian and arbitrary
management style of his predecessor, the founder of the firm,

and hoped that if he helped them to develop, regain their independence and self-confidence, they would be able to apply their rich experience to rehabilitating the firm. He told them that until the firm's most pressing problems had been solved and until he properly understood the workings of the firm, he would be keeping a tight hold on the reins. He defined his job during his first 2 years as that of "student" and begged everyone's indulgence for interfering in the execution of their work in these early stages. As soon as he finished learning about the firm, he promised, he would return the reins to them and would stop interfering.

Josh turned out to be a brilliant, fast learner. Before long he mastered the major functions of his new organization. "He can do in minutes what takes us hours," we were told by his immediate subordinates. In close cooperation with his organizational consultants, Josh carried out a survey on his firm, after which he initiated a comprehensive program for management training and development. Later the effort was extended to the lower managerial levels of the organization and was linked to such procedures as performance appraisals, advancement programs, and incentive plans. This process of changing-while-learning was conducted in a top-down manner, starting from Josh and his senior managers and gradually going down the hierarchy as a "waterfall." This method of change became an object lesson for the organization and gained a place of honor in its culture. Josh very soon implemented the turn-around plan, significantly reducing manufacturing costs and substantially improving the quality of the goods, changes that led to a steady increase in profits.

The board of directors, delighted with the results, gave Josh a free hand to invest in new production lines, to provide the employees with material rewards, and to give them the feeling that someone was taking care of them. On top of all this came an award granted by the Manufacturers' Association for "substantive improvement in production and perfect maintenance of labor relations." His subordinates began to perceive him as a management wizard—very different from what they had known before—brilliant, effective, courageous, determined, and firm in his decisions. Josh himself, with his typical understatement, responded to the praise heaped on him with: "It's just a question of proper procedures."

The Trap

As long as the conditions that led to the creation of the enchanted world continue to prevail and the reality in which this world operates remains relatively stable, the wizardry of the magician works. Continuing success turns this world into a closed system in which actions reinforce perceptions. However, only too often the conditions change and the stability of the enchanted world is upset. One such source of change is the need for rapid growth and disturbance of the existing status quo—that is, precisely the conditions that led to the emergence and success of the magician in the past. Another source of change is the competitive environment, which may change in a way that makes the old wizardry obsolete. Yet other reasons for the decline of wizardry are the magician's fatigue or his subordinates' dissatisfaction. Under such circumstances the enchanted world becomes an obstacle to the changes demanded by the situation, and the role of the magician turns into a trap. He is likely to find himself collapsing under the burden of decisions he has to make. Having no one to challenge his judgment (who questions magicians?), the scene is set for wrong, and sometimes even disastrous, decisions. The many possibilities have one important common denominator: the paradox that it is precisely the strategy that in the past succeeded so well now turns into a trap for the magician and his organization.

As a natural response to David's initial success in developing his company, the management of the parent concern incorporated under his control more and more new businesses. A professional team was brought in to support him and to handle the day-to-day aspects of the business. But the "method" and the "new order" (especially the new deputy for finance and systems) that were imposed on David against his will turned out to be a real nuisance to him. He continued to manage the growing establishment by means of telephone conversations with the various managers, making calculations on the backs of cigarette packages, and using his intuitive judgment. Very soon he began to feel weary. He would describe himself at the time as a genius surrounded by fools who drove him crazy with their inability to perform the simplest of tasks in the areas for which they were responsible.

A labor relations crisis very quickly developed into a debilitating 4-month strike with no satisfactory outcome. For the first time since David had been appointed its general manager, the firm registered heavy losses in its financial statements. In fact, the situation was even worse than reported in the financial statements. The chief accountant of the firm, so it emerged later, had managed, by means of "accounting exercises," to paint a much rosier picture of the firm's financial status than was actually the case. The accountant later explained, "It was David's wish that I do it. He never actually said so in so many words, but I sensed that that was what he wanted me to do."

After taking full responsibility for the crisis, David submitted his resignation, but it was not accepted. However, although it decided to keep him on, the board of directors limited the scope and freedom of action he had enjoyed in the past. David's immediate response was to fire several of the managers who were directly subordinate to him, to transfer others to other positions, and to recruit new managers from outside. But he quickly came to realize that the performance of the new managers was little better than that of their predecessors. The firm lurched from one crisis to another, and David's magic aura began to fade away.

Josh, by contrast, was quick to detect the dangers inherent in the magician's role. As soon as he took up his post as chief executive of the firm, he made clear his intention of building a strong management team. He encouraged his managers to learn all they needed to know to fulfill the various facets of their jobs, so that he would be able to devote his time to long-term policy considerations. Despite his good intentions, he found it extremely difficult to shake off the magic myrtle that was constantly being thrust on him. The gap between Josh and his managers, in terms of knowledge, education, and decision-making skills, was indeed vast. It was clear that despite his commitment to his team's development, his subordinate managers were dependent on his wizardry in performing their duties. He believed that he already knew the system and was ready to delegate more and more responsibility for the ongoing operation of the firm. He was also proud of his middle managers who had made remarkable progress in assuming their leadership roles, but he was deeply disappointed with his senior managers' behavior. They were not developing into a cohesive team and, individually, still depended on him for all major decisions and their implementation. Josh thought he was constantly investing in them and getting no results.

Attempts to Get Out of the Trap

When a magician becomes aware of the trap he is in danger of falling into, he tries to change his behavior pattern, but this change is usually very difficult. The awareness of the danger inherent in his position is likely to motivate the magician to play down his special status and deny, for example, the magic qualities attributed to him. He is likely to say, as David and Josh did, that he wants his subordinates to share the responsibility for managing the firm and develop the managerial expertise that he himself has. In certain cases his subordinates may try to meet his declared wishes. However, the two sides tend to go on behaving in a way that makes implementation of the desired change difficult or impossible.

After the severe crisis in his firm, David declared a new policy of decentralization and delegation, but despite his efforts to the contrary, he still carried on with his unilateral decision making. His subordinates, like those of other magicians, insisted they were striving to acquire for themselves a larger share of responsibility and at the same time continued to avoid making any decision that had not received his explicit blessing.

Although both parties really wanted to free themselves from the magician's trap, their basic behaviors did not change. They were, in fact, blind to the inherent reasons underlying their behavior and the values and needs that led them to create and preserve their enchanted world.

David's blindness to the pitfalls of his wizardry in the end cost him his managerial career. Three years after the first crisis, his firm again ran into serious difficulties that arose from significant changes in the markets of their products and that David and his subordinates failed to foresee. The board of directors relieved him of his position, and he has not since then held a senior management post.

Another possibility open to the magician is to withdraw from his key position and refuse to continue playing his magic role. This retreat, he believes, will create a vacuum into which his subordinates are likely to be drawn. When this expectation is not fulfilled, however, he loses patience and responds with anger and frustration.

Josh, for instance, as a response to an increasing load, demanded more responsibility from his managers. He got to the point where he would send subordinates out of his office if they came asking him for a decision that he thought they should be making themselves. This tactic helped for a while and for a very narrow range of decisions. However, patience not being one of his strong points, Josh began to lose his temper more and more readily with them. He went back to doing things himself without waiting for his subordinates to do them, and they, in turn, became increasingly passive. They began to complain that he always knew better and more quickly what had to be done and that there was no way they could keep up with him. By this time Josh already had mastered the operations of the firm so well that even though he was doing all of the ongoing control himself, by noon he had finished his day's work and was looking bored and irritable.

Breaking Up the Enchanted World

Changes in organizational structure, job definitions, incentive systems, or the application of new technologies are necessary conditions for a smooth transition from the enchanted world to a more rational and professional one. But they are by no means sufficient. First, the magician has to develop an awareness of his spontaneous "theories of action" (Argyris & Schon, 1978)—that is, all of those deep-rooted premises and opinions that we all have concerning the effect of our action on others (e.g., "what you don't do yourself, no one will do for you"). Second, he must learn how to serve as an effective trainer who can help those around him understand and replicate his special talents and performance ability. He must make obvious what had in the past been shrouded in mystery, to provide clear and detailed explanations of his understanding and strategies and what it is about his way of thinking that produces the organizational magic.

The magician can attain these two objectives by developing a better understanding of his part in creating the magician's trap. It is not enough to analyze his intentions and declarations. He must learn to reflect on the details of his behavior in practice. A good way of doing this reflection is to identify the gaps between what he does in practice and what he says he is going to do. More often than not, the magician himself understands no better than anyone else how he works his magic, though if pressed for an explanation, he very likely will attribute it to intuition. He is at even more of a loss to explain what is happening when his magic powers begin to fail.

To better understand what it is that endows him with the power of magic, the manager must provide detailed, precise, and usable descriptions of his actions. He must ask himself, as though he were an impartial observer: What is it I actually do that endows me with my magic powers? He almost surely will discover that the more interesting and important part of his work cannot be described in terms of a list of tools or procedures, but rather in terms of concrete behavior that gives an indication of his theory of action (Argyris & Schon, 1978). This process of self-interrogation in real time is called "reflection in action" (see Schon, 1983). The manager can be helped to develop such an awareness by outside consultants who are not involved in the enchanted world that surrounds him.

Indeed Josh was helped by us in this way. Following work sessions we attended, together with him, we would analyze his concrete behavior during the session: his way of arguing, his fast responses, the impatience he radiates when listening, the fact that he always has more information than the other participants, and, in conclusion, the fact that all too often he is right. We showed him how this style of his, however efficient, stultifies the others. We also analyzed how his behavior contributes to the jealousy among the managers subordinate to him and how their battling for his attention and esteem adversely affects the relations among them. Together with him we tried to work out how to prevent this effect. Josh was surprised and doubtful, but curious, eager to learn and willing to try a new tack.

At this point Josh took yet another initiative, leading his firm into a 3-year period of rapid growth. New partnerships with external parties were formed, production facilities were added, and new technologies were introduced. To control the growing enterprise, Josh decentralized its structure and delegated more responsibility to his subordinates. Josh closely controlled the various aspects of the expansion program. He was involved personally in all stages, drawing the others along in his wake. For the first time in a long time, he stayed at work until midnight. Finally he had what he wanted—time pressure and a real challenge. The positive side effects were technical improvements throughout the system, a tremendous upgrading of the workforce (professionalization of the recruiting system, training, follow-up), and greater upward mobility of young staff members. Morale was high, but so was the tension because of the pressure Josh put on those who were doing the work. And the minute the enterprise started operating, Josh went full steam ahead into a new project—export.

To us it was clear that under the pressure of these new activities, Josh was reverting to his old habits and doing everything himself. His reaction to our observation on this point was, "It's just temporary—till the new operations start going." But indeed delegation of authority went from bad to worse, perhaps because staff members had begun to develop expectations of a certain degree of independence. Some of them began to oppose him openly, and it was precisely these whom he began to respect. Slowly we began to get from them a more human picture of their general manager. The profound admiration for his abilities still remained, but it was accompanied by a measure of criticism.

Josh gradually became aware that his style often stultifies any initiative in others, but at the same time he began to question the wisdom of his decision to retain all of the staff when he took up his position as head of the firm. Indeed over the course of the next years, Josh did let several of his management team go. In their stead he promoted young managers and took on several senior managers recruited from outside the firm. He thus was able, to some extent, to reduce the competence gap between himself and his subordinates and to create a better team spirit. Josh's management style is still too centralized, but not intolerably so. The firm continues to thrive, and Josh is now trying to cope with a new dilemma: preparing an heir to succeed him when he retires.

Conclusions: Magicians as Human Beings

What are the main lessons to be learned from these stories? Three entities contribute to creating the enchanted world: (a) the *manager* with the extraordinary talents, (b) his *subordinates and colleagues* "who see the pictures and hear the voices" and attribute them to the powers and competence of an unusual person (the magician), and (c) the *organizational setup,* which demands wizardry of the kind that the individual heading the organization is able to produce and that his subordinates and colleagues want to see. When one of the three factors changes significantly, the power of the magician is likely to evaporate.

The magic is first and foremost a means of reducing uncertainty or a substitute for the more conventional means of dealing with it. The paradox of wizardry arises from the fact that the answers given by the magician to the existing situation do not necessarily fit other situations that develop sooner or later, after the current uncertainty has been dealt with. In other words, today's wizardry may well be tomorrow's stumbling block. This is perhaps the main reason for the painful falls from grace of many magicians who starred in organizations operating in a turbulent environment.

The magician may be spared from falling into the trap if he is replaced in good time by another magician better suited to the new conditions. However, magicians and those around them tend to adhere to tried and tested spells that have worked in the past, and they only discover their weaknesses when it is too late. David's story might have turned out differently had he been replaced in time, and he and those around him would not have had to pay such a heavy price. The magician may be able to prevent the development of the trap by trying to share his expertise and abilities with his colleagues and subordinates. The fact that Josh still holds his position as a reputable general manager heading a successful organization may be attributed in no small measure to just this. Sharing the ability to perform magic is a process of teaching and training. The magician must describe how he operates, let his subordinates observe how he puts his extraordinary ability to work, and help them understand how he thinks. Then he will free himself of the aura of mystery that envelops him and be able to become an effective trainer of generations of managers who will learn to develop their own versions of his basic expertise to the benefit of the entire organization.

In the last analysis, the roots of wizardry are planted deep in the set of values and beliefs held by the manager-magician and those around him and relate to questions of power, influence, responsibility, and authority. Dismantling the enchanted world thus requires access to the underlying strata of the world of values of the individual and the organizational culture created around it (Etzion, 1990; Schein, 1992).

David, for instance, had to put up for scrutiny his claim that there are "two kinds of people in the world." He also had to relinquish his inner conviction that everything can be done by intuition alone. He had to realize, moreover, that he could not manage a large and complex organization solely by means of direct and informal contacts even though these were the source of his satisfaction and pride in his work. Had he done so, he might have avoided stepping into the waiting trap.

Josh had to come to terms with the fact that not all people are able to learn everything if they are only given the chance. He also had to acknowledge that he might have been wrong when he decided, after taking up his position, not to replace any of the managers and that perhaps it would have been better for him and for the organization to let some of them go. Furthermore he had to recognize his own part in creating the dependence and lack of initiative of his managers that he complained about and that, in a sense, the dependence and accompanying admiration were a source of much pleasure and pride to him.

Clearly the magician needs to learn to recognize the pitfalls that his behavior creates and to enlist the help of his subordinates in avoiding them. Indeed developing learning ability in the difficult conditions of a turbulent environment and rapidly changing organizations is today a central issue in research on organizations and their managers (McCall, Lombardo, & Morrison, 1988; Senge, 1990). The lessons to be learned from these studies are likely to broaden the understanding of the magician's trap as a special case of learning on the part of managers.

From a methodological point of view, our decision to employ a narrative, "clinical" approach in studying the effect of our own interventions as organizational consultants was fortunate because it gave us access to material that otherwise would have remained undetected. Like many other personal/organizational phenomena, the rise and fall of "magicians" can be detected only over time, from a longitudinal perspective, and sometimes only in retrospect.

The case study method, which is a traditional research and teaching device in the area of management and organization development, offers us a way of seeing individuals, groups, and total organizations within a meaningful context and from a longitudinal perspective, rather than in a limited, ahistorical snapshot way, as cross-sectional research often does.

There is no better way to understand a complex phenomenon than to tell the story of the parties involved in it, particularly when the "life course" of the organization is linked closely with that of the individual heading it. Indeed the magician phenomenon cannot be presented properly from only one party's perspective, be it the manager's personality and personal experience or the organization's culture and its struggle with environmental pressures. To understand the development of the phenomenon, one needs to integrate the stories of both parties against the environmental context in which they are embedded.

Epilogue

At the time of publication of this chapter, several years after we conducted the original interviews with our manager-magicians, Josh is still keeping a tight hold of the reins in the firm he now has been heading for many years. Over the course of the years, he has, no doubt, learned the importance of wizardry in management and the pitfalls awaiting those who practice it. David, who fell into the trap of the wizardry he performed with such telling effect, has not returned to the manager's chair. He embarked on a new career and now serves as a much sought-after consultant in the areas of the technologies and businesses in which he gained expertise during his good years.

Note

1. Because no women chief executives were included among our interviewees, the masculine gender is used throughout the chapter. But women-magicians

may also be a rarity. Women's style of management tends to be more cooperative than that of men (see Rosener, 1990); thus successful women managers may be less susceptible to the magician predicament than their male colleagues.

References

Adizes, I. (1979). *How to solve the mismanagement crisis.* Tel Aviv, Israel: Goma, Tcherikover. (in Hebrew)

Argyris, C., & Schon, D. A. (1978). *Organizational learning: A theory of action perspective.* Reading, MA: Addison-Wesley.

Bass, B. M. (1985). *Leadership and performance beyond expectation.* New York: Free Press.

Burns, J. M. (1978). *Leadership.* New York: Harper & Row.

Conger, J. A., & Kanungo, R. (1987). Toward a behavioral theory of charismatic leadership in organizational settings. *Academy of Management Review, 12,* 637-647.

Etzion, D. (1990). Burnout in management positions: Causes and consequences. In A. Globerson, A. Galin, & E. Rosenstein (Eds.), *Human resource and industrial relations in Israel: New horizons* (pp. 271-285). Tel Aviv, Israel: Ramot. (in Hebrew)

Greiner, L. E. (1972). Evolution and revolution as organizations grow. *Harvard Business Review, 50,* 37-46.

House, R. J. (1977). A theory of charismatic leadership. In J. G. Hunt & L. L. Larson (Eds.), *Leadership: The cutting edge* (pp. 189-204). Carbondale: Southern Illinois University Press.

Mann, S., & Pedler, M. (Eds.). (1992). *Biography in management and organisational development.* Lancaster, UK: Centre for Study of Management Learning.

McCall, M. W., Lombardo, M. M., & Morrison, A. M. (1988). *The lessons of experience: How successful executives develop on the job.* Lexington, MA: Lexington Books.

Morgan, G. (1988). *Riding the waves of change: Developing managerial competencies for a turbulent world.* San Francisco: Jossey-Bass.

Quinn, R. E. (1988). *Beyond rational management: Mastering the paradoxes and competing demands of high performance.* San Francisco: Jossey-Bass.

Rosener, J. B. (1990, November-December). Ways women lead. *Harvard Business Review,* pp. 119-125.

Runyan, W. M. (1982). *Life histories and psychobiography: Explorations in theory and method.* New York: Oxford University Press.

Schein, E. H. (1987). *The clinical perspective of fieldwork.* Newbury Park, CA: Sage.

Schein, E. H. (1992). *Organizational culture and leadership* (2nd ed.). San Francisco: Jossey-Bass.

Schon, D. A. (1983). *The reflective practitioner.* New York: Basic Books.

Senge, P. M. (1990). *The fifth discipline: The art and practice of learning organizations.* Garden City, NY: Doubleday.

Torbert, W. R. (1987). *Managing the corporate dream: Restructuring for long-term success.* Homewood, IL: Irwin.

Tushman, M. L., Newman, W. H., & Nadler, D. A. (1988). Executive leadership and organizational evolution: Managing incremental and discontinuous change. In R. H. Kulmann & T. J. Covin (Eds.), *Corporate transformation: Revitalizing organizations for a competitive world* (pp. 102-130). San Francisco: Jossey-Bass.

Vaill, P. B. (1989). *Managing as a performing art: New ideas for a world of chaotic change.* San Francisco: Jossey-Bass.

Weinshall, T. D. (1975). *Management and organization in Israel.* Tel Aviv, Israel: Massda.

Yukl, G. A. (1989). *Leadership in organizations* (2nd ed.). Englewood Cliffs, NJ: Prentice-Hall.

❧ 6 ❧

Personal Rites of Passage

Stories of College Youth

Sherry L. Hatcher

The Background

Not long ago I asked a class of some 80 women and men, college juniors and seniors, what event defined for them the passage from childhood to adulthood. Not surprisingly for this population, the greatest number, 34%, wrote that it was their leaving home for college. A close second, 24%, identified physiological puberty as their perceived rite of passage. The next 34% were about evenly divided among the following events: obtaining a driver's license, their 18th birthday, graduation from high school, working at a paid job, travel abroad, a blossoming romance, a broken romance, and a traumatic family happening such as an acrimonious parental divorce. A notable 8% wrote that they did not yet feel as if they had passed through a transition from childhood to adulthood or, if

AUTHOR'S NOTE: I wish to thank the many undergraduate students who participated in this study, most particularly those who contributed expanded narratives. Credit is also due to Lisa Walsh, Meredith Reynolds, Jerry Galea, and Missi Nadeau, who helped code a portion of the data, some of which are destined for a more statistically based study. Finally, thanks are due to Ruthellen Josselson for her support and fine editorial suggestions, to Robert Hatcher for his helpful suggestions, and to Linda Ludwig for typing the manuscript.

they had, that they were not sure what event(s) might have served as a vehicle for their passage or indeed how to recognize it if it had or would yet occur.

I have assigned this exercise to numbers of college classes over the past 20 years and, not surprisingly, the findings are reasonably consistent across these two decades. The only expectable variation in such responses is that in a high school and/or non-college-bound population (Fasick, 1988), youth are more apt to identify either graduation from high school or the world of work as their perceived passage. As the anthropological and sociological literatures on this subject suggest, the cultural context is crucial in defining which social customs aid youth in achieving their transition to the adult world, with its attendant privileges and responsibilities.

One can conclude from the response of my college classes that there is consistently a quite varied response to the question, What event defined for you the passage from childhood to adulthood? This finding is surely a comment on the lack of uniform initiation rites in modern society. In earlier eras and in other cultures, where there existed consensually determined rites of passage, both youth and their elders recognized exactly what it was that signaled incipient adulthood.

For example, in the days of the agrarian Plymouth Colony, the child was an apprentice to the parent, a kind of "miniature farmer," wrote Kett (1977). In such systems of apprenticeship that were prevalent both in preindustrial America and in many parts of Europe, elders defined an obvious transition for their youth—that is, a pathway from the role of a child to that of an adult. Elders even prescribed the time and manner in which youth were expected to leave the parental home. Writes Kett:

> The older and larger a child, the more space and food
> he took up, and the greater the economic incentive to
> send him elsewhere to live. . . . A second form of
> homeleaving was for a young person to go out on a
> seasonal basis in search of work or perhaps advanced
> education. (pp. 17-18)

It is a fairly unusual and dubious distinction that our current society's definition of passage from the last official stage of childhood into adulthood is frequently a prolonged time of confusion (Blos, 1962). Such is not the case for societies in which the transitional markers between childhood and adulthood are relatively uniform, specific, and consensually validated.

From the days of Aristotle's observation that youth are "passionate, irascible, and apt to be carried away by their impulses" (Kiell, 1967), a frequent perception has been espoused by such luminous theoreticians as G. S. Hall and Freud that adolescence is a stage of life characterized by emotional Sturm und Drang. Such a conclusion, however, may be too general and culturally nonspecific. In the past 25 years, beginning with the psychosocially based work of such authors as Offer (1969) and Adelson (1980), a strong argument has been made that rumors of adolescence as a stage of turmoil have been greatly exaggerated. These researchers emphatically state that the adolescences of most American youth are relatively nonrebellious and that the existing deviations from the family norms are relatively minor and superficial, having more to do with fashion and curfews than politics and values. Whether or not this more recent assessment of modern American adolescence is correct (Hatcher, 1989), few writers would deny the complexity of roles and choices available to youth, a virtual potpourri of options.

Considering that rites of passage are social customs designed specifically to aid people in their transition from one developmental stage to the next, we find important differences between societies that have clearly prescribed passages from youth to adulthood and our own increasingly vague culture, which offers its adolescents such a plethora of choices that there is little uniformity or clarity in the perception of what constitutes a rite of passage.

Society's looser social fabric further increases the challenge to the adolescent in his or her progression to adulthood. Widespread alcohol and drug abuse, an increasingly high rate of divorce, and, in many instances, prolonged financial dependence on the family of origin make lasting commitments to love and work difficult indeed for the young to accomplish. Few have argued against the notion that the bridges connecting adolescence and adulthood are delicate ones, but still fewer have suggested means by which such bridges may be constructed so that the pathway between childhood and adulthood becomes clearer and smoother.[1]

Although only sparingly cited in the sociological and psychological literatures, the bible on "rites of passage" is a book by that title by Arnold Van Gennep (1908/1960). A theorist who stressed development throughout the life cycle, Van Gennep discussed rites of passage in terms of individual life crises and the ceremonies designed by a society to aid and commemorate such transitions.

According to Van Gennep, the *ceremonies of passage* are those rites that (a) mark the end of a developmental stage, (b) note the process of transition, or (c) denote one's entry into a new stage of development. He labeled these three stages of passage "rites of separation, "transition rites," and "rites of incorporation," respectively (Van Gennep, 1908/1960). Although the conceptualization of "adolescence" as a unique developmental stage had barely begun in the early 20th century, Van Gennep discussed the transition from childhood to adulthood in terms of ceremonial initiation rites that led youth to an adult status. In the formulation of this theory, Van Gennep is respectful of the complex and wide-ranging nature of his topic, and he appears more cognizant than some later writers of the multiple contributions to this subject of those working in related disciplines.

Quite intriguingly, Van Gennep saw the particular transition from adolescence to adulthood as a collection of rites of separation from the "asexual world" to the "world of sexuality" (p. 67). Nevertheless he stated clearly his belief that there is no absolute correspondence between physiological puberty and what he calls "social puberty." This uncertainty exists because ceremonies defining the passage from childhood to adulthood are quite lengthy, in some cultures extending over a period of months or even years, and also because the event of female menarche does not have a clear parallel in males' pubertal onset. Van Gennep's original distinction between physiological and social puberty was the precursor of a widely used modern definition of adolescence as "psychological puberty" (Conger, 1973).

Because rites that initiate the adolescent to the world of adulthood vary so widely across eras and cultures, and because such rites may or may not be correlated with physiological puberty, the distinguishing factor between those rites that simplify the adolescent's passage to adulthood and those that complicate the process is how expectably, clearly, and consistently a rite is ceremonialized.

Examples of those societies that have tended to prescribe quite specific and consistent ceremonies are found in many preliterate cultures. Such groups are discussed by Brown (1969); she differentiates societies wherein initiation rites are clear from societies wherein such passages are defined vaguely. Brown writes: "All those who have been initiated, have the privileges and responsibility of adults, and those who have not been initiated, do not. Those who have been initiated are adults by definition; those who have not been initiated, are not" (p. 59).

Like Van Gennep, Brown notes that initiation rites have been difficult to study across societies because the ages of adolescence, as cited in the literature, span the years from 8 to 20 and because the duration of ceremonies defining this passage ranges from single events to occasions lasting many years. In addition, some initiation rites are joyous and aim to celebrate, whereas others are known to be quite painful, with the function of negatively reinforcing taboos. Similarly, whereas some puberty rites are quite public, others are private, some even cloaked in secrecy. Finally, whereas some rites of passage are what we today might call "unisex," others traditionally have been gender-specific.

The Theory

It is the thesis of this chapter that in the absence of clearly prescribed rites of passage for adolescents, youth in our society will individualize and create what I call their "personal rites of passage." These rites are individually created substitutes for the limited and culturally prescribed rituals of the past. Such individualized rites may range from dating, to obtaining a driver's license, to graduating from high school, or, in the case of many postsecondary students, they will be defined by the youth's leaving home for college.

In a society that neglects to offer well-defined transitions from one life stage to the next, it is possible to create personal rites of passage that are maladaptive, even self-destructive and/ or antisocial: Gang memberships (Brown, 1969), substance abuse, eating disorders, and other symptomologies of separation that occur with unfortunate frequency among today's youth are examples of "negative" personal rites of passage. In such instances youth define their transitions by a negative identity, often with maladaptive and/or self-punitive features.

It would be interesting in future work to compare some of the preliterate puberty rites discussed by such anthropologists as Brown and Mead with those self-invented by modern adolescents to fill the void left by a lack of societal prescriptions. This comparison could be done with those personal rites of passage that are positive and developmentally progressive and those that, like the "Symbolic Wounds" described by Bettelheim (1962), are punitive, superego-ridden, and frequently rebellious in their appearance and psychological intent.

In discussing the "rebellion, philosophical perplexities, conflict and struggle of the adolescent," Margaret Mead posed the following question in her famous ethnography *Coming of Age in Samoa* (1928/1961): "Were these difficulties of youth due to the nature of being an adolescent in America?" (p. 19). Mead contrasts the American adolescent with Samoans who, at a year or two postpuberty, are assigned to adult groups, given a name for their transitional organization, and "who are invested with definite obligations and privileges in the community life" (p. 65). In Samoan culture, rites of passage are ones of privilege—in the context of a society that has few taboos.

One surely can argue about the virtue or failing of a society that mandates fixed rites of passage for their youth. Nevertheless most social scientists, regardless of their discipline or theoretical persuasion, generally agree that adolescent rebellion and turmoil tend to increase where passages are unclearly defined and where there may be an overabundance of perplexing choices. Mead said:

> [A society] which is clamoring for choice, which is filled with many articulate groups, each urging its own brand of salvation . . . will give each new generation no peace until all have chosen or gone under, unable to bear the conditions of choice. . . . (p. 170)

> Samoa knows but one way of life and teaches it to her children. Will we, who have the knowledge of many ways, leave our children to choose among them? (p. 179)

Consider the present thesis: *In the absence of clear societal initiation rites, youth invent their own positive or negative rites of passage into adulthood*—as a partial response to Mead's poignant question. However, the current theory also implies that an adolescent's choice of personal passage may occur outside of his or her conscious awareness; that is to say, in the absence of clear and consciously prescribed societal rites of passage, adolescents will invent their own personalized and psychologically overdetermined ceremonies.

In his introduction to Van Gennep's book *Rites of Passage,* Solon Kimball writes:

> Rites of passage deserve attention within themselves. The critical problems of becoming male and female, of relations within the family, and of passing into old age are directly related to the devices which the society offers the individual to help him (her) achieve the new adjustment. Somehow we seem to have forgotten this—or perhaps the ritual has become so completely individualistic that it is now found for many only in the privacy of the psychoanalyst's couch. . . . One dimension of mental illness may arise because an

increasing number of individuals are forced to
accomplish their transitions alone with private symbols.
(p. xviii)

The Stories

To illustrate how personal rites of passage may be understood, we will examine the stories of 82 college students who
were asked: "Please describe what it was like for you to leave
home." In studying the resulting narratives, one can observe that
in the absence of clear rites of passage, each student creates his
or her particular way of negotiating the transition from the
parental home to the college campus. Each person's "story"
appears to be variously shaped by circumstances of family life,
by cultural experiences and values, and, of course, by personal
psychodynamics.

In a best-case scenario, the resulting passage is, if not without
bumps and detours in the road, at least successful in ultimately
introducing the adolescent to mastery of some adult roles. In a
worst-case situation, the resulting passage goes awry and offers
instead dysfunctional, even symptomatic, solutions to the search
for safe passage to the adult world.

Because most colleges in America today function free of any
concept of "in loco parentis," the substitute parentalism that
preoccupied many college administrators in the 19th century,
more personalized solutions and often confusion about how to
grow up have resulted. The rules and regulations of an "in loco
parentis" philosophy, though frequently mocked by students,
nonetheless offered a standard of curfews, chaperons, sanc-
tions, and "peer loyalty" (Kett, 1977, p. 58), which clearly
defined the boundaries and expectations of college life. As noted
earlier, such clear-cut rites tend to universalize a sense of passage to adulthood. College life today, rather different in this
regard, creates a smorgasbord of choice even within the educational setting. Van Gennep makes the point that as societies and
institutions develop, their ceremonies often become less clear.

It is worth noting here that a number of papers, like this chapter, express fascination with Van Gennep's early model for rites of passage. Most of these researchers (Barry & Schlegel, 1980; Fasick, 1988) appear to be trying to isolate a "one and only" rite of passage to characterize our youth's transition from adolescence to maturity. A typical choice in this regard is the passage through secondary school to graduation. The present theory, with its emphasis on personal rites of passage, with their various choices and multiple themes, takes exception to this univocal position. Even as we focus here on a single illustration of "personalized rites," in reviewing the stories of youth leaving home for college, one is struck by the variety of interpretations of such an experience and the wide-ranging functions they may serve.

A final theoretical question must be addressed here in relation to the neurotic psychopathology not infrequently observed during the adolescent years. One might ask whether some or all of such deviance can be conceptualized as "personalized rites of passage gone awry." For example, we know that anorexics' eating disorders most often erupt around a major separation from home. Thus, barring the presence of gross psychopathology such as psychoses or psychopathy, a theory of personalized rites of passage permits a useful conceptualization of the complex transition from adolescence to adulthood in our society with all of its attendant advances and pitfalls, including some neuroses that have a special relationship to separation anxiety.

Here, by using examples in the voice of the late adolescents on the subject of their personal rites of passage to college, I wish to illustrate how rites of passage have become personalized in modern American society. Because leaving home for college is a most frequently cited passage to adulthood, I chose this example in its modal forms: those rites that celebrate, those rites that punish, and those rites that teach or from which one learns. Although each of these types of passage may serve as a transition to adulthood, the success and quality of the transition is determined, in part, by the choice of a personalized rite of passage and, in part, by the way that particular choice is experienced.

That is to say, not only may the choice of a particular rite be observably positive (say, obtaining a driver's license or graduating from high school) but also the quality of the experience of whatever rite is chosen may subsequently be positive or negative or even "false positive." A narrative format seems to be natural for describing these kinds of data. As president Hyde of Bowdoin College wrote in his 1898 book *The Evolution of a College Student:*

> The college student is a being of infinitely complex and swiftly shifting phases which external description is powerless to catch and reproduce. The only way to portray his deeper natures is to place him in intimate and confidential relations and let him "give himself away." (Kett, 1977, p. 177)

In asking 82 undergraduates at a large Midwestern university to describe what it was like to leave home for college, and because these students often had cited college as a primary personal rite of passage for themselves, their various responses to this task are quite intriguing. Approximately one-third of the data that follow is from males; the remaining two-thirds are stories of college women. Although occasional gender differences will be noted, it was, interestingly, not a striking feature in these narratives. Those of us who worked from the numerically coded narratives in sorting out the data were struck by the difficulty in correctly guessing gender of the storyteller; we had to go back to a master list of names and code numbers to assess this correctly. It appears that a good deal of commonality is in this particular rite of passage for both women and men in our society.

The data were examined in two ways: (a) to assess the frequency of particular responses and (b) as narrative data coded for themes and for sense of qualitative experience. Using the schema of those rites that celebrate, those that punish, and those that one learns from, we can analyze, as an example, the experience of leaving home for college and assess how this experience relates to Van Gennep's paradigm.

On the surface it might seem that leaving home for college is an event that would fall only in the first and last of these three categories. But we shall see that although a rite of passage may be classified as generally positive or negative, the personal translation of a (presumably positive) rite such as going off to college may indeed be experienced as a celebration, a punishment, and/or a learning experience. In this latter regard, I refer to adjustment to college life as a potential learning experience in itself; this is over and above the fact that the college experience is, by definition, educational.

To begin with an overview of the data, 36% of the 82 participants experienced leaving home for college as a positive event, 32% experienced it as "difficult," and 32% experienced it, in one student's words, as "two-sided." Examples of such two-sided responses were embedded in characterizations of leaving home for college as "frightening but exciting," "sad but positive," and "psyched but scared."

Celebrations

The more thoroughly celebratory college-goers write rather differently. Often they refer to earlier leave-takings from home— that is, "bridges" that provided a transition experience preparatory to leaving home for college. It is important to note that, in this sample, no one lived at home while attending college, although in theory this is possible, usually at a "commuter-type" school.

Those who celebrate their chosen rite as a truly positive passage stress excitement at having increased responsibility and independence as a developmental milestone, rather than as escaping from an unpleasant surrounding. Says one such celebratory student, "It was a real joy just to be responsible for myself." "I loved it immediately," wrote another. Others in this "positive" category wrote that they saw college as a "challenge . . . a logical next step." Still others wrote such comments as, "It was really nice to be independent on my own and to be able to take charge of my life. I felt stronger and more comfortable with myself."

Most of those who celebrated their passage to college life spoke of bridges, what Van Gennep referred to as "transition experiences," that smoothed the way from home to life away from home. Such "bridges" mentioned in this sample include boarding school, camp, and travel. For others it was, "pick[ing] a school far enough away that my parents wouldn't visit and yet close enough that friends could and that I could . . . drop in at home." Others mentioned that it helped their adjustment if parents were supportive, if there were no obvious financial worries or sibling or parental problems. A secure family back home most often obviated the need for guilty feelings about being away. Said one student who cited a secure sense of family, "I felt that my family would not abandon me. . . . I refer to both places as home." A male student wrote along similar lines:

> My parents were supportive and never cut down my ideas. Therefore, I have many creative ideas about what I want to do in life. My sister was tired of living in my shadow so I felt comfortable about leaving the door open for her.

Another woman who celebrated her collegiate rite of passage wrote:

> I really was not apprehensive about leaving home because I knew that my family would not abandon me . . . they were very supportive and excited about seeing me grow. I had also been away for summers . . . so it was not a traumatic event. I think this is very important.

And a student who describes the value of "bridges" wrote:

> When I first went away to summer camp for 6 weeks when I was 14, I was very homesick. I thought a month and a half was a very long time. . . . My family has

always been very close, and I was afraid something would happen to them and I wouldn't know. . . . When I first left to college, I wanted to get away from home. I felt confident and mature and able to make it on my own. . . . I left for school 10 hours from my home. I fit in okay—I met people, had fun, did well in my classes. I feel I was able to do this because I learned from prior experience.

In a similar vein a male student wrote: "I had infinite freedom from my parents in high school, so I did not have a hard time adjusting to college life." Still another celebrator wrote:

I loved [leaving for college]. It couldn't have happened too soon . . . [there were] amazing new friends, radicalization, growth of personal experience and tremendously improved senses of self confidence and self awareness.

And yet another in this group: "I enjoy seeing my family when I go home . . . because I feel more proud and confident about myself."

Finally, a number of students in this celebratory group reported practicing a kind of cognitive role play preparatory to their leaving home. An example cited by one male student: "I had mentally traveled all over the country before leaving"; and in similar fashion, a female student wrote: "I had left home without physically leaving it. Therefore, it was very natural to physically separate. . . . Actually I never thought about it until now." From such narratives it would seem that the bridges that can facilitate separation-individuation may be imaged or fantasized as well as acted out.

Punishments

Those who had not "built bridges" seemed to feel the lack. Said one such student, "I'd never been away from home for more

than a week, so it was a big adjustment." Said another, "Though
I went to college in my hometown, I visited my parents in their
offices on their birthdays in order to stay away [from home]."
And finally, a rather poignant remark from a foreign student on
campus without benefit of bridges: "When I came to college, I
had splitted up my heart."

The students who did not seem to have a reference point for
"leaving home" from their previous experience did not discuss
the kinds of transitions that mark a comfortable and successful
rite of passage. Indeed one group seemed to experience the
college send-off as a negative, even punishing, rite of passage.
Some of these individuals simply wrote of feeling "homesick,"
"frightened," experiencing "culture shock," and feeling that
they were "not ready to go away." As one student wrote, "If you
do things before you're ready, then it usually isn't a good experience." Another female student commented, "It was a lot harder
to turn off the life that I had known with the friends I had shared
things with for over 10 years. . . . It's almost like living a double
existence and I just cannot live in [both places]."

Others in the negative group reported guilty and conflictual
responses to family problems at home, particularly if there was
now a question of parental separation or divorce. Another concern mentioned several times was the illness of a sibling, especially if it was serious; such known distress in the family back
home often made the student want to call home every day.
Sometimes a situation in which the student had been fighting
bitterly with a parent—a situation that led some in the first group
to want to "escape"—induced those in this more overtly con-
science-ridden group to feel guilty about leaving.

One female student told her story with a focus on her feelings
about leaving her family without her historical presence as the
family's "mediator":

> Leaving home is an experience that everyone must face
> at some point in their lives. For most people, that time
> is when they leave for college. Many factors affect
> whether this experience will be a positive one. In my

personal situation, my family relationships and other support systems influenced how I dealt with the separation and my new-found independence.

On September 1st, 1990, my mother, father, and I drove from Lansing to Ann Arbor to move me into the dormitory. As we faced the routine difficulties (long check-in lines, minuscule dorm rooms), we all tried to ignore the overwhelming sadness we were all facing. We spent the day moving furniture and meeting my new roommates, and then we celebrated the move-in by going out to dinner. Because I had left a few extra things at home, we drove back [home] that night. My boyfriend would drive me to Ann Arbor to stay 2 days later.

Those next 2 days were very interesting. My youngest sister, age 9, was very upset by the whole situation. We have a very close relationship, so it was also very difficult for me to deal with the fact that I was going to miss a substantial part of her life. My other sister, at that time 14, was pretty involved in being a sullen, avoidant adolescent and didn't seem to care about the situation. My parents were dealing with things in their own ways. My mother seemed depressed as she made numerous references to how lonely she would be without me at home. My father just talked a lot about the school, what classes I would take, et cetera. I, while dealing with the fact that I was moving away from my family, was also facing a long-distance relationship with my boyfriend. Because of this, I didn't give a lot of thought to how I would handle actually leaving my home of 17 years.

The day came when I was to leave for school [to stay]. My boyfriend came to pick me up, and my family assembled to see me off. The actual good-byes seemed pretty easy, and soon I was in the car, ready to go. The minute we started the car and began pulling out of the driveway, I realized what was happening: I was leaving home and would never live full-time with my family again. The sadness and apprehension I had been experiencing for weeks came out in a rush of tears. My boyfriend was stunned and incapable of consoling me. It must have taken me a full 20 minutes to calm down.

While my initial reaction to leaving home was pretty dramatic, the following months are a more accurate reflection of my experience. After my boyfriend left, I had the chance to sit down and have the reality of the situation sink in. I was on my own, responsible for myself, and beginning a new chapter of my life. I adjusted quickly to dorm life, making a lot of friends and having a great time. Classes also went well, but although these areas of life were satisfying, I was still dealing with the emotions that leaving home had stirred up. While this was somewhat a reaction to the actual separation from my family, I feel that it was also a reaction to the family situation I had left behind.

I don't believe that it is simply moving away from home that affects people, but unresolved issues that they leave behind. This was definitely true in my case. My family life is a typical dysfunctional family; my parents don't communicate, my 14-year-old sister and my father can't stand one another. My role in the family was always as the mediator. Whomever the argument was between, I was required to step in and resolve the conflict. My other, more difficult role was that of a confidante. Everyone in my family came to me to discuss their problems. What made this difficult was the fact that usually their problems were with other members of the family. I was forced to take sides and was given information that I should not have had to hear about the people that I love. These family dynamics weighed heavily on my mind during those first few months I spent away from home. I felt that now that I was gone, my family wouldn't know how to function. This fear is one I face even today, 2 years after leaving home.

It is because of these residual feelings that I have begun to view leaving home as a process rather than as a singular experience. Even now, as I approach my junior year, I still do not feel that I have really left home. I go home quite often, and when I'm there, I fall right back into the same patterns as I left. Recently, as I have begun to face some of the more difficult decisions that come with "growing up," I have realized that it is time for me to break those patterns and "leave" my family, in order for them to adapt and function without my interference. It has been difficult, and I still have a long way to go, but I feel that as my attitude towards my family situation has begun to change, I have become a more mature individual. Someday soon I will really leave home, not just in the literal sense, but psychologically as well. It won't be easy, I'm still very afraid of the changes that must be made, but I realize that the only way for me to grow and to become my own person is to break away from my family of origin. Only then can I maturely face the decisions that lie ahead.

Although this student's story focused on her sense of responsibility to her "dysfunctional family," others felt impeded in their adjustment to an illness or mishap of their own in their early college life. Said one woman on this subject: "[College] was difficult and frightening . . . this was complicated by a kidney infection I had where I was almost hospitalized. I am still very close with my family. I speak with them on the phone almost every day." A male student who reported moving back home due to financial difficulties and poor grades wrote of the return to the family: "I have 'regressed' in a way back to my older, more dull personality. Now that I am away [at college] again, I'm trying to change back to a more exciting personality, similar to my first year away from home."

Once again, the self-report data can become a bit misleading in that the ostensibly "positive" group, which emphasized the joy of coming to college to "escape" from home, is really more similar to the negative group, which felt punished; thus the group that is running away from an old experience, rather than tilting toward a new one, is clearly different from the relatively positive and celebratory group described earlier.

To round out a discussion of the self-punishing subjects, the occasional student reported becoming symptomatic around his or her entry to college life. Psychosomatic symptoms, eating disorders, and overindulgence in drugs and alcohol were some of the problems mentioned. Some of these students were doing poorly or left college altogether. Others were simply unhappy at a particular institution and successfully transferred to another college that better met their needs.

Two-Sided Learning Rites

One of the more prevalent sets of responses that I liken here to Van Gennep's rite of passage as a learning experience is the group that was openly ambivalent, "two-sided" as one student put it. This is a group in which students started out scared or homesick but worked through and mastered their mixed feelings to land on their feet, in some cases with insight in the balance. Such students describe how it took time to adjust. One described having "college shock." Another said she felt as if she was being "torn from [my] parents and thus my childhood." A typical two-sided protocol reads as follows:

> When I first thought of leaving home, I was very excited. Being on my own seemed like a dream come true. I was a little mistaken. I found that leaving home meant feeling alone sometimes. I was homesick for a while. I not only missed my buddies but mostly my family. My parents are very important to me, and not seeing them daily was hard to adapt to. As the days went by, I met new people and began to explore my new surroundings. Pretty soon I felt like I was home, at my new home.

Another story in a similarly ambivalent mode reads:

> It was quite difficult to leave home. Part of the difficulty stems from the fact that I am the oldest of five

daughters and neither of my parents left home for college. I was navigating uncharted [*sic*] waters, and that caused me much anxiety. . . . It was difficult to leave my family because of the support I could count on from them. . . . I was actually surprised and relieved to find that their support was unconditional in that no matter how badly I thought I was doing on my own, they still had confidence in me.

Finally, a more detailed story from a male student whose initial adjustment to college life was quite rocky—only much later followed by a sense of adjustment and success:

When I remember how happy I felt when I was accepted to college, it seems a little strange to think of how different I felt when [actually] getting ready to go to college. I left home a week early to start athletic practice, and I was living off-campus in an apartment which my family owned. I was the last of five kids to go to college, and having an apartment saved my parents the costs of dormitory living.

I remember the night my parents dropped me off at "my apartment." I was terrified. Neither of my brothers were around, and so I was left alone to think about the new world I was suddenly dumped into. I tried unpacking my things and getting used to my new room, but I couldn't. I just sat on the couch and felt homesick.

For that first week, I was alone, walking the 4 miles to athletic practice in the morning and walking back again at night. I barely spoke to anyone, and ate little; my checking account wasn't opened yet, and I depended on my [older] roommate to buy food for me. I didn't want to ask too much of him, so I spent several weeks surviving on bagels, milk, cereal, and Hi-C.

I was really miserable, even after school started. I thought I'd enjoy the new-found "freedom": nobody telling me to do my homework, staying up as late as I wanted, eating what I wanted. But compared to the responsibilities I faced, the freedom didn't mean as much. I had a lot of trouble coping with the difficulty of classes and how much was expected of me. I wasn't used to having to work for grades, or getting grades lower than a B. On my first English paper I got a C and was pretty shocked. Somehow that set off a weird chain reaction where I got bad grades and did nothing about it. Somehow, over the course of that first term, I gradually got used to living away from home, doing laundry, cooking, and shopping, but not studying. There was something in me that resisted taking adult responsibility, something that told me that I'd never had to work for success before, and I wasn't about to start.

Strangely enough, even though I was living in a new town, I never referred to my apartment as "home." I always differentiated between going to "my place" and "home." When I was at home, I wasn't very truthful about my grades—my parents had and still have a lot of faith in me, and I didn't want them to know that I was failing their expectations. They didn't necessarily pressure me to succeed, but they expected that I'd try my best in everything that I did, and I wasn't even trying. It's taken me a long time to act responsibly about my school work, and I still don't put in all the effort I should, but I've made a lot of progress in the realm of caring about how I do.

At the end of the first semester, I got in some serious academic trouble—I don't like talking about it, but suffice it to say that I was in jeopardy of being suspended. This was the culmination of a miserable semester; I felt friendless, and I felt like a complete failure already, and this was the icing on a really bad-tasting cake. Fortunately I received no punishment from the college, but it changed me. I'd lost all vestiges of the cocky high school student who didn't have to study or try hard to do well—now I was a college student, more serious and a little more mature. The second semester was a complete reversal of the first. I did well in school and for the first time began to question the life goals that for years I had thought irrevocable.

So much has changed from that first year in college; I've learned some very painful lessons, but have also learned some wonderful ones. Most importantly, I've learned a lot about myself and what I feel my future should be. My apartment is "home" now. Of course, my permanent home is home too, but I can accept having two "homes." Things aren't black or white anymore, and I've become able to see things from different perspectives. From eagerness to fear and homesickness, to surprise, to humiliation and depression, and finally to maturity and contentment, college has taught me a great deal about myself and the world, lessons not found in books. In a way it's painful to recall that first night here at school and the fear I felt; it brings back a lot of memories about many unpleasant events in my life. Yet in a way, it's comforting to know that even though these feelings and memories will always be a part of me, they're part of my past. Thinking about my future still makes me a little afraid, but what I've learned about myself gives me the courage to face whatever the future holds, and face it happily.

As illustrated by the above narrative, the characteristic that members of this "learning" group seem to have in common is that, in time, they adjust to their leave-taking and come to feel as positively about college life as do their peers who were enthusiastic from the start.

False Positives

Further complicating this classification scheme is the observation that a self-reported positive rite of passage may not truly be experienced in that way. To borrow a phrase from medical terminology, I refer to this group as "false positives"; that is, students in this category report the college experience as positive;

however, the underlying motivation does not suggest a developmental advance from adolescence to adulthood, but rather escape from unpleasant situations. As one woman student wrote:

> I was very excited to leave home to attend college. I have never had a close relationship with my mother, and I could no longer endure our vicious arguments. Therefore I was looking forward toward my independence and having a life revolving around me and my peers, the only people to whom I revealed my innermost thoughts and feelings.

Another "escapee" wrote: "I left after my stepfather beat me up. He was an alcoholic, and I had no tolerance for his lifestyle and I refused to be controlled by it." Although such narratives are self-classified as positive by the storytellers, they are examples of what I call "false positive" rites of passage. Such an assignment was made when the narrative suggested that the late adolescent's primary motivation for leaving home was in running away from something. To further illustrate this point with a narrative of one male student in this category: "I always wanted to get out of the house ever since I could remember; living in the house was beginning to be unbearable for me. . . . I didn't want to have anything to do with the family."

Despite such strong words, there is some evidence that some "escape" students set up similarly negative transferential relationships with peers at college, thus illuminating the false positive aspect of the ostensibly positive self-report. An example of this is found in the words of a male student: "I wanted to leave home because I had to get out of the house. But my three good friends here at school . . . are stifling me in [the same] way that I think friends back home did." Others claimed to have formed more positive relationships at college than they had experienced with those whom they were leaving behind. As one woman wrote:

> When I left home, I felt relieved to be away from my mother—we fought a lot. I felt guilty because she made me

> feel like I shouldn't be looking forward to leaving . . .
> my coach [at college] taught me what . . . commitment
> means and how to look in the mirror and say, "I did my
> best and that's all I could do" or face up and say, "I
> could have done more."

As illustrated by the example above, some students who begin
as false positives seem to end up more genuinely adjusted. The
following story, written by a female student, makes this point
clearly:

> I was very happy to leave home and come to the
> university. Living at home with my mother was starting
> to suffocate me. Since she married when she was 19
> years old, I feel she never fully matured. She never
> understood my need for independence and the need
> not to be supported by a man. . . . I relish the
> independence of living on my own.

Some Conclusions

We have examined the departure for college as one example
of many possible "personal rites of passage." In applying Van
Gennep's suggestion of individualized rites of passage, we have
highlighted a problem indigenous to our complex society, one
in which our youth often find no clear apprenticeships and no
clear mentors for learning how to become grown-up. This problem is complicated by frequently prolonged financial dependence on the family of origin.

A question that naturally evolves from such observations is,
How can we move closer, if not to uniform rites of passage, then
at least to a more generally positive experience of such individualized rites? And, how can we learn from those more homogeneous societies that prescribe clear rules for passage from childhood to adulthood without compromising precious cultural
diversity and technological advance?

As societies become more complex, they shift from common support of one clear rite of passage to greater personal freedom of choice for the individual. Our examples show that strong and positive family support may enable the adolescent to make best use of the freedom to choose and find his or her way through a personal rite of passage. When this family support is lacking, the process is much more difficult, and there are few social supports to aid the transition.

One alternative is to make more uniformly available some opportunities for peer communication on the subject of modern "initiation rites." Increased opportunities for "families of youth" to be trained in and practice peer facilitation skills might create an environment that nurtures empathic listening about those complex choices leading to adulthood. In this way we could offer our youth a supportive forum in which to discuss each other's personal passages without a sense of secrecy, aloneness, or diminished self-esteem as unwelcome concomitants to the process.

A Final Thought

We could as easily have studied the stories of those who had selected as their personal rites of passage their obtaining a driver's license, experiencing a first date, or graduating from high school. The principles and problems discussed here likely would be quite similar regardless of the particular modern-day rite we focused on. The question remains how we in the late 20th century may better help our youth know when their elders will welcome them as adults, and thus when they may regard themselves as having successfully negotiated the adolescent years.

Note

1. Over the past three decades, intriguing and important theories have been advanced to account for the pathway that connects adolescence and adult life. Some of these have emphasized the role of cognitive development, most particu-

larly the appearance of formal thought during the adolescent years (Elkind, 1968; Piaget, 1972); others have proposed related theories of moral development (Gilligan, 1984; Kohlberg, 1964); and still others have discussed conceptions of identity formation as bridges between the adolescent and adult years (Erikson, 1956; Josselson, 1973; Marcia, 1967). A rich companion literature discusses development during the college years and makes much use of the major theoretical paradigms cited above (Coburn & Treeger, 1988; Madison, 1966; Perry, 1968).

References

Adelson, J. (Ed.). (1980). *Handbook of adolescent psychology.* New York: John Wiley.

Barry, H., & Schlegel, A. (1980). Early childhood precursors of adolescent initiation rites. *Ethos, Journal of the Society for Psychological Anthropology, 8,* 132-146.

Bettelheim, B. (1962). *Symbolic wounds.* New York: Collier.

Blos, P. (1962). *On adolescence.* New York: Free Press.

Brown, J. (1969). Adolescent initiation rites among preliterate peoples. In R. Grinder (Ed.), *Studies in adolescence* (pp. 40-52). New York: Macmillan.

Chodorow, N. (1978). *The reproduction of mothering.* Berkeley: University of California Press.

Coburn, K., & Treeger, M. (1988). *Letting go.* Rochester, NY: Adler.

Conger, J. (1973). *Adolescence and youth.* New York: Harper & Row.

D'Andrea, V. J., & Salorey, P. (1983). *Peer couseling: Skills and perspectives.* Palo Alto, CA: Science & Behavior Books.

Douvan, E., & Adelson, J. (1966). *The adolescent experience.* New York: John Wiley.

Elkind, D. (1968). Cognitive development in adolescence. In J. Adams (Ed.), *Understanding adolescence* (pp. 128-158). Boston: Allyn & Bacon.

Erikson, E. (1956). The problem of ego identity. *Journal of the American Psychoanalytic Association, 4,* 56-121.

Fasick, F. (1988). Patterns of formal education in high school as rites of passage. *Adolescence, 13,* 457-468.

Gedo, J. (1984). *Psychoanalysis and its discontents.* New York: Guilford.

Gilligan, C. (1984). *In a different voice: Psychological theory and women's development.* Cambridge, MA: Harvard University Press.

Hatcher, S. (1989). Aspects of turmoil and self-containment in the adolescent psychotherapy patient. In E. Stern (Ed.), *The self-contained patient* (pp. 73-83). New York: Haworth.

Josselson, R. (1973). Psychodynamic aspects of identity formation in college women. *Journal of Youth and Adolescence, 2*(1), 3-52.

Kett, J. (1977). *Rites of passage.* New York: Basic Books.

Kiell, N. (1967). *The universal experience of adolescence.* Boston: Beacon.

Kohlberg, L. (1964). Development of moral character and moral ideology. In M. Hoffman (Ed.), *Review of child development* (Vol. 1, pp. 383-431). New York: Russell Sage.

Loughlin, E. (1979). Family rites of passage: A study of ritual and the school entry transition in five healthy families. *Dissertation Abstracts International, 48,* 1391-1392.

Madison, P. (1966). *Personality development in the college student.* Reading, MA: Addison-Wesley.

Marcia, J. (1967). Ego identity status: Relationship to change in self-esteem, "general maladjustment," and authoritarianism. *Journal of Personality, 35,* 118-123.

Mead, M. (1961). *Coming of age in Samoa.* New York: William Morrow. (Original work published 1928)

Offer, D. (1969). *The psychological world of the teen-ager: A study of normal adolescence.* New York: Basic Books.

Perry, W. (1968). *Forms of intellectual and ethical development in the college years: A scheme.* New York: Holt, Rinehart & Winston.

Piaget, J. (1972). Intellectual evolution from adolescence to adulthood. *Human Development, 15,* 1-12.

Quinn, W., Newfield, N., & Protinsky, H. (1985). Rites of passage in families with adolescents. *Family Process, 24,* 101-113.

Van Gennep, A. (1960). *The rites of passage* (M. Vizedon & G. Caffee, Trans.). Chicago: University of Chicago Press. (Original work published 1908)

Weiner, I. (1970). *Psychological disturbance in adolescence.* New York: John Wiley.

❦ 7 ❦

A Woman's Story

E Pluribus Unum

Jill F. Kealey McRae

The universe is made up of stories, not atoms.
Muriel Rukeyser

The following analysis draws on sources other than an interview with Louisa Rogers Alger. There exist in the Schlesinger Library, Radcliffe College, the *Alger Family Papers,* which were furnished by Louisa several years ago. They include an interview that her mother gave in the 1960s and also an account entitled *A Day in the Life of A.L.A.,* who was Louisa's aunt, Abby Langdon Alger.[1] I refer to them throughout, wherever they substantiate or otherwise illuminate aspects of Louisa under consideration at the time.

The fact that Louisa is not a run-of-the-mill subject has inclined me to adopt a broader perspective than is usual. It seemed that dealing with an extraordinary person called for extraordinary measures. To meet the situation sufficiently, I have developed, though tentatively, a hypothesis of my own concerning the ways story serves to reveal and construct identity, whether through anecdote or as folkhistory; as well I have incorporated Carolyn Heilbrun's analysis of the relationship women have with autobiography because it amplifies our understanding of how and why Louisa's story is told as it is.

Throughout the interpretation I have been at pains to place Louisa in a proper perspective, one that takes full account of the many forces that have shaped her identity. If nothing else, I hope I have explored, however modestly, a being about whom, alas, we know so very little:

> Biographers often find little overtly triumphant in the late years of a subject's life, once she has moved beyond the categories our available narratives have provided for women. Neither rocking on the porch, nor automatically offering her services as cook and housekeeper and child-watcher, nor awaiting another chapter in the heterosexual plot, the old woman must be glimpsed through all her disguises which seem to preclude her right to be called a woman. She may well for the first time be woman herself. (Heilbrun, 1988, p. 131)

I came to America because I live in times that recognize this nation as among the great. Those of us who inhabit the corners of the Empire once looked to Britain for the imprimatur that Oxford and Cambridge have stamped on generation after generation of colonial hopefuls. I am not of their number; if such it can be called, my quest is otherwise.

Gifted with so much boisterous history, America emanates a radiance for those farther from the mainstream; it has produced men and women who have held the world in a thrall. In contrast, and for all its vigor, Australia is a country that has chosen to exalt the maverick and the heller: "Waltzing Matilda" celebrates sheep stealing, and, in our meager catalogue of heroes, a bushranger hanged for murder is king. Founded as a Gulag, we have no Declaration of Independence, replete with cherished verities, to separate us from our genesis as a penal colony, and neither have we any statesmen of renown whose words have been for all humankind. Curious, speculative, I came here intending to encounter for myself the national enterprise that is America and the energy that has generated prominence on a scale unexampled in the modern era.

I began by looking in the phone book. Why not? Boston has been home to an impressive array of founding persons; one need look no farther than Harvard Yard to sense their substance; in creating this, the emblem of their ideals, they built to last.

On the trail of an interest in Native Americans, I had come across the work of a Bostonian named Abby Langdon Alger; *In Indian Tents* (1897) is a collection of Passamaquoddy and Penobscot tales. The book is aberrational because, alone among fin de siècle mythologies from New England, this contribution is from a woman. A mention in *Allbone's Critical Dictionary of English Literature* ascribes to her a modest list of accomplishments, translations in the main, though on closer examination one is surprised to discover a catchment of French, German, and Italian authors, even a Norwegian. At the very least, a superior facility with languages is indicated; add to this Penobscot, Passamaquoddy, and Romany, and you are looking at a woman educated beyond the conventions of her day.

Curious, I telephone the listed Algers and leave a message on answering machines but, when nobody responds, let the matter fall to the wayside. Then comes a call to say my number was mislaid, but yes, descendants of Abby Langdon are around, and do call Uncle Johnny, and so on and so forth.

The upshot is that 2 weeks later I find myself up by Dartmouth, seated before Louisa Rogers Alger, Radcliffe alumna (class of 1922), cousin once removed of Horatio and great-great-grandniece of President Zachary Taylor. Louisa is, she says, pleased to place her memories of Aunt Abby at my disposal, should I care to listen. And most certainly I do. This is the WASP ascendancy; at last I am to be face to face with that mythologized species, *an American of family.*

In the throes of setting up the interview, I ask Louisa to speak to me of her own life. Although it is on behalf of an interest in Abby Langdon that I make contact, it is out of curiosity about Louisa herself that I request an interview; without consenting to or declining this line of inquiry, she agrees to my visit.

History is often dark and vague concerning women, even those from recent eras. I intend the encounter with Louisa to provide a chance to sharpen the picture, to explore the dichotomous hierarchy of gender and class. In recent years theorists have forwarded the idea that women's accounts of their lives differ markedly from masculine self-disclosure not only in subject matter but also in form and structure. Where Louisa is concerned, it is my intention to tease out these differences, to ascertain those things in her usable past that reflect a particular sense of rhythm—that is, the less linear, more open-ended accretion of details and events that might reveal the truth of the moment if not the truth of fact. I must use every means at my disposal.

As we begin, I early decide to follow Louisa, rather than to lead. It is not merely her age that compels this deference. Born in one of the politer periods of history, when the 20th century ruled in name only, its beginnings overshadowed by that near-imperishable dowager, the 19th, Louisa is possessed of that hauteur that is the perquisite of her class; one might as well attempt frivolity with the Queen of England. If I choose not to regard this as an impediment, it is because I understand that Louisa is of an era and type not given to introspection in a large way, just as its rank and file do not favor the very modern notion that private life is something to be picked over by all and sundry. (Even my own grandmother, remote though she was from the Social Register—colonial version, circa 1900—thought it common to make the newspapers at all, and to be in the social pages plain vulgar.) Privacy is sacrosanct; it is the example to which Louisa still attends, with a cast of mind bordering on reverence:

> One thing I can tell you about her [Abby Langdon's]
> personal life . . . *I wonder if I'm betraying a*
> *confidence* [italics added] . . . I found a little diary of
> hers, and I had it in my room in Annapolis, and I looked
> at it and it had just a few notes here and there, but one
> very important note which I'll tell you. And my mother
> came and took it away. She said, "That's not for you." I

think she thought it was private with Aunt Abby, but
there was one note on a certain date. "This day my
darling mother died and left me alone in the world."

Let it not be said that Louisa has me overawed, however; if I
pay my dues, it is because to do otherwise would plunge me into
the depths of indecorum. In any case, whether Louisa elects to
share with me details of her own life, I reason that they are
bound to feature, however obliquely; caught in the act of scor-
ing glimpses into a vanished world, I am not so much the voyeur
as to lose sight of my quarry or to believe my expectations will
not be allowed into play, eventually.

And what, you ask, does Louisa look like? There's a dowager
hump, yes, though I suppose that is in the cards at 93, and some
ordinary old lady troubles with arthritis. The skin, creamy and
unlined, is regally wattled (*very badly* I want to ask for some
beauty tips). For all their dimsightedness, the eyes are clear and
their gaze direct. A flirty twinkle whenever there's a joke about.
Hair bobbed, thickish, and gray. The features are pert; a looker
in her palmier days, let me surmise. Never married (Papa died a
bleeder, is there a rogue gene?). Louisa is elegant in a pleated
skirt of charcoal wool, creamy blouse, and sage cardigan. A ring
or two. Uses a walking frame; exercises daily. No trace of age in
her voice. Mother and sister lived to be 95.

And what does Louisa make of me? To be sure, achieving 93
years must focus one's mind on endings quite wonderfully, so
the cultivation of new friends would hold few attractions. Suffice it to say that ours is a conjunction founded on opportunism;
I am edged on by love of a good story, Louisa by someone to tell
it to, which is not to say that we are either of us undiscriminat-
ing. Whereas I want a tale ever marvelous, Louisa wants an
audience up to the task. I have other agendas to pursue, of
course, to which we shall come duly.

"Lincoln," she announces, "will be left until after lunch." By
this stratagem, Louisa reveals an investment in her audience qua
audience, and I am in her capture because, of course, I cannot
forget that it is Lincoln who anchored me in this country.

Washington is where I began, the first days there a confusion of people and events. "It's no good," I said to my friend. "I cannot feel as though I am *in* America—too much like home, except the trees and accents are wrong. Take me to Lincoln." It is such a long fall to his feet, to where I planted myself underneath that face that showed to me a century-old fatigue and sadness. Overwhelmed, I wept, untidy and very public sobs that startled the Japanese tourists and myself. My eyes became American that day.

But I digress. All too few of us are destined to achieve almost a century of living with our wits and organs in sound repair. Until a year ago, Louisa lived alone in Cambridge, though even in the rural retirement complex that is her present home, independence is far from extinguished and metropolitan standards are insistently maintained: "Old as we are here, there are lots of opportunities for volunteer work." Louisa putters about on an electric vehicle that transports her hither and yon, takes *The New York Times* (large print edition), and advises one to phone during the evening because she is about her business during the day.

Louisa is purposeful. As a concession to her failing sight, she knits more simply now, squares of a thick skein joined up to make afghans for the needy, on whose behalf she has mobilized what appears to be an army of knitters. Industry of this order bespeaks a lifetime's habit:

> For many years I worked in the Quaker clothing center at the Cambridge Friends Meeting, and when I came here I was still knitting . . . those squares are not knitted by me but put together by me. . . . It's a beautiful gift . . . so we have turned in 31, no, 41 afghans to local organizations where they're needed. It's quite a satisfaction. . . .

> I remember during the war, the Second World War, I would spend my summer vacations with my Navy family in Newport . . . and I served as a volunteer a couple of days a week in the delivery wing of the maternity part of the big hospital there . . . and my job was to sit and sew and mend things and thread beads for necklaces.

With a sure sense of her own rank, Louisa is doing now as she has always done, setting aside a portion of her time and energy for the common weal. And in such rituals we recognize the Puritan ethic at work, part of which is disposed to civic mindedness and its concomitants. More generative than *good works,* I would claim it to be a manifestation of *e pluribus unum,* but more of this later. Indeed there is ample evidence that Louisa has caught the habit of service from elsewhere, from the aunt who died 90 years ago:

> Aunt Abby was very much interested in the Italian immigrants. She would go to their tenements, and my mother told me, "I said Abby, why do you do that? Go up all those steps, that's very fatiguing." And Aunt Abby said to her, "If I don't go on payday, the rent is not there the next day." And she took money from them and established savings accounts for them and she taught them what a savings account was and she put the money in for them. . . . In those days the Italians had fruit barrels. The cart would be about perhaps that square . . . and the man would push it and he'd sell his fruit. They had to have licenses, and Aunt Abby would help them [the men] get licenses.

Abby Langdon herself has left us an account of a day in her life. Here we have *caritas* with its sleeves rolled up, in its matter-of-factness a resolve from which any grudgingness or the taint of the self-righteous is signally absent. It is worth noting that Abby Langdon was not in the business of handouts; it was thrift she was encouraging, and legitimate business enterprise, schemes that have had their impact. A hundred years later, her niece is able to report that Boston is "the first American city to have professional social services, and the reason they did that was that the ladies of Boston used to do things."

The compass of Abby Langdon's world may seem overly invested in others; these days it is common to ascribe to do-goodishness motives that are less than noble, but the inventory

of tasks and routines is a far cry from cold charity. On the
evidence of these crowded few hours in the middle of her day,
one is left with the impression of rigor and reward, of connection and of caring:

10.30 am

To Mrs Colorusso, 54 Prince Street, took savings (10
cents) & Mrs Bevilaqua's (5 cents) and began to teach
Narinccia (7) and Philomena (4) to sew patch work
which it had taken all my leisure moments for three
days to prepare. Had to wait while Narinccia sent out to
buy a thimble for a cent, although she promised last
week to have it ready. Mrs C. begged me to send the
dispensary doctor for Vicenzo (10 months) who has
convulsions.

10.50 am

Went to Eames, apothecary, corner of Hanover and
Carter Sts, to leave the order, found Dr Henry Jackson
would not be there again till Monday, but moved by my
representations, the man told me that the doctor had to
call at 20, 64 and 116 Prince Street, all up two flights,
and I might catch him at one of these places. Very hot
and hurried, but went. At first place met two most
common-looking men on the stairs, whom I took for
lodgers, but on getting up stairs, found it was the
doctor and his friend, ran after them but they had
disappeared. To other places, in vain. At one a German
woman with a swarm of dirty naked children insisted
on thinking I was the doctor and telling me her woes
(in German). Sympathized, told her the baby was
teething and advised as well as I could. Left a note in
case the doctor called.

11.15 am

Back to Hanover Street, took a car to Scollay Square and
another to 225 Marlborough Street.

11.45-1.00

Read Ruskin's *Fors Clavigera* to Mrs Blake, and wrote a
note to Dr Jackson asking him to call at 54 Prince Street
today if possible.

9.30 pm

Home and bed, reflecting that Mrs Colorusso would
never know what a chase I had for the doctor, who
would probably never go there and she will think that I
forgot all about the baby's convulsions. (*A Day in the
Life of A.L.A.*)

Is it open to accusations of lowering the feminist colors?
Abby Langdon's talents as a translator, linguist, and ethnographer were relegated to the sidelines and serving others to the
fore. Her mother died early in the 1880s, when Abby Langdon
was 30 or so; thereafter she dedicated herself to attending her
father, a prominent Bostonian minister, Mason, orientalist, theo-
logian, card-carrying Abolitionist, tractarian, orator, literary critic,
and occasional writer. Papa died in 1905, Abby Langdon 3
months later. We have little but *A Day in the Life of A.L.A.* and
Louisa's reminiscences to judge her on, though there is her
literary output, which is, it must be said, as much as many
writers achieve in a lifetime, and Abby Langdon's covers 30 years
only. Louisa reports that as her schemes prospered, so did she:

> She made a good deal of money out of her books I
> guess, and Mama told me that Aunt Abby had said to
> her, with annoyance, that if she hadn't listened to her
> brother Arthur's advice on investment that she would
> have had a lot more than she did.

Abby Langdon's scrapbooks (*Alger Family Papers*), which
are collections of her reviews, occasional pieces, and a series on
refined pastimes for young ladies (published in the *Boston
Globe*–her embroidery was a local sensation), do not indicate a
life that is stalled and frustrated, merely one that is circumscribed

by the conventions of the age. Indeed, viewed from a distance, Abby Langdon seems animated by a talent for industry and enjoyment rather than sacrifice or a compulsion to please; she carved for herself a niche as a competent careerist in times notoriously ungenerous to the breed, full-time or part.

I have a friend in Cambridge, one of the brahminical Cabots, who sets out in fair weather and foul to clean up the neighborhood. Representing the antithesis of those who are devoid of responsibility because their ties to any one place are so attenuated, collecting litter is one of the ways she serves the community. My friend has supported Boston opera for half a century, the American Repertory Theater, the ballet, and so on, patronage a deal costlier than trash collecting, as well as participating in the Host Family Program that Harvard runs for its overseas students (how we met). These are not mere gestures, but ingrained lifetime habits based on the postulates of belief. I mention this because it taps a hidden vein of sameness connecting Louisa's knitting-bees and Abby Langdon's penny-scouting rounds among her unlettered tenement dwellers, to a belief that service, like virtue, is its own reward. It is born of the dogma of secular enlightenment. Neither to be advertised nor applauded, it is part of the ledger of daily work, regardless of one's station; "It's quite a satisfaction," reminds Louisa, and this is also, is it not?, the kind of ethic we recognize as a cornerstone of the Puritan legacy. My friend is part of a line that stretches unbroken through Louisa's generation, Abby Langdon's, and her mother's, and so on, back to Plymouth.

Louisa's runabout comes equipped with a basket on the handlebars, where a half dozen or so pennies jingle about (we are off to lunch, and I must stride out to keep abreast). "These are for Amanda," explains Louisa, "donated by my kind friends here towards her education. Amanda is 9 months old. I have started a fund for her college years." I do hope I look impressed. Only later does it occur to me how much Louisa's thrift subscribes to the popular view of Horatio Alger. Previous to our meeting, I asked whether he were a relation. "Yes. Grandfather's cousin, though we in the family do not talk much of him." The embodiment of a quintessential American dream, a Horatio Alger is he who by sheer dint of effort prevails, be he ever so humble.[2] The pennies assume a larger significance.

Without sentimentalizing the past or attributing to it any special valor, it serves us usefully as a framework in which to couch the values and habits of women such as Louisa, at the same time drawing to our attention the role, largely unapplauded, they have played in upholding and transmitting the received secular orthodoxies central to American life.

Perhaps it is well to pause here to give time and consideration to these orthodoxies per se, with a view to apprehending them in relation to ethics as a governing idea in society. "Ethical thought consists of the systematic examination of relations of human beings to each other, the conceptions, interests, and ideals from which human ways of treating one another spring, and the system of value on which such ends of life are based." These words of Isaiah Berlin (1988) commend the notion of a code of conduct (an individual's ethical map) with conceptions, interests, and ideals as constituents (*conduct,* by the way, can be defined as human actions carrying value and responsibility). In spirit the Puritan ethic is founded on the inventory of homely virtues enshrined in such teachings as the Sermon on the Mount; at its best and broadest, it values courage, thrift, religiosity, truthfulness, sobriety, self-reliance, forbearingness, honest labor, and the sacramentalization of private property; at its narrowest and most pejorative, it espouses a reverence for work that borders on the fanatical, is hypocritical, rigid, priggish, and self-righteous. Fundamental to the connection between Puritan ethic and conduct is a notion of personal and civic responsibility within the inclusive terrain of community, to which end are forwarded the desiderata of dignity, decency, and freedom. That these truths are held to be inalienable is nowhere more evident than in the Declaration of Independence. Exclusively and suggestively American, ratified by statute, the fixed moral universe of the Pilgrim Forebears is fundamental to the nation they began.

Most certainly it is germane to the rank and file of Louisa's gender and class, who more than any other are its heirs. Legitimized by time, these values may never be postulated as such, but in sum and substance, they are an indelible impress informing conduct, shaping the character and expectations of social relationships, including a belief in *e pluribus unum*. We are obliged to give these values due consideration in our efforts to understand the severity with which Louisa stays subject to the world they represent. Indeed her remarks do not notice any other.

Before we part company, Louisa tells of Helen Keller (Radcliffe, class of 1902):

> Bernice and I (Cronkhite, that is) wrote the words that
> are in Braille on the garden wall of the Graduate Center.
> It is a memorial for Ann Sullivan. As I walked with
> Helen around the garden on the day she came to visit, I
> said to her, "You have given us the legacy of your great
> courage."

Here we have the unlabored rightness of the plainspoken. What more could any of us have said to Helen? More pointedly, Louisa's anecdotes of Helen Keller strike me with their difference; in every instance it is Helen, and not Louisa, who stands revealed. Very properly, it is Helen she wants me to know, and I do, because something of Helen's great courage transmits itself. I am moved to wonder how a man would handle such stories, whether he would keep his distance, as it were. Louisa is one for women; it is women who are the stanchions of what is remarkable and remarked upon throughout this account; it is they who are memorable. I shall return in a moment to this very issue.

Of course, things about the interior woman invite endless speculation. How did Louisa encounter life as a single woman during times notorious for disparaging this state? What importance have her women friends had? How frankly has she dealt with misogyny? What is it like to have half your life to get on with after your 50th birthday, and, luminously sane yourself, to watch one's flock of friends lose their wits? And what of the things that have held her life together?

Displaying her mettle, Louisa is adroit at keeping this private self beyond my reach: "Oh look, let's deal with Aunt Abby. Don't deal with me," she cautions, and means it. Having elected to be interviewed, she treads a tactful line between demonstrating a responsibility to scholarship (a respectable arena, self-evidently worthy) and revelations that are of personal, rather than historical, interest. Watching her observe the separation of these domains is not without its excitement. Louisa is not gossipy, she goes in for decorum instead, but a sense of *noblesse oblige* tugs away at her.

Over lunch, when Louisa asks me about myself, she means *family;* quite deliberately I choose to tell of a convict past attached to one of my great-grandmothers, even though it is a tenuous connection at best (they say her brother was a felon). Louisa loses interest immediately. As it happens, I have a raft of exotic progenitors, but parading them is not something I do on command, perhaps because (unlike Louisa) of belonging to a people who are not improved by an escutcheon over the mantlepiece. Parenthetically, a friend has chastised me for this niggardly stand, saying that my raft of exotica might have served to interest. But. I am the organ-grinder, not the monkey.

Insofar as this aspect of Louisa bespeaks the primacy of the *Mayflower* mob and its indelible cachet, plus, if you please, a lineage that includes Robert the Bruce, it may also be seen as the camouflage for a concept of self-narrative that is, at base, impoverished. Heilbrun (1988) poignantly alerts us to the way women, deprived of a paradigm for the self-told story that is unique to their gender, either model theirs on the archetypal male version that, it need not be said, "typically embodies his strength," or that:

> fail directly to emphasize their own importance, though writing in a genre that implies self-assertion and self-display. . . . And in all of them the pain of lives is, like the successes, muted, as though the women were certain of nothing but the necessity of denying both accomplishment and suffering . . . the self-discovery of female identity seems to acknowledge the real presence

of another consciousness, and the disclosure of female self
is linked to the identification of some "other." . . . Well
into the twentieth century, it continued to be impossible
for women to admit into their autobiographical narratives
the claim of achievement, the admission of ambition, the
recognition that accomplishment was neither luck nor the
result of the efforts or generosity of others. (Heilbrun,
1988, pp. 22-24)

In speaking of her life, Louisa confirms Heilbrun in every
respect. That she is invested in the *other,* being *family,* lineage,
and men of derring-do, is an inescapable conclusion. It may be
women who have been the lodestars in her firmament (Aunt
Abby, Mama, and Grandmama aside, the *Alger Family Papers*
include copious correspondence with notable women intellec-
tuals), but it is *men* who are the confidants of princes and
presidents, *men* who are the cynosures of ambition and strength,
whose careers are forwarded as the proper measure of achievement. Vigorously committed to hiding her own light under a
bushel, Louisa is almost dismissive of herself as a teacher and a
scholar. I have troubled to browse through the wad of essays she
wrote during her Radcliffe days, to find in them a fine, able
intelligence and breadth of scholarship that embraces two classical languages and one modern European. She allows herself to
applaud Aunt Abby's achievements, but cannot her own:

My mother, who was devoted to Aunt Abby, said that Aunt
Abby spoke 12 languages. . . . My mother's dealing with
numbers was very poor, so I suspect the 12. I'm sure that
there were several and that Aunt Abby was interested in
Romany. . . . Aunt Abby was very much interested in the
Indians who came to her house there in Maine. . . . She
understood their vocabulary and recorded it and listened
to their stories. . . . Somewhere in the 1880s or possibly
the 1890s, the premier association of intellectual people,
the American Academy of Arts and Letters, something like
that . . . invited Aunt Abby to come and speak to them
about her Indian vocabulary.

Her father spontaneously read at 4, yet the early manifestation of her own numeric talent (the word is precise), which led to tutoring young Charlie-from-across-the-street, is reduced to a charming anecdote:

> But I remember, when I was about 10, the little boy Charlie . . . was maybe 7, and Mama said to me one day, "What are you doing with Charlie?" "Nothing." "Something to do with numbers?" "Well, Charlie wants to know the answers to the multiplication tables, and I've been telling him." . . . "Mrs. Milkwater says you must stop doing that or Charlie will have brain fever." . . . I certainly walked out of that room saying to myself, "He knows them all anyway now."

I know from the *Family Papers* that Louisa was engaged as mathematics consultant to a reputable encyclopedia publisher for a decade or so. The career that Louisa has couched in terms pragmatic and terse belies the success and pleasure it brought her; according to Louisa, opportunities opened up because others made it so, with her abilities playing no part of consequence:

> But my father died when I was 11, and very soon I realized we didn't have as much money as before, and it became clear to me that I was going to have to support myself, and in those days the only things that a lady could do—she could run a boarding house or she could teach or she could be the poor cousin who lived with the family and scrubbed. . . . Not one of those occupations appealed to me . . . so I made up my mind I would have to have an education. This meant that I would be going to boarding school.
>
> I remember the first interview because I said cheerfully to the Prefect of Studies . . . "I intend to go to college." "Oh, but we don't prepare for college." "Well," I said, "you teach Latin and mathematics?" "Yes." . . . "I will take care of it." . . . Well, I passed the necessary exams. . . .

> When I was in college, there was a very gifted teacher
> . . . she laid her eye on me and later on sent me a letter
> . . . offering me a job. . . . I was to be apprenticed to
> Dorothy Jones, and I found out that she was a
> remarkable teacher. So that was how I learned to
> teach. . . . The next year, somebody else in the faculty
> dropped out, and Frances had the courage to put me in
> charge of the middle school.

And though never one to linger on her pain, the 30 classics she termited through at 11 are overshadowed by a dying Papa:

> He gave me books to read. . . . I went to him once, and
> I remember how his shoulders looked and know now
> that he was going to die within 2 or 3 months. Anyway,
> I went to him and said, "Papa, I haven't anything to
> read." He looked at me and put down his pen and said,
> "Come with me," and took me to a bookcase. . . .
> Anyway, he went and he ran his finger along a set. . . .
> "Begin with this one." It was Dumas, and I was like a
> termite. I went right through from one end to the
> other. . . . I was bitterly upset when I discovered that
> number 30 was missing.

What the Schlesinger collection reveals is a woman who has cared deeply and consistently for others, who has been a loyal, valued friend, sometimes to persons as known as those courted by the Alger men, those hallowed others who are sashayed about, caught in the limelight because evidently it is beyond Louisa to take what is her due or to accord her losses their proper voice.

Hidden in all of this restraint is the lonely little figure who watched as her Papa bled slowly to death and who, like the missing 30th volume, remains a mystery. "He died when I was 11," Louisa says, not once but several times, until it becomes a refrain. There are no amusing anecdotes about Papa because Papa never outlived her adoration. Near to a montage of Great-Grandpapa Meigs, his photograph ornaments the wall, eternally handsome and splendid in Naval togs. "The relation with the father will be less complex, clearer in its emotions and desires, partaking less of either terrible pity or binding love" (Heilbrun, 1988, p. 27).

But if the father dies before a daughter has time to see him as fallible, then what? You idealize his memory with an ecstatic's blind fervor because no supplementary vision of him exists. And here a demurrer must be added: Because my real father died when I was 4, I know too much about the business of loving dead fathers to make objective sense of Louisa's predicament. As in the matter of parading my lineage, I must declare my hand as one aware that my own issues are intruding, regrettably to no useful end.

Rather than focus on what Louisa cannot comfortably make explicit, I must work with what she can, and that is substantial. Although the remainder of my analysis will concern itself with story as a means of organizing experience and of verifying identity, it has touched already on issues of identity, of Louisa *as a female narrator,* as well as those aspects of her personality and character that reflect the American ethos at large and that, in its finer moments, has given rise to what is remarkable. On another occasion I wrote:

> It is story which has linked the continents and the ages; wherever people have walked, stories have gone with them. Alone among the animals, these story-makers have thus imposed unanimity upon chaos and the divergent. Our very nature is predisposed to story, for here all is invented and explained. Story is that medium by which we know ourselves.

As a means of objectifying existence, the creation of narrative must rank among the earliest expressions of the psyche. We need look no further than the cave paintings of Spain to see the beginnings of story as a pictorial. Like the bison of Altamira, *story is not the experience itself, but a representation of it.* For reasons that we must assume drew as much on need as on whimsy, no sooner had the evolutionary mills produced *Homo sapiens,* the ape who walked and talked, than this creature used language to place him- or herself *at a distance from experience.* I have always been quietly amazed by the daring of this application of intelligence; where others have admired our progenitors as toolmakers, I own I am captivated by them as storymakers and artists. Adaptive in essence and in effect, the persistence of the pictorial and of narrative is such that now we recognize both as means of organizing experience. It behooves us to remember that a culture has never existed that did not express itself in story and in art.

One need only place oneself at a remove from Western civilization, as I have done, to understand how inextricably story and identity, whether individual or tribal, have ever been companions. It has been my privilege to spend time with the Warlpiri Aborigines in the Tanami Desert of northern Australia. The Warlpiri are a people whose ceremonial life has been preserved largely by virtue of remoteness and the hostility of their environment (nobody else has wanted to live there). Maintaining traditional lifeways that have gone virtually uninterrupted for some 80,000 years, they are a living stone age culture. My interest in storymaking took me out into the Tanami with the women, who gave me tales from the *Jukurrpa,* or Dreaming. It is in the Tanami I learn that the Dreaming is a living mythology, a generative body of spiritual belief, story, and law that is continuous in its growth, even now being added to.

An important feature of the Dreaming is that it is founded in real events. Of course, over time the names of protagonists may drop away or be subsumed by the generic "my ancestor," locations may become generalized, and the story attached to some mythological creature, but the sense of connection to, and immediacy with, the past is maintained through story. Of endings that have no calculated finality, every story has a hard-and-fast beginning because it must be prefaced by a statement of ownership: "This story is from my father's father" (or it may come from the matriline); only those to whom the story belongs may tell it. Here we have genealogy as a mnemonic, as a means of accessing not only systems of social relations but also the stories that validate these structures. In other words, for every tribal Aborigine, the Dreaming provides a means of recording and mirroring the individual and the society:

> *Mordja Amari Boaradja*
> *Ngu Borngga Amari Mordja.*
> Forgotten I lost Dreaming
> Country I left forgotten lost. (literal translation)
> Those who lose their Dreaming are lost. (paraphrase)
>   (McRae, 1991, p. 64)

I took from my experiences with the Warlpiri an understanding of Warlpiri women as capable sustainers of ritual, independent of men. Storytelling, a ritual activity, is one way the women strive to keep the country around Lajamanu productive, in a fertile state, nourished, and the people who live there harmonious. Although men and women are involved jointly in maintaining country, the significance of women's role in this deserves our closest scrutiny.

I believe that the importance of Warlpiri women as cultural agents has been underreported and undervalued. Among them, one has confirmed again and again the notion that they have independence and autonomy in both ritual and secular realms. Nor is their broader role in society a submissive one, confined to childraising and domestic concerns. While acknowledging their economic usefulness, many ethnographers would have us believe that the power base of women is decidedly limited, a conviction arrived at, one assumes, because for the most part it is men who have written about Aboriginal society. One has only to read the few women who have made contributions to the study of Aborigines to appreciate the extent to which the views of male ethnographers have dominated. The indigenous men and women of central Australia inhabit largely separate worlds, with substantially independent economic and ritual lives; corresponding to this separation is a reluctance on the part of both sexes to share information, particularly that which is regarded as significantly the domain of the other, with a member of the opposite sex. In terms of the importance of this division to ethnographic studies, it has meant that women from this region would communicate little, and possibly nothing at all, to a male ethnographer. Of course, until recently, this reticence has not prevented these scholars from forwarding male ritual activity as representative. Perhaps it should come as no surprise that, by and large, Aboriginal women share with their Western counterparts an enforced silence, an exclusion from recorded accounts.

It occurs to me that the distance separating the Lajamanu women from their Boston sisters is not as great as is at first apparent. Both groups are fearful of discontinuity, both conscripted by tradition and the common good. If ever a group dedicated its considerable talents to keeping the past and the present meshed and vital, to preserving intact lineage and sundry other manifestations of cultural inheritance, it is the women of Lajamanu.

Narrative comes in many forms, and the saturation of the media is so inevitably a part of life that it seems as ordinary to us as breathing. Personal narrative, or one's life story, unless it finds expression in diaries or autobiography, is similarly persistent, though a deal less accessible. We strive to give our lives coherence not only in the stories we tell about ourselves but also in the way we tell them. Each of us has a private store, a mythology that operates much as the *Jukurrpa;* it is generative and continuous, and we do not cease adding to it for as long as we live. Like the Warlpiri, and like Louisa, it is in the stories we tell about ourselves and our "tribe," be it family or community, that we seek to unite the separate domains of private and public self, the sacred and the profane, past and present, our feelings and thoughts, as well as to bring into consciousness all of those many things, unknowable but insistent, of which the self is, in part, constructed. Storymaking presents a genuinely clarifying means of pursuing these connections. When the ability to compose narratives is damaged by neurosis and other psychopathological phenomena, or by neurological disorders, such that our ability to define and redefine ourselves atrophies or is marred by confusion and neglect, we understand immediately that the self has been impoverished in a fundamental way.

This poverty I know firsthand because I come from a family whose manifest destiny has been located at the bottom of a whisky bottle. Having one parent an alcoholic is unfortunate, but having two is *un vraie catastrophe.* Recently I have been compelled to bear witness as my mother's brain is eaten alive by alcoholic dementia. Long-term memory has permitted her visitable past to live on, but now that it is dying off, there is a silence she more and more retreats to. Obscurely ashamed, she is a woman no longer able to salvage the self because she cannot remember the stories that might retrieve it. Hers is a terrible decline into anonymity.

Psychotherapy is another dimension of story. Having just emerged from a longish bout of psychotherapy, it has occurred to me that it was through shaping my life into a narrative that the levels of interacting complexity, the contradictions, the events that otherwise lay too deep for exhumation or self-recognition, came together once and for all to be acknowledged as part of the one account. It is not just that someone was there to hear it through to the utter last word, but *the act of telling was itself a healing thing to do.* Memory is where the self is captive, specialized, intense, and unamenable to any disposition but its own. Viewed in this light, personal narrative is a source of empowerment because, in shaping it, one is able to acknowledge the self who stands revealed and to benefit one's sense of identity from this congruence. If identity is the opposite of anonymity, and if identity is strengthened through the self-narrative, then *telling one's story is a means of becoming, just as much as is having a story to tell.*

I hope to show that this procedure serves us well as a vantage point in understanding Louisa and, in particular, her sense of who she is. When her interview is read at a sitting, and read again, the way Louisa is invested in her stories is as significant as their focus.

We sense that, in telling of her family, Louisa is speaking of herself; she has projected onto them not only the values and traditions that have upheld her but also her sense of identity. A case in point is the following extract:

> So my father went into the Naval Academy and became the leading expert on ballistics in the Navy. When I sponsored a ship named after him, the Navy Department sent along a young lieutenant, and he said to me, "Did you know what your father's work was?" I said, "No, my father died when I was 11, and I don't really know." He thought, and he said, "At the beginning of the First World War, the English, the French, and the Germans were astounded at the accuracy of American Naval gunfire. That was your father's work." And he didn't live long, died in his early 50s. Now my parents were married in 1891. In 1892 along came my sister Mary, in '94 my brother Philip, in '96 my brother Mont, and then in those summers . . . my father had transferred from the line in the Navy, regular Navy, into . . . the corps of professors of mathematics.

Father is uttered here five times, *brother* twice, and *sister* once. Familial relationship is rubric and matrix both, as clearly as if Louisa were saying to us, "I am them, and they are me." By this means she connects the past and the present, and also her public and private selves. Louisa could not join the Navy, but she did the next best thing in sponsoring a ship that bears her father's name. It is a commemorative act above the ordinary, yet she did not attend the ceremony of commission; though the *Alger Family Papers* have letters of invitation from the Navy (1967; Louisa was then in beginning old age) and also a medal struck for the occasion, it was left to nephew Johnny to do the honors.

In addition, Papa was a mathematician, a field in which Louisa herself has excelled. Has she adored him more than can be said, her grief gone so unresolved as to blur the distinction between her identity and his? I think these are the conjectures we are left with. Louisa's feelings about Papa, her past and present, her public and private selves, are captioned in this excerpt. Complex and even contradictory (why didn't she attend the commission ceremony?), they indicate a stratum of grief and loss that may never have been healthily confronted. And although this story and the way Louisa has shaped its elements is perhaps prompted by a desire, albeit unconscious, to reconcile complex feelings and events, the result is disturbing for the extent to which it raises more questions than it answers.

And like the Warlpiri, though with pedantic exactitude, Louisa retrieves people through their genealogy:

> She was the daughter of William Alger, a Unitarian minister well known in his day. They said that he could fill Tremont Temple when he preached. There were a lot of children. I think Aunt Abby must have been the oldest, and then there was Arthur, who became a judge; Henry was accepted at Harvard and died before he got there of typhoid fever: and then there was William, who became a Consul for this country in Central America; and then there was my father, and apparently Mrs. William Alger was not well after the birth of my father, Philip.

Whoever Abby Langdon was in private is left in abeyance; instead she is obscured by a confusing caravan of siblings of the first rank. So much is this retrieval a trait of Louisa's, we are obliged to see it as illustrative. Tribal genealogies operate as mnemonics and as a record of kinship moieties in preliterate societies, but that hardly describes the Algers of Boston. Perhaps the explanation runs along these lines: Louisa is unable, or unwilling, to attribute individuality except within the matrix of the familial. We must ask ourselves whether that is also the way she sees herself. Certainly, in choosing to present Aunt Abby thusly, Louisa seems to subscribe to this view. In providing a world of reference rather than of reason, if story reflects the social ascription of identity, we are left to assume that, for the Algers, identity is essentially corporate in nature. I think we must assume also that, far from regarding this as a diminution of Aunt Abby, Louisa would believe it to be empowering. In this family the process of becoming is inextricably a corporate enterprise; identity is derived from the congruence achieved by individuals perceiving themselves as inseparable from the many.

For most it means a great deal that their lives will have a resonance beyond the here and now; if in no other way, we are immortalized in the memories of those who are our friends and neighbors, kith and kin. There is such a thing as family lore, a body of oral literature handed down the generations while ever it has meaning and significance for the living. Mostly it comes to us in *anecdote* ("a short account of an amusing or interesting event, often connected with a particular person" [ML, from Gk: things unpublished] *Macquarie Dictionary,* 1982). Understanding it as a sensible activity and without effort or qualm, we are accustomed to knitting these fragments until they provide us rotundity, making what we will of the gaps (the lacunae that are themselves telling, as we have seen already), those many things that are left in estrangement because that is the way of an oral tradition. And like the Warlpiri, we hold no particular brief for a calculated finality. Often reckless of the details, neither do we care when certain errors of fact creep in. It seems neither a strain nor unusual to be composing our picture of others over many years and episodes: Constantly being trued up, identity is not all-of-piece, and I daresay hardly ever are we.

"History is bunk!" cried Henry Ford. Scholarly in domain and factual in purpose, history concentrates on a linear representation of events. There is another kind however, with which poor Henry might have felt more at home. Charles Hudson has defined *folkhistory* as "the historical beliefs of other societies and cultures" (Hudson, 1966, p. 53). It is worth striving to understand the philosophy that informs this genre. The 18th-century German thinker Johann Herder tells us that every society has:

> its own center of gravity, which differs from that of others. If . . . we are to understand . . . the ways in which men live, think, feel, speak to one another, the

> clothes they wear, the songs they sing, the goods they worship, the food they eat, the assumptions, customs, habits which are intrinsic to them—it is that which creates communities, each of which has its own "life-style." . . . Members of one culture can, by the force of imaginative insight, understand the values, the ideals, the forms of life of another culture or society, even those remote in time and space . . . if they open their minds sufficiently they can grasp how one might be a full human being, with whom one could communicate, and at the same time live in the light of values different from one's own. (Berlin, 1988, p. 14)

Composed of narratives that are for the most part shunned by historians for being imprecise (and for whom *methodology* means the simplifying certitudes of fact), folkhistory is a form of orality that relies on naught but a capacious memory to transmit the atmosphere, texture, character, and flavor of particular social enclaves *at the time of first telling*. Rather than instruct us on the specifics of beliefs, folkhistory places them within a story, or anecdote, much as a parable is suited to a moral theme. A difference of folkhistory is that its contents are selected intuitively and impressionistically, without any particular regard for verification outside itself. When we talk of the assassination of Kennedy, for example, we are more likely to give an account of where we were at the time, or the seismic shock it brought us, and to leave out our opinions of assassination as a premeditated evil, although that is what our story demonstrates. Rather than situate it exactly in this year or that, we are inclined to donate it to the forever of here and now. Folkhistory tends to ignore linear time in favor of synchronistic time, wherein it is generalized and subsumed as the past; this placement endows it with no particular remoteness because we will always exercise the wit and wisdom of the raconteur, who cannot resist the immediacy of today.

Both Louisa's interview and her mother's are folkhistory, insofar as beliefs and attitudes of their times are represented. Here, for example, we have Louisa's mother's account of the beginning of the Civil War:

Now when Lincoln came in . . . (His first public appearance in Washington was also at St. John's Church there on Franklin Square and my mother was there on that occasion too.) . . . She was sitting at a pew with my father, everybody was on tenterhooks—the President was somewhere—that side door on H Street opened and in came a remarkable-looking man—extraordinary height, carrying in his hand that queer stovepipe hat he used to carry; immense feet, immense shoes, and she said on his face was an inexpressible, tragic sadness, with wonderful eyes, great shaggy brows, great gravity, accompanied by the Secretary of State, Seward, who took him up to the Secretary of State's seat which then, in those days, was at the end of the chancel. . . . Dr. Pine was in the middle of his sermon, and a soldier came in and gave a letter to Secretary Stanton and another man came in and gave a letter to the Secretary of the Navy, and they got up and walked slowly out, followed by their wives. . . . Dr. Pine said, "The blow has fallen. That of which we have all been apprehensive has happened. The sermon is closed, the congregation dismissed."

They went out there on that great brick pavement next to Lafayette Square. They all fluttered out there . . . and there she saw for the first time the animosities of the two different philosophies. Mrs. Robert E. Lee, who had been a lifelong friend of my grandmother's, my grandmother spoke to her cordially, she looked at her haughtily and cut her dead . . . face after face froze as people passed each other without speaking who had known each other all their lives. That was the beginning.

The picture is so colorfully alive that it seems a shame to complicate it. Louisa's mother's story is remarkable for the ease with which it allows us to make sense of the occasion *in her terms,* as someone who signally represents the mores of her society, class, and gender, while at the same time sacrificing nothing of immediacy. A hinterland of antagonism and conflict that lived on to tear this nation apart is demonstrated by the expedient of reducing it to the anecdote of Mrs. Robert E. Lee, taking its flavor and color from the frozen faces of the congregation; moreover, the account is particularized by the female emphasis it places on the way two absolutely top-drawer women behave toward each other. It is worth noting that nothing here is trivialized; all *dramatis personae* are accorded their due place, and though the picture is impressionistic in composition, it is sublime in its authority. We care not whether it is factual in every detail, for here momentous events are caught up and uttered as seldom before; *never has the outbreak of the Civil War stood on a nearer plane.*

Just as importantly, as soon as she has spoken, we know something of the storyteller, of her relationship to these events qua events, but also of herself as a woman who endured the aftermath, in the process internalizing the social relationships that pervade this account. We may know these elements intuitively, but we know them nonetheless, because they surround the story just as surely as an eidetic image. From this we may postulate that whereas *history,* concerned with precision and rational interpretation, is *intellectual* in its apprehension of events, *folkhistory* relies on an intuitive, impressionistic organization of the same material. It is another way of knowing, but its lack of reputation should not blind us to its merits; Louisa's stories, and her mother's, have credibility and value as a means of understanding the individual in the context of a particular event. And if the personal is political, as it is currently the fashion to claim, so too the personal is historical. We are each in some relation to the march of events; most live at a distance, some nearer the epicenter. I say our understanding of both is enhanced when we encounter the past through the experiences of eyewitnesses, regardless of their gender, race, or class, a view capably upheld by the success of the PBS television series *The Civil War.*

And if we choose to smile at the account of the day the Potomac ran uphill, at Mrs. General Meigs and her tears of utter relief, it is because the historicity of the occasion is framed more humanly by the emotions of an anxious wife. She may be Louisa's great-grandmama, but she is also every woman who has turned up, dressed to the nines, for a public occasion where she can expect to see her husband either lionized or pilloried. And here, although at a remove, we have something of Louisa's spirit because she would not have included the anecdote without it saying something of her own investment in the events:

> That is the montage, and it shows Meigs and the dome of the Capitol. . . . He was a remarkable engineer . . . he put all those columns in place, and he had only a little donkey engine. . . . There was never an accident. He also perceived that there would be a civil war. Washington at that time had no public water system. . . . If that continued, the Confederates (my grandmother never said *Confederates,* only *Rebels*) . . . could have taken Washington. So Meigs persuaded Congress to grant him enough money to build Cabin John Bridge, which at that time was the longest bridge in the world of its sort.

> When the 100th anniversary of that bridge was celebrated, a couple of water commissioners came down from Washington to interview my mother, who by that time, in her 90s, was pretty frail and wasn't much use to them, but they talked with me . . . and were very admiring of the work. . . . It's called Cabin John Bridge because it was built over where an old black man had his cabin. . . . On the risers is written either MCM or M. C. Meigs. It was his way of signing his work, and he claims he did. . . . My grandmother remembered that.

> One day he said to his wife, "I want you to take the children down. . . . The water is going to come in at noon." . . . There was a great deal of talk at that time about Meigs's Folly (people said he couldn't make water run uphill from the Potomac), and there was a huge crowd gathered, Grandmama said. It was a beautiful, sunny blue-sky day, and all the talk was of Meigs's Folly, and just about noon a plume of water went up. The

whole crowd was absolutely silent. Must have been a
satisfaction to Mrs. Meigs, and then she burst into tears.
And that was the beginning of the water system for
Washington.

And it is precisely this investment that holds true for the
closing chapter of the interview, where we are once more in the
capture of our endless fascination with that epic event, the death
of Lincoln. Every time we encounter such happenings afresh,
there exists a pious hope that this time it might be explained. In
addition is the chill excitement of confronting once more the
eternal verities evoked by the spilling of the blood Royal:

> That night Hallack was ill and in the suburbs and Taylor
> was in command. Well, the family was expecting him
> back for dinner, which apparently was going to be . . .
> in the middle of the evening. Anyway (a soldier) came
> in and immediately asked to speak to General Meigs in
> the hall. My grandmother said his tone was such that,
> "we all went into the hall."
>
> He said to General Meigs, "I saw a soldier running; I
> stopped him. 'Why are you running?' The soldier says,
> 'The President has been shot and has been carried into
> a house across the street from the Ford Theater.' " He
> turned at once, started to go back to his headquarters,
> which was very near (though I was never able to see
> quite where). Mrs. Meigs said to her husband, "Oh,
> Mont, don't go until you have changed into civilian
> clothes; they will be looking for you."
>
> (People in Washington were well aware that the
> Southerners had a conspiracy in which they hoped to
> eliminate a number of important people.)
>
> But Meigs put a pistol in his pocket and left. He spent
> the night in the room where Lincoln lay dying. There's
> a picture—you'll see him there. Grandmama (she had a
> new baby, she'd only been married a short time) could
> go down to the front of the house and see in the light of

the flambeaux which the soldiers had set up, her husband walking to and fro. Now Grandmama said he was not wearing his cap. (I don't understand that, and why didn't I ask because it shows by the braid who is the one in authority.) Well, anyway, she said he was walking to and fro, and there was a howling mob. Of course, she didn't know then what was happening, but she found out the next day that [it was] one of the conspirators, a stupid boy who had torn the sleeve from his jacket and put it over his head in an attempt to disguise himself. He was in Grandfather's office.

Whether he was brought there by the crowd or whether he took refuge there I do not know. I do know that he had worked on a plantation of one of the Taylor cousins, so that [Zachary] Taylor knew this man and this man knew Taylor, and whether that is why he took refuge I don't know, but he did take refuge and hid under the desk, or under the table while Taylor kept the mob at bay. I suppose they wanted to lynch him; I do not know. Anyway Grandmama said there was a howling mob and that her husband walked to and fro in the midst.

And then you see General Meigs came home very early, let's say 7 o'clock, and said, "The President is dead."

At the beginning I said of Louisa that she is one for women. What is remarkable is the degree to which this particular account reflects a tension that pervades Louisa's interview in toto. On the one hand is her implacable guardianship of lineage (and all that it represents), the public face of which is the achievements of men; on the other is very often the women who make the story memorable. And if we remember General Meigs's adventure with the Potomac, it is because we cannot help but see it through the eyes of his wife. Far from being an unjust handicap—or a handicap at all—women donate to these events a palpably human touchstone. It is the picture of young, anxious Mrs. Meigs at the fence, peering through the rings of light cast by the flambeaux, that dominates. For the life of me, I cannot fathom the remark about changing into civvies because "they will be looking for you." I expect this means that, in uniform, General Meigs would have been spotted more easily by the conspirators. Perhaps these details matter less for their plausibility than for the very human dimension they bring to the death of kings. It is veracity of another kind, deftly and identifiably female. I think we understand that it would not have featured in husband Mont's version of that terrible night. My point is that in shaping this batch of stories, and in the matter of her family's inestimable reputation (being its most jealous guardian), Louisa habitually illuminates events through the eyes of women. I believe this to be inadvertent on her part. Yes, she speaks as a born admirer of men, in particular as achievers earmarked in the history books, but it is her women we remember:

> And 2 or 3 days later my grandmother learned of Fannie Seward, the daughter of Secretary Seward, one of the people in the Cabinet, of what happened to her. Her father had been in a carriage accident and thrown out and had broken his collarbone, so he's lying in bed, on the bed, heavily bandaged . . . and Fannie Seward was reading to him. Well, a man came, rang the bell. The butler answered the door and the man came in, knocked the butler down. And he stormed up the steps. Seward's son came out, hearing the ruckus, and he knocked the son down too. He charged into the room where Seward was lying on the bed. And Fannie Seward, seeing his knife, flung herself across her father's body. She deflected the knife, so that although Seward was cut, it was not serious. . . . And by this time the son and the butler had got to their feet and they got hold of the man and he was held for police.

We are left to conclude that this tendency of Louisa forcibly suggests a central ambivalence concerning the relationship with her own femininity. For all that her life has demonstrated outwardly an investment in career, in independence, and in useful activity (presumably rewarding, because she has kept this up), Louisa espouses a distinctly nonfeminist bias. Pointing to a snapshot of two toddlers that has caught my eye, she provides a caption: "My English twins. . . . You see the eternal feminine and the eternal masculine, she is giving, she is beaming. He is receiving, and he is beaming. That's the way they are." Oddly enough (or is it?), Louisa then allows me to lead her into talking of her career, something she had sidestepped before lunch. In speaking of this career, Louisa does not subscribe to the conventionally founded roles that most women modeled themselves on in the 1920s and 1930s. Although she claims that her vocation was dictated by necessity, nonetheless she exercised substantial effort to make sure it provided her with choices and opportunities. Here she is again:

> And right now, women, I'm sorry to say, are making a fuss because they think Mr. Clinton has not named half of his Cabinet as women. That's stupid because there are not nearly as many women as men who have had administrative and business experience. . . . He hasn't got as many able women for his Cabinet as men because women's lives are different and I do not care what you say. In my opinion, 1,000 years from now it will still be true.

It seemed impolitic to contradict this point of view, but I thought at the time, as I do now, how often Louisa's life story and the women who fill it demonstrate a different reality. Her opinions we are obliged to accept at face value, but we should remember as we do so that there is ample evidence to the contrary: Women have populated Louisa's account with such verve that their difference (in her sense of the word) is oftentimes confounded by manifestations of real ability. We need only recall Aunt Abby's financial acumen; she would have made more money (yes?) had it not been for her brother, of the same sex here paraded as possessing business experience.

Just as Louisa is unable to acknowledge the dimension of pain and loss over her father's death, except in an oblique manner, and just as she cannot claim for herself the merit she consistently awards others, except obliquely, there is a concomitant failure to align her femininity with any paradigm that might be seen to detract from glorious men. Throughout her account, tension runs high between what is upheld (family and position) and what is demonstrated (a tendency to focus on women, their achievements, influence, abilities, and presence), such that we are left with no conclusion but the obvious: The tension is evidence of unresolved contradictions within Louisa herself, contradictions that inevitably have found their way into her narrative because she is, in effect, still trying to come to terms with the issues they raise. The way she has gathered her tales together is an attempt, probably unwitting, at rapprochement—that it does not quite achieve that end is our gain because a deeper, more complex understanding of Louisa is donated to us. The tales constitute the things she has kept in estrangement, the revealing lacunae, that contribute so satisfyingly to the whole.

It matters not that our picture of Louisa is incomplete; hers is the kind of story that comes back unbidden, as the meaning it has for us changes in the light of our subsequent experiences. It is not a narrative to be read once and then forgotten. For one thing, it particularizes events that, for most of us, belong in history books; for another, it provides us proximity to an enclave from which much that is unique to this country has come.

Everybody's moral and social universe, carefully anatomized, comes to be identified with who he or she is, and so presents us with an abridged form of autobiography. In pursuing something of the bracing ethical doctrines that are the inheritance of Louisa's class (of which she is both exemplum and steward), I have benefitted also from an expanded understanding of Louisa's private stream, the habits of mind and values that inform her view of herself and the world, and that are part and parcel of the sinuous path to identity.

Similarly, in interpreting her narrative within the context of folkhistory, of story as an age-old arena in which events are impressionistically arranged and recorded, I have gained an insightful picture of Louisa individually and in membership with the women of her family, insofar as she stands in particular relation to the events portrayed. It is a picture replete with teasing paradoxes. These have been a valuable entrée because they have directed us beyond the specifics of a story and into the heart of the matter. As often as not, we are confronted with contradictions that indicate a lifelong antipathy toward issues of gender. The tension between what is said and what is demonstrated is characteristic of the narrative as a whole; in essentials there are, as it were, warring factions that Louisa cannot readily acknowledge because they are in the nature of unsettled accounts.

In addition are those elements that verify the difficulty women encounter in constructing a self-told story that is not congruent with the hard-and-fast horizons by which the male version has dominated for 500 years. That Louisa has been no more successful at providing herself an alternative paradigm is not to be wondered at.

Finally, there remains the larger picture, the verification of Muriel Rukeyser's truth: The world is made up of stories—not atoms. Privy to a moment in history that has lost nothing of its power to enthrall us, we have encountered the death of Lincoln through the eyes of a young wife. Something of great moment has been freshly illuminated, and we are the richer. I expect, in after years, it is this I shall remember. For a brief while I stood close to the death of a man whom I hold to be this nation's greatest son. If encountering Louisa is a question of value received, then I am the beneficiary of her considerable largesse.

Notes

1. Portions used with permission from the Schlesinger Library, Radcliffe College, Cambridge, MA.

2. Horatio Alger (1834-1899) was a best-selling author for more than 30 years at the end of the 19th century. His influence over his own generation began with the publication of *Ragged Dick: Or Street Life in New York* (1867), which provided him with the prototype "Alger hero" germane to American life and language, and the focus of all of his books. It is said that no other figure has exerted so much influence on the popular imagination as the cheerful, persevering boy who proves that virtue will have its just reward.

References

Alger, A. L. (1897). *In Indian tents.* Boston: Roberts.

Alger Family Papers, A-103: Box 1: Folio 3 and Folio 6. Box 3: Folio 34, Schlesinger Library Collection, Radcliffe College, Harvard University, Cambridge, MA.

Berlin, I. (1988, March 17). On the pursuit of the ideal. *New York Review of Books,* pp. 11-18.

Heilbrun, C. G. (1988). *Writing a woman's life.* New York: Ballantine.

Hudson, C. (1966). Folkhistory and ethnohistory. *Ethnohistory, 13*(1-2), 52-70.

Macquarie dictionary. (1982). Brisbane, Queensland: Jacaranda Press.

McRae, J. F. K. (1991). *Story as sovereignty: A study of the relationships between the Warlpiri Aborigines and their country.* Sydney, Australia: University of Technology Press.

❦ 8 ❦

The Women's Movement and Women's Lives

Linking Individual Development and Social Events

Abigail J. Stewart

Social events and movements serve as sources of flashbulb memories (Brown & Kulik, 1977) and political ideologies (Mannheim, 1928/1952). They also may serve as sources of self-definition and personal meaning. Stewart and Healy (1989) proposed a general developmental model for understanding how social experiences take on individual meanings over the life course. This model

AUTHOR'S NOTE: The research with the Radcliffe Class of 1964 has been supported by grants from the Boston University Graduate School, National Science Foundation Visiting Professorships for Women in Science, the Society for the Psychological Study of Social Issues, the MacArthur Network for Research on Successful Midlife Development, and the Radcliffe Research Support and Midlife Program Grants from the Henry A. Murray Research Center. Computer-accessible data and copies of some of the raw data for several waves of this study have been archived at the Center, at Radcliffe College, Cambridge, MA. I am particularly grateful to the three women who were such articulate collaborators in the process of understanding different meanings of the women's movement. Correspondence may be directed to the author at the Psychology Department, University of Michigan, 580 Union Dr., Ann Arbor, MI 48109-1346.

230

begins with the assumption that one important factor in the attachment of individual meaning to social events is an individual's age, because of the connection between age and stage of psychological development, at the time of the social event. A second important factor is the degree to which an individual is identified with a cohort, or what Mannheim (1928/1952) called a "generational unit"—that is, a group of people of roughly the same age who shared some crucial experience. In the United States, people who experienced the Depression or who were born during the baby boom belong to cohorts with strong "cohort identities," though clearly some subgroups have stronger identities than others (e.g., belonging to the baby boom generation may be a more central identification for white and middle-class people than for people of color or those from working-class backgrounds).

In this chapter I first outline Stewart and Healy's model, along with some quantitative evidence about the impact of the women's movement on one cohort of women. This evidence provides broad support for the developmental model proposed by Stewart and Healy. Then I turn to interview data from three women, which will show how even among women in the same cohort, the women's movement had very different meanings tied to individual development. Thus the interview data illuminate some important ways in which a normative developmental model—even though broadly accurate—conceals individual developmental processes. I conclude with a discussion of how the normative developmental model could be expanded to incorporate attention to personal developmental timetables.

A Model Linking Social Events and Individual Development

The broad outlines of Stewart and Healy's developmental model are presented in Table 8.1. The fundamental assumption of the model is that social experiences can be important influences on personality at any age but that the precise form or nature of the influence may be a function of broad developmental periods.

232 THE NARRATIVE STUDY OF LIVES

TABLE 8.1
Links Between Individual Development and Social Events

Age When Social Event Is Experienced	Focus of Impact of Event
Childhood	Fundamental values and expectations (e.g., family values, assumptive frameworks)
Adolescence/early adulthood	Opportunities and life choices; identity (e.g., vocational identity)
"Mature" adulthood	Behavior (e.g., labor force participation)
Later adulthood	New opportunities and choices; revision of identity

First, according to many theories about the links between the sociocultural context and personality development (Adorno, Frenkel-Brunswik, Levinson, & Sanford, 1950/1954; Bowlby, 1969; Erikson, 1950/1963, 1968, 1980; Mannheim, 1928/1952), the domain most likely to be affected by major social historical events for young children is broad values and expectations about the world (see especially Elder, 1974; Jones, 1980). Children's experience of social historical events is, of course, filtered through their experiences in their own families. Some families—and therefore some children—are more directly affected by social events than others, and the specific kinds of effects also may vary. Elder (1974; Elder, Caspi, & van Nguyen, 1986; Elder, van Nguyen, & Caspi, 1985) has shown that the degree of economic loss experienced in particular families was an important factor shaping the effects of the Great Depression on children.

In general, ignoring temperamental or family-level influences, children raised in periods of stability and prosperity should develop relatively positive and optimistic views of the world and social institutions, expecting that basic needs can and will be met. Such secure children often later develop an interest in personal development and self-definition, as well as in intimate interpersonal relationships. However, children raised in hard times more often develop pessimistic views and assume that life will be difficult, perhaps even a struggle for subsistence. Values deriving from these fundamental views also may develop: Just as those raised in prosperity come to value self-development, those raised in hard times may come to value self-reliance, autonomy, and security. Although these values are normally quite conscious, the worldview that shapes them is often out-of-awareness; it is made up of a nonconscious set of background assumptions about the way the world does, and should, work.

Social-historical events experienced in late adolescence or young adulthood are likely to have quite different effects (see Braungart, 1975, 1976, 1980; Erikson, 1968, 1975; Mannheim, 1928/1952; Stewart & Healy, 1986). First, unlike young children, adolescents bring a set of experiences and already-formed world-views and values to any historical event. Events they face may, then, be ones that can be assimilated to these preexisting views, or they may not. Events that are not radically discrepant with their life experience to date may not have much impact; thus children from economically deprived families may not experience the advent of a national depression in their late adolescence as demanding revision of their values. However, if events occur that are radically discrepant with their life experience to date, those events may have enormous power in shaping the newly developing personal identity of the adolescent. Thus young men and women raised in turn-of-the-century England were faced suddenly, in 1914, with international conflict and violence on a massive scale; many in this generation grounded their identity formation in their experience of World War I—an experience utterly discrepant with the period before (see Wohl, 1979). Similarly, many children raised in the prosperous and confident 1950s and early 1960s in the United States, when faced in their late adolescence with the Vietnam War of the later 1960s, defined themselves in terms of their experience fighting or protesting that war (see Braungart, 1975; Jones, 1980; Wilson, 1980). However, children who were raised in the United States during the grim years of the Depression and World War II but who came of age in the sharply contrasting postwar years, with a booming economy and new superpower status, defined themselves in those new terms—of affluence and global responsibility (see Whyte, 1957). In general, then, when events discrepant with childhood values and expectations occur in late adolescence, those events may become central features of an individual's conscious identity.

When a substantial part of a cohort defines itself in terms of a single social experience, we may think of it as having a "cohort identity." Individuals in that cohort vary in the degree to which they share that cohort identity; in fact, within a birth cohort there may be several subgroups with cohort identities. Thus, within the cohort that came of age in the 1960s are individuals with strong identifications as Vietnam veterans and as war protestors, as well as some with identifications as civil rights, gay rights, or women's movement activists. Gender, race, class, and sexuality, as well as many other differences, crucially structure and organize individuals' experiences within particular age cohorts.

Social and political events arising during early "mature adulthood" (the period when individuals have first made commitments to work identities and/or personal lives) have very different consequences. During this period of creation of an adult life structure, adult commitments operate as a pressure to limit drastic self-definitional change (Jacques, 1965; Levinson, 1978; Osherson, 1980; Vaillant, 1978). Social events during this life stage may have profound effects on options available in the job and housing markets, the educational opportunities available to their children, and so on; but individuals are not likely to change—at least immediately—either basic values and expectations about life or their "identity." Social events during this life stage, then, may affect adults' behavior—what they actually do—but not how they understand or think about what they are doing. For example, Chafe (1972, 1977, 1983) argued that (contrary to the historical stereotype) many young middle-class mothers returned to the labor force while their children were still young, during the 1950s and early 1960s. The white, middle-class women doing this had formulated identities as "culture bearers" in the context of postwar pressures for such women to leave the labor force and ·provide secure homes for husbands and children. Their new labor force participation, at odds with their self-definition as good wives and mothers, was not accompanied by change either in values or in identities. Instead, the work outside the home was construed as behavior for the family—behavior that was not undertaken out of personal need or desire, but for the sake of children's education or family vacations. Thus the expanding labor market of the time affected adult women's opportunities and behavior, but did not affect their personal identities or their beliefs about what was proper behavior.

This relative imperviousness of basic beliefs and identity to social experience may change some time later in adulthood, probably beginning around "midlife" (Gould, 1978; Jung, 1931/ 1960; Osherson, 1980). Whether due to the accumulation of life experiences that cannot be accommodated by earlier perspectives and identities, or to internal developmental pressures we do not fully understand, at least some individuals do experience radical revisions of their beliefs and identities when faced with significant social events in middle adulthood. For example, women who raised children at home during the 1950s and early 1960s sometimes were moved by the women's movement of the later 1960s and 1970s to reconsider the structure of their lives— to go back to school, abandon a marriage, or find a career. These women sometimes reconstructed their worldviews, and their personal identities, in radical ways.

Implications of the Developmental Model

Several implications for exploring the meanings of social and historical events can be derived from this model. First and most obviously, *the same events should have different effects on different cohorts;* cohort analysis within age-heterogeneous samples permits examination of this possibility. Thus Stewart and Healy (1989) carried out secondary analyses of Ginzberg and Yohalem's study of women who were graduate students between 1945 and 1951 (Ginzberg & Associates, 1966; Yohalem, 1978). They demonstrated that when the sample was disaggregated into separate age cohorts on the basis of their experience of social history, the different effects of World War II and the postwar "feminine mystique" on the different cohorts could be seen. For the oldest cohort (already adults during the Depression), work and family roles were viewed as incompatible; women in this cohort made personal choices (e.g., remaining single) that assumed that incompatibility. For the middle cohort, work and family roles for women also were experienced as incompatible in childhood, but World War II offered labor force opportunities and experiences that helped them develop vocational identities that quietly persisted throughout the 1950s "feminine mystique." The different ages of these cohorts at the time of World War II shaped not only the degree to which they consciously "felt" affected by the war but also the degree to which wartime experiences provided powerful counterpressures to earlier socialization pressures.

Second, *the experience of psychologically significant social events at different stages of adulthood should have different consequences not only for the individual person but also for his or her children.* Thus women who are parents may (because they are "mature adults") change their behavior in response to dislocating social events, but not their attitudes and values. This discrepancy between worldview and behavior may, in turn, have complex consequences for their children. It certainly will make it more difficult for researchers to decide what a parent is "modeling" (attitudes or behavior) and what a child is internalizing or learning.

In another secondary analysis, Stewart and Healy (1989) showed that the women who participated in the classic Sears, Maccoby, and Levin (1957) study of patterns of childrearing provided very different messages to their daughters about employment, despite the fact that during their daughters' childhood in the early 1950s, none of these mothers were employed. At the time of the initial study, mothers were asked about their feelings about leaving the labor force; in a later follow-up, their daughters reported on whether their mothers eventually resumed labor force participation. Daughters of mothers who had felt regret and later were employed were significantly more likely than other daughters to combine motherhood and employment when they were in their early 30s. These daughters, then, despite being raised during the "feminine mystique" years by mothers who were not actually employed, nevertheless apparently were exposed to some positive valuing of employment for women from their mothers.

Finally, *the same events should have different effects within cohorts, depending on the particular experience of the individual.* Individual differences in a social experience (e.g., the presence or absence of family hardship) in childhood and/or adolescence should have consequences for the impact of certain events (e.g., the Depression) both at the time and later (see Elder, 1974, for confirmation of this notion). In addition, individuals may vary in the degree to which they expose themselves to or focus on a given event. Thus individuals play an active role in selecting and avoiding influences in their lives, as well as in timing their responses to those influences.

Meanings of the Women's Movement for One Cohort

For nearly 20 years, I have been following the lives of a single cohort of women who graduated from Radcliffe College in 1964 (see Stewart, 1975, 1978, 1980; Stewart & Salt, 1981; and Stewart & Vandewater, 1993, for detailed descriptions of the sample and earlier analyses). These women were born during World War II and were raised in the postwar era. Their college years coincided with the Kennedy administration and assassination. Their immediate postcollege world—often mentioned in their questionnaire responses at earlier data collection points—included the Peace Corps, the civil rights movement, and the women's movement.

In the fall of 1986, the women were 43 years old, and my colleagues and I asked them to rate a series of social events in terms of their "personal meaning" for them at the time they occurred and in the present. We provided 26 events, ranging from the Depression (occurring before they were born) to Three Mile Island, Watergate, and the oil crisis. We then asked the women to choose a single event, from the list, that was "particularly meaningful" and to explain its significance. Our expectation was that meaningful events (events that were consciously felt to be personally important) would more often be drawn from the late adolescent/early adult period. As was reported in Stewart and Healy (1989), 61 of the 91 women who rated all 26 events also described one particularly meaningful event. Of these, 11 discussed events that had occurred during their childhood or early adolescence, and 6 discussed events that had occurred during their mature adulthood; 44, or 72% of the women, chose events from their late adolescence or early adulthood. For this cohort, then, those social events that were felt to have special personal meaning did, in fact, cluster during the identity-formation period. Stewart and Healy pointed out evidence that these same events were not widely cited as important by a national probability sample (see Schuman & Scott, 1987, 1988), so they are not simply more meaningful to all people, regardless of age, who lived through them.

Overall, this sample of women may, then, be differentiated from cohorts before and after in terms of the particular social events that shaped their identity. They also differ from other men and women in their cohort in terms of the particular cohort-relevant events that meant the most to them (see Schuman & Scott, 1988). As described below, the women's movement was identified by this sample as a very important influence, though few people identified it that way in Schuman and Scott's national sample.

In this sample, 91% of the women rated the women's movement as at least somewhat meaningful to them, and 62% rated it as "very personally meaningful" now and/or selected it as particularly meaningful. In fact, the women's movement was one of only six events that were seen as more meaningful now than at the time (mean difference = .22, N = 93, t = 3.92, p < .001) and the only event drawn from that time to show that pattern. In contrast, for example, the Vietnam War was rated as significantly less meaningful now, and the civil rights movement as about the same. Moreover, when we look at the 10 most highly rated

TABLE 8.2
Ratings of "Personal Meaning" Associated With Selected Social Events
for Women Born During World War II (Class of 1964)

Social Event	Meaning Rating[a]	Percentage Choosing as "Particularly Meaningful"[b]
Great Depression	1.62	< 2
World War II	2.16	5
Eisenhower presidency	1.24	0
Korean War	1.29	< 2
Kennedy presidency	2.07	5
Martin Luther King, Jr.	2.27	< 2
Civil rights movement	2.42	8
Vietnam War	2.38	8
Women's movement	2.51	30
Nixon presidency	1.82	0

a. N = 90 women.
b. N = 61 women; no other event listed was selected by more than 8% of the sample.

events (see Table 8.2), fully 30% of the women selected the women's movement as the event that was particularly meaningful to them, and that choice was by far the most frequent.

But just what does the women's movement really mean to these women? Considering quantitative data first, we can ask whether those women who claimed to have been affected by the women's movement in fact have led lives that reflect the values and goals of that movement.

Most broadly, the women's movement can be construed as advocating women's right to equal opportunity in the workplace and to an expanded range of personal sex-role definitions. Thus it provided encouragement of women's vocational self-definition, as well as women's consideration of alternative role structures. Stewart and Healy (1989) reported that higher levels of felt meaning associated with the women's movement were correlated with combining employment and family roles in midlife, nontraditional occupational choice, and pursuit of a career in a traditionally male pattern (continuous or continuously advancing education or employment after college).

Stewart and Healy also used data from the Radcliffe sample to address the issue of cohort identification and the impact of the women's movement. We have seen that the importance of parent models may depend on the power of an individual's cohort-linked social experiences. A sense of disjunction with the previous generation is likely to be enhanced by strong cohort identification, while a sense of continuity with the previous generation may be supported when cohort-identification is weak. According to this reasoning, in the case of women in the Radcliffe class of 1964, mothers' employment history should be a particularly significant predictor of women's own employment among those women relatively unaffected by the women's movement and therefore not cohort-identified. In fact, Stewart and Healy reported a strong positive correlation between maternal employment and several daughter employment variables among women who did not find much personal meaning in the women's movement; and virtually no correlation was found among those women who were influenced by the women's movement.

These analyses suggest not only that the women's movement was felt to be personally meaningful by a substantial number of women in this sample but also that demonstrable life consequences flowed from those meanings. Nevertheless the clearest evidence of the centrality of these experiences in women's personality and worldview comes from interviews with them. At the same time, examination of their accounts suggests some important developmental differences among these women in the same cohort.

Meanings of the Women's Movement in Individual Women's Lives

During the summer of 1988, I interviewed several of the women in the sample who reported that particular events had been meaningful, including three women (identified below with pseudonyms) who rated the women's movement as a significant event in their lives and who also chose to write about it as "particularly meaningful." All three women, then, seemed to be good examples of women who were identified with a social historical event (in this case, a movement) that took place during their late adolescence or early adulthood. Thus they seemed to "fit" the normative developmental model. The interviews made it clear, though, that for Carla Ehrlich the impact of the women's movement took place during college, though not precisely in the way the model suggests; for Nina Jacobs the women's movement's impact coincided with her early adulthood—the period when social events are hypothesized to influence behavior but not conscious values or identities; for Sarah Turner the women's movement's impact came at midlife. These women's accounts of their experience with the women's movement and its effects on their lives posed valuable challenges to the normative developmental model.

Carla Ehrlich: The Women's Movement in College

Carla Ehrlich was raised in a working-class, Boston-Irish neighborhood. By the time she went to college, she knew she was relatively uninterested in both marriage and motherhood. She said:

> I never could understand why people thought women
> would be happy to find their identification through
> their husbands and children. I thought, "That sounds
> stupid." I want people to be interested in me for
> me. . . . I was not interested in having children, and I
> knew that very early on. . . . I saw that as not full adult
> status, being a mother. . . . It seemed to me they're
> always on the losing end. You've gotta bow to daddies,
> you've gotta bow to kids . . . and nobody respects
> you. . . . Also, I did not have any romantic image. I grew
> up in a double triple-decker [apartment building], with
> triple deckers [apartment buildings] stacked along, and
> everyone was having babies. This was the 50s! And
> they cried all the time. And people yelled all the time.
> That was my view of kids—they cry all the time, they

trap you, they foreclose options, and they're a heck of a lot of trouble, and they drive you nuts.

Up comes the women's movement with women should not be satellites of their husbands, women should have freedom of choice whether or not to have children, women should have careers, and I thought this sounds good!

I came across *The Feminine Mystique* . . . very early and I thought, Oh, this is it! Because I couldn't really articulate these things very well, but everything she [Betty Friedan] said—my God, here for the first time is somebody who knows exactly what I'm saying.

For Carla, then, exposure to the women's movement *confirmed and supported a worldview that predated it. There was no experience of transformation or conversion, but a tremendous sense of resonance and validation.* The women's movement did not challenge, but confirmed values and assumptions that developed early and have been retained through midlife. It is probably important that during Carla's years of identity formation in college, she did not feel at all identified with her cohort. In fact, she felt rather alienated from many students. As she put it:

I didn't go through that bit where you've-got-to-have-a-man-to-have-your-identity, and yet as I got older and moved in more middle-class circles in college, I was exposed to that kind of thinking, and I found it repulsive that anybody could buy into that kind of life.

Carla saw the women's movement as articulating a critique of middle-class gender roles in a way that fit her own personal perspective.

Nina Jacobs: The Women's Movement in Early Adulthood

In contrast to Carla Ehrlich, Nina Jacobs described the importance of the women's movement for her as coming more in the late 1960s and early 1970s (when she was in her late 20s) in a very personal form. Still, she clearly felt very much a part of her cohort. As she said:

> It's so hard to sort out the social from the personal here. In some sense every one of us is part of a big wave. You don't necessarily experience it yourself as an outside force acting on you. You think you've originated it, you think you've come to these conclusions yourself. . . . In fact, you're part of a large social trend.

Nina married early and was a young mother in the late 1960s; she found herself increasingly unhappy with her marriage. As she put it, "All sorts of women were looking at the relationships they were in with men, and saying, Wait a minute, this isn't very fair and I don't like it." Eventually she concluded that "the problem is pervasive, it's everywhere, it's in small-scale events."

For her the importance of the women's movement was that it provided validation for a new set of understandings she was evolving at that time. As she said:

> Knowing there were other people helped, because sometimes when you have sort of confusing experiences you don't trust your own reactions. If it's in the air, that this goes on all the time, it helps you solidify your own interpretation of something, what's happening in your own personal life. It reinforces you and gives you confidence to make that judgment of it, rather than some other one.

For Nina, then, the impact of the women's movement coincided with its most vigorous period (the early 1970s) and her early adulthood; it resulted in her assumption of a new and significant worldview. As she said:

> I'm not sure I had an explicit ideology before. I think if you had asked me any number of questions, I probably

would have given you the correct feminist answer even at the age of 17, but did I really believe it? I mean, it wasn't very vivid to me, and I think you're very protected when you're in school; you don't have this sense of what it's really going to be like, and when you get into the shock of the real world, that's when your consciousness gets raised. I don't think my explicit views changed that much as much as that I realized that these were important–that these were issues that were really important.

Nina's sense of being part of a "cohort" phenomenon was very strong. She said:

I mean I couldn't explain how it happened. It's just as if everybody–you had the feeling other people were feeling the same thing. Why everybody should have suddenly realized it then as opposed to earlier–I don't know what made the difference. But certainly you had the sense that there were other people, other women out there, you weren't alone.

Sarah Turner: The Women's Movement at Midlife

Interestingly Sarah Turner was exposed to the women's movement at a very similar time in her own development. But the exposure had a very different effect.

Let's see, in 1969 . . . there was the beginnings of some women's groups. . . . I remember my daughter was very young and there was this other woman who was sort of marginally involved with the movement at the time, and she had a daughter who was my daughter's age, and we started this sort of women's discussion group, very rudimentary consciousness-raising. This group actually split up because two of the members of it were in love with the same man!

At about the same time, she said:

> There was this convention . . . and I actually spoke, not
> on sexism—we didn't like the use of the word *sexism;*
> we preferred *male chauvinism*—and so I gave this talk
> about male chauvinism to 1,500 people. And I could
> have said anything because every time I opened my
> mouth . . . our faction would yell and scream "Yay!" and
> the other faction would yell "Boo!" I mean the whole
> thing was a complete zoo.

In the end, though, Sarah concluded that this encounter with
the women's movement did not have much impact on her, in
part, because of her preoccupation with her family life:

> I tried to sort of deal with . . . very rudimentary issues,
> you know, "Why do I always have to do the dishes?"
> kind of stuff with my husband, not to any particular
> avail. I remember when I was recovering from the birth
> of my daughter, a friend of mine who was a little bit
> more feminist than I was, bringing me a copy of this
> article about "The Myth of the Vaginal Orgasm." And I
> remember looking at this thing and thinking, "Joan,
> you don't get it. I just had a baby. It really hurts. I don't
> want to think about this. Take it away." And then I
> remember reading it later. So it wasn't transformative at
> all. It was sort of like, "Oh, this is kind of interesting,
> male chauvinism is a terrible thing," but it didn't really
> change my sense of myself.

More than a decade later, though, something powerful happened
after Sarah had divorced her husband but was still parenting
teenage children:

> I found myself with a brand new degree and a single
> life, teaching at [a women's college]. . . . A friend of
> mine asked me to join a study group on feminist theory
> in June of 1982 . . . [when she was 40]. . . . And the

world just fell apart. It was extremely exciting. It didn't
fall apart in a bad way. I mean, for the first time,
everything came together for me. . . . I've been working
off that ever since, in my personal life, and it's the
center of my work life.

For Sarah, feminist theory encountered in midlife provided a
radically reorienting perspective on herself and the world. As
she put it:

The most exciting thing about it is that in a way in which
nothing else in my life ever could have done it has given
me an explanatory framework for my past as well as my
present experience. It's enabled me to look back at
[college] and explain things about that experience that
would been permanently obscured from my gaze. . . . Not
only have I got a lens to look at my experience, but that
lens has been validated and worked through in the
context of a community. . . . It's something I can use to
make sense of my own life and the world. . . . It's
frightening to think that if it hadn't been for the women's
movement, I would've [done the same things], and not
had a handle on what was going on!

It is clear, then, at the time of the major writings and activism
in the women's movement in the early 1970s, Sarah was aware
of and interested in the movement, but not very engaged in it.
The women's movement acquired meaning for her much later,
when it fit into her own developmental timetable better.

The Development of Individual Meanings

In some ways, then, these three interviews simultaneously
confirm and disconfirm the general developmental model in women
who were all the same age at the time of the social "event"—the
"women's movement." According to the general model, late
adolescents ground their identities in social-historical events

when they encounter discontinuity between their earlier experience and the social world of late adolescence. Carla Ehrlich found the Radcliffe social milieu both new and aversive; the women's movement provided welcome validation for her view of it. It provided conscious articulation of her previously only vaguely articulated values—an articulation that was crucial if she was to succeed in resisting the middle-class gender role pressures she found at Radcliffe. Carla's identity formation as a feminist resulted from a process of self-recognition, though for others it entailed self-transformation.

Nina Jacobs felt the women's movement to be a shaping force, partly because she was a young adult identified with her cohort when she encountered it, even though she was building her family at the time. It was probably crucial that Nina was, as a young mother, experiencing her new family as disappointingly different from what she had anticipated; the women's movement helped her understand, accept, and act on her disappointment. Perhaps because of her young marriage, Nina had deferred some aspects of identity formation. As she realized that her marriage, work, and family life were not what she wanted, and worked toward freeing herself from unsatisfying commitments, she found real meaning and support in the views she now realized had been empty rhetoric before. Nina's story makes clear that although early adult commitments may often constrain and limit the impact of social events, when those commitments are mistaken they provide little resistance to the pressure of events.

Finally, despite earlier exposure to it, Sarah Turner's response to the women's movement really came in midlife. At a time when she was making many changes in her life, she experienced "the biggest moment of truth." She felt that "the scales just fell from my eyes," and as a result she reshaped her personal and professional identity around feminism. For Sarah the early adult encounter with feminism came at a time in her life when her family and work commitments were sufficiently involving and satisfying that the admitted insights of feminism seemed beside the point. Later she found herself ready to rethink not only her present but also her past, not only her own life but also "the world."

These differences show, in part, how three women in the exact same cohort could experience and derive personal meaning from the same social experiences differently and at different times in their own development. The ways they did that confirm the broad outlines of the model, but they also point to the need for a fuller, richer understanding of the processes of engagement with social events at the individual level.

First, we need to understand better what determines when an event experienced at one time in life is retained and reworked at a later time. Clearly Sarah Turner was exposed to the women's movement in the late 1960s, but as she put it, "It wasn't transformative at all." Was that early exposure actually consequential? Or is it crucial that the women's movement is a social event associated with a body of theory that could be encountered at any time? Or is it crucial that the women's movement, unlike some other social events, has (despite media pronouncements of its "death") endured and changed shape since the late 1960s? Was it the women's movement of the late 1960s that influenced Sarah Turner, or was it the 1980s movement?

Second, we need to understand better why different aspects of their experience of the women's movement were important to different women. Features that emerged in these three women's accounts included (a) validation of the self, (b) the sense of community and similarity, and (c) the acquisition of a useful explanatory framework. These elements were present in varying degrees in each woman's account, but they may have been associated with particular developmental stages. Among these three women, self-validation was most prominent for the woman (Carla Ehrlich) at the identity formation stage of late adolescence; the sense of community and similarity was more central for the woman in early adulthood (Nina Jacobs); and the pleasure in a better explanatory framework was most intense for the midlife woman (Sarah Turner). This pattern makes sense in terms of the normative needs of individuals at each life stage (adolescence for validation of identity; early adulthood for connection to community; midlife for a renewed sense of meaning), but these three cases cannot provide evidence for the generality of the connections between these meanings of the women's movement and developmental needs. What these interviews can do is provide clear evidence that we must explore further the simultaneously personal and social meanings of social events if we are to understand how social-level phenomena both shape a person and remain in an individual's consciousness to be used by her for her own personality development ends.

References

Adorno, T. W., Frenkel-Brunswik, E., Levinson, D. J., & Sanford, R. N. (1954). *The authoritarian personality.* New York: Harper. (Original work published 1950)

Bowlby, J. (1969). *Attachment and loss: Vol. 1. Attachment.* London: Hogarth.

Braungart, R. G. (1975). Youth and social movements. In S. Dragastin & G. Elder (Eds.), *Adolescence in the life cycle* (pp. 255-290). Washington, DC: Hemisphere.

Braungart, R. G. (1976). College and noncollege youth politics in 1972: An application of Mannheim's generation unit model. *Journal of Youth and Adolescence, 5,* 325-347.

Braungart, R. G. (1980). Youth movements. In J. Adelson (Ed.), *Handbook of adolescent psychology* (pp. 560-597). New York: John Wiley.

Brown, R., & Kulik, J. (1977). Flashbulb memories. *Cognition, 5*(1), 73-99.

Chafe, W. H. (1972). *The American woman: Her changing social, political, and economic roles, 1920-1970.* New York: Oxford University Press.

Chafe, W. H. (1977). *Women and equality: Changing patterns in American culture.* New York: Oxford University Press.

Chafe, W. H. (1983). The challenge of sex equality: Old values revisited or a new culture? In M. Horner, C. C. Nadelson, & M. Notman (Eds.), *The challenge of change: Perspectives on family, work, and education* (pp. 23-38). New York: Plenum.

Elder, G. (1974). *Children of the Great Depression.* Chicago: University of Chicago Press.

Elder, G., Caspi, A., & van Nguyen, T. (1986). Resourceful and vulnerable children: Family influences in hard times. In R. K. Silbereisen, K. Eyferth, & G. Rudinger (Eds.), *Development as action in context* (pp. 167-186). New York: Springer Verlag.

Elder, G. H., van Nguyen, T., & Caspi, A. (1985). Linking family hardship to children's lives. *Child Development, 56,* 361-375.

Erikson, E. (1963). *Childhood and society.* New York: Norton. (Original work published 1950)

Erikson, E. (1968). *Identity: Youth and crisis.* New York: Norton.

Erikson, E. (1975). *Life history and the historical moment.* New York: Norton.
Erikson, E. (1980). *Identity and the life cycle.* New York: Norton.
Ginzberg, E., & Associates. (1966). *Educated American women: Life styles and self-portraits.* New York: Columbia University Press.
Gould, R. (1978). *Transformations.* New York: Simon & Schuster.
Jacques, E. (1965). Death and the midlife crisis. *International Journal of Psychiatry, 46,* 502-513.
Jones, L. Y. (1980). *Great expectations: America and the baby boom generation.* New York: Coward, McCann & Geoghegan.
Jung, C. G. (1960). The stages of life. In *Collected works: Vol. 8.* Princeton, NJ: Princeton University Press. (First German edition, 1931)
Levinson, D. (1978). *The seasons of a man's life.* New York: Ballantine.
Mannheim, K. (1952). *Essays on the sociology of knowledge.* London: Routledge & Kegan Paul. (Original work published 1928)
Osherson, S. D. (1980). *Holding on or letting go.* New York: Free Press.
Schuman, H., & Scott, J. (1987). Problems in the use of survey questions to measure public opinion. *Science, 236,* 957-959.
Schuman, H., & Scott, J. (1988, August). *The intersection of personal rational history.* Paper presented at American Sociological Association, Atlanta, GA.
Sears, R. R., Maccoby, E. E., & Levin, H. (1957). *Patterns of child rearing.* Evanston, IL: Row, Peterson.
Stewart, A. J. (1975). *Longitudinal prediction from personality to life outcomes among college-educated women.* Unpublished doctoral dissertation, Harvard University, Cambridge, MA.
Stewart, A. J. (1978). A longitudinal study of coping styles in self-defining and socially defined women. *Journal of Consulting and Clinical Psychology, 46*(5), 1079-1084.
Stewart, A. J. (1980). Personality and situation in the prediction of women's life patterns. *Psychology of Women Quarterly, 5*(2), 195-206.
Stewart, A. J., & Healy, J. M., Jr. (1986). The role of personality development and experience in shaping political commitment: An illustrative case. *Journal of Social Issues, 42*(2), 11-31.
Stewart, A. J., & Healy, J. M., Jr. (1989). Linking individual development and social change. *American Psychologist, 44,* 30-42.
Stewart, A. J., & Salt, P. (1981). Life stress, life-styles, depression, and illness in adult women. *Journal of Personality and Social Psychology, 40*(6), 1063-1069.
Stewart, A. J., & Vandewater, E. A. (1993). The Radcliffe class of 1964: Career and family social clock projects in a transitional cohort. In K. Hulbert & D. Schuster (Eds.), *Women's lives through time* (pp. 235-258). San Francisco: Jossey-Bass.
Vaillant, G. (1978). *Adaptation to life.* Boston: Little, Brown.
Whyte, W. H. (1957). *The organization man.* Garden City, NY: Doubleday.
Wilson, J. P. (1980). Conflict, stress, and growth: The effects of war on psychosocial development among Vietnam veterans. In C. R. Figley & S. Leventman (Eds.), *Strangers at home: Vietnam veterans since the war.* New York: Praeger.
Wohl, R. (1979). *The generation of 1914.* Cambridge, MA: Harvard University Press.
Yohalem, A. M. (1978). *The careers of professional women: Commitment and conflict.* Montclair, NJ: Allenheld, Osman.

Index

About the Contributors

Dan Bar-On is the Head of the Department of Behavioral Sciences at Ben Gurion University of the Negev. He received his PhD in 1981 at the Hebrew University of Jerusalem. In 1985 he launched a pioneering field research in Germany, attempting to understand the psychological and moral aftereffects of the Holocaust on the children of the perpetrators. His resulting book is *Legacy of Science: Encounters With Children of the Third Reich.* In 1992, during his sabbatical at Harvard and MIT, he started a group composed of children of Holocaust survivors and children of perpetrators from Germany.

Lyn Mikel Brown is an Assistant Professor and Cochair of the Program in Education and Human Development at Colby College in Waterville, Maine. She received her PhD in human development from Harvard University. She is coauthor (with Carol Gilligan) of *Meeting at the Crossroads: Women's Psychology and Girls' Development* and has published articles and book chapters on girls' development, narrative, and feminist research methods.

Dalia Etzion is a tenured faculty member at the Faculty of Management, Tel Aviv University, Israel. She received her PhD in psychology from the Hebrew University of Jerusalem in 1975.

257

She headed the faculty's Organizational Behavior Programs during
1979-1981 and 1988-1992. Her main areas of teaching and research
are consulting behavior and organization development, coping
with stress and burnout, and work/nonwork adjustment. Her current research focuses on burnout of people in managerial and
technical careers in Israel and in the United States.

Noga Gilad was born in Israel and grew up in a kibbutz. She
completed her BA at Ben Gurion University, Israel, where she
participated as a research assistant in Dan Bar-On's study of the
families of Holocaust survivors. At pesent, she is in graduate
school at Tel Aviv University.

Sherry L. Hatcher is an Adjunct Associate Professor in the Department of Psychology at the University of Michigan, where she received her PhD in 1972. She has authored a number of articles on
female adolescent development, on the development of empathy,
and on self-understanding during the adolescent years. She is currently editing a book about the teaching of peer counseling skills for
prevention in college populations. She developed a college-level
course on this subject and also supervises the Peer Advising Program
in the Department of Psychology at the University of Michigan.

Ruthellen Josselson is currently Forchheimer Professor of
Psychology at the Hebrew University of Jerusalem. She is also
Professor of Psychology at Towson State University, where she
is the director of the Clinical Concentration Program. She is the
author of *Finding Herself: Pathways to Identity Development
in Women* and *The Space Between Us: Exploring the Dimensions of Human Relationships*. She is currently at work on a
book entitled *Revising Herself*.

Amia Lieblich is a member of the faculty of the Department of
Psychology at the Hebrew University of Jerusalem, where she
served as chairperson in 1982-1985. She is the author of several
psychology books that deal in narrative form with specific issues
of Israeli society, such as war, military service, and the kibbutz.

Her most recent work is *Seasons of Captivity: The Inner World of POWs.*

Jill F. Kealey McRae is on leave from her job managing part of the Australian government's program of international development assistance. Her work entails extensive contact with Pacific island states. She is completing doctoral studies at the Graduate School of Education, Harvard University. Her intense interest in narrative grew out of fieldwork completed among a remote Aboriginal group, the Warlpiri, who live in the deserts of central Australia.

Amittai Niv is a Senior Lecturer of Organizational Behavior and General Management at the Ruppin Institute in Israel. He received his DBA from Harvard Business School and is a consultant to and a researcher of fast-growing organizations. His main interest is the interface between strategy formation and organizational development.

Richard L. Ochberg is Assistant Professor of Psychology at the University of Massachusetts, Boston, where he teaches the course Interpretive Research. He is coeditor of *Storied Lives* and *Psychobiography and Life Narratives* and the author of *Middle-Aged Sons and the Meaning of Work.*

Shulamit Reinharz is Professor of Sociology and Director of the Women's Studies Program at Brandeis University, Waltham, Massachusetts, where she initiated the Women's Studies Graduate Program in 1992. She is the author of *On Becoming a Social Scientist* and *Feminist Methods in Social Research* and coauthor of two other books. Her biographical research centers on women in the history of sociology, and early feminist Zionists. She is coauthor (with her husband, Jehuda Reinharz) of an analysis of Manya Shohat's writings.

Annie G. Rogers is a developmental and clinical psychologist who earned her PhD at Washington University and an Assistant

Professor in the Human Development and Psychology Program at the Harvard Graduate School of Education. Her writing and research include gender differences in ego development, psychoanalysis, the development of courage in girls and women, and the prevention of developmental difficulties. She has coedited (with Carol Gilligan and Deborah Tolman) *Women, Girls, and Psychotherapy: Reframing Resistance*, and is finishing a book, *A Shining Affliction: Trauma in Psychotherapy*.

Abigail J. Stewart is a Professor of Psychology and Women's Studies at the University of Michigan. She has directed the Henry A. Murray Research Center at Radcliffe College, as well as the Women's Studies Program at the University of Michigan. Her research has focused on the longitudinal study of women's lives and the psychological meaning of changes experienced at the individual, family, and social levels. She is coeditor (with Carol Franz) of *Women Creating Lives: Identities, Resilience, and Resistance*, a collection of psychological life histories of women.

Mark B. Tappan is an Assistant Professor and Cochair of the Program in Education and Human Development at Colby College in Waterville, Maine. He received his PhD in human development from Harvard University. His primary areas of scholarship include moral development and education, narrative, gender differences in social and personality development, and interpretive research methods. He is coeditor (with Martin Packer) of *Narrative and Storytelling: Implications for Understanding Moral Development*.